THE JAPANESE PSYCHE

Major Motifs in the Fairy Tales of Japan

HAYAO KAWAI

Translated from the Japanese by
Hayao Kawai and Sachiko Reece

Spring Publications, Inc.
Dallas, Texas

Published 1988 by Spring Publications, Inc.;
P.O. Box 222069; Dallas, Texas 75222
Printed in the United States of America

This book is a translation of *Mukashibanashi to Nihonjin no Kokoro*
by Hayao Kawai, Copyright © 1982 by Hayao Kawai,
published in Japanese by Iwanami Shoten, Publishers, Tokyo, 1982.

On the cover is an Oni, rendered by the Japanese painter
Osamu Tsukasa (and commissioned by the author).
Cover designed and produced by Bharati Bhatia.

International distributors:
Spring; Postfach; 8803 Ruschlikon; Switzerland.
Japan Spring Sha, Inc.; 12-10, 2-Chome, Nigawa Takamaru;
    Takarazuka 665, Japan.
Element Books Ltd; Longmead Shaftesbury;
    Dorset SP7 8PL; England.
Astam Books Pty. Ltd.; 27B Llewellyn St.;
    Balmain, Sydney, N.S.W. 2041; Australia.
Imagenes y Libros; Apto. Post 40-085;
    México D.F. 06140; México.

Library of Congress Cataloging-in-Publication Data

Kawai, Hayao, 1928–
    The Japanese psyche, major motifs in the fairy
tales of Japan.

    Translation of: Mukashibanashi to Nihonjin no
kokoro.
    Includes bibliography.
    1. Fairy tales—Japan—History and criticism.
2. Fairy tales—Japan—Classification.   3. Folk
literature—Themes, motives.   4. National characteristics, Japanese.   I. Title.
GR340.K3713 1988   398.2'1'0952   88-11383
ISBN 0-88214-336-0 (pbk.)

CONTENTS

ACKNOWLEDGMENTS

I would like to express my deep gratitude to the following persons without whom the translation and publication of my work *Mukashibanashi to Nihonjin no Kokoro* (Fairy Tales and Psyche of the Japanese) would have been impossible.

The idea for this project was initially set forth by Dr. James Hillman who made all of the necessary arrangements. Although I was enthusiastic about his proposal, I did not think that I could find the necessary time and space to devote myself to this project. Understanding my plight, Mrs. Gilda von Franz, former president of the C. G. Jung Institute of Los Angeles, created an ideal situation for me. She scheduled a lecture series on Japanese fairy tales at the institute in the fall of 1984, enabling me to devote myself to the translation during my stay in Los Angeles. Mrs. Joyce Ashley, a friend of Mrs. Franz, was truly kind and offered to let me stay at her splendid home while she was away in New York. Dr. Marvin Spiegelman, my former analyst, Dr. Mokusen Miyuki, Mr. Gerow Reece and his wife Sachiko attended my lectures and stimulated me to think in English; this proved to be an invaluable aid in my translation efforts. Special thanks are due to Mr. Reece who checked my English sentence by sentence and to Mrs. Reece who translated the Japanese fairy tales which appear in the Appendix. I am also greatly indebted to Ms. Mary Helen Sullivan of Spring Publications for her editorial and publication expertise.

My heartful acknowledgments are due to everyone involved, and it is my earnest hope that this work will serve to further the mutual understanding of the Japanese and the peoples of the West.

NOTE TO THE READER

The translators and editor remind the reader that the main fairy tales discussed are printed in full in the Appendix. He or she may wish to review these first for orientation.

The context determines whether a Japanese word is singular or plural. Hence, Yama-uba and Oni—for example—can be either. Japanese consonants are pronounced as in English, the vowels as in Italian—e.g., *saké* (rice wine) is "sah-keh," *-hime* (princess) is "hee-meh."

ONE
The "Forbidden Chamber" Motif

The Bush Warbler's Home

The motif of the "forbidden chamber," widely spread in fairy tales throughout the world, appears in stories collected in various parts of Japan. A good illustration is "The Bush Warbler's Home," 196A in Keigo Seki's monumental *Nihon Mukashibanashi Taisei* (Compilation of Japanese Fairy Tales, hereafter CJFT).[1] It runs as follows:

A young woodcutter went into a forest and came across a splendid mansion that he had neither seen nor heard of before. Entering the mansion, he met a beautiful lady who asked him to watch over it while she went away briefly. As she was leaving, she forbade him to look into the next room, and he promised her not to do so. Once she was gone, however, he broke his promise. He found three pretty girls sweeping that room; but upon see-

ing the woodcutter, they immediately disappeared, gliding away
quickly like birds. The woodcutter then went on into one room
after another and saw that they contained many treasures. In
the seventh room there was a bird nest with three small eggs.
Picking up the nest, he accidentally dropped them. Three birds
hatched from the eggs and flew away. Just then, the lady came
back and blamed the woodcutter for breaking his promise, causing thereby the death of her three daughters. Transforming herself into a bush warbler, she too flew away. When the man became aware of himself, he was standing alone just where he had
found the mansion, but the mansion was no longer there.

Let us consider for a moment the structure of this story. The
forest, the story's locale, was familiar to its hero, but he found
there a fine mansion about which he had known nothing. Sometimes we are surprised to discern completely new features in a
reality which we had believed to be entirely familiar to us. An
ordinary, accustomed scene may suddenly seem brilliant or like
an abyss. A beautiful woman may appear ugly or even like a
witch. Reality consists of countless layers. Only in daily life does
it appear as a unity with a single layer which will never threaten
us. However, deep layers can break through to the surface before our eyes. Fairy tales have much to tell us in this regard: the
mansion that suddenly appeared and the beautiful lady who
lived there are good examples of that type of experience.
Heroes of fairy tales often encounter curious existences when
they have lost their way or when they have been left by their
parents.

Reality's multifariousness corresponds to that of human consciousness, or—if we follow the thought of analytical psychology—it corresponds to the human psyche which contains
conscious and unconscious layers. If fairy tales tell us about the
structure of reality, it may as well reflect that of the psyche. Take
"The Bush Warbler's Home," for instance: the mansion, the
lady, the forbidden chamber—they are all manifestations of
something existing in deep layers in the psyche.

"The Bush Warbler's Home" has variants that are spread all
over Japan, as may be seen in Seki's CJFT. Aside from the prob-

lem whether these variants originated independently or were disseminated from a common source, it is interesting to try finding a common pattern. In table 1, which shows the variants found in Seki, one can detect a basic pattern in stories 1–13: (1) the hero meets a young woman; (2) he looks into a room when she forbade him; (3) the woman disappears with a grudge; and (4) the hero is left alone, finding himself in the same situation as at the beginning. (In story 10, however, the young man has become old.) Stories 14–18 have some different variations.

The pattern in which a man from daily life space meets a beautiful woman from non-daily space occurs frequently in fairy tales and legends throughout the world. We may interpret the structure of daily and non-daily spaces as the structure of the conscious and the unconscious in the psyche. Then one can say that in man's unconscious there exists a woman of a special kind, and an encounter with her is a highly universal event. The existence of such a universal pattern shows, as C. G. Jung pointed out, the existence of a collective unconscious in the human psyche. This pattern, however, has variations peculiar to the cultures in which it is revealed. While fairy tales have a universal nature, they concurrently manifest culture-bound characteristics. This chapter aims to demonstrate the latter point regarding Japanese fairy tales.

First, I should like to draw attention to some special features of "The Bush Warbler's Home." The bush warbler is a bird especially loved by the Japanese as a harbinger of spring. The earliest anthology of Japanese poetry, *Man'yōshū*, compiled in the eighth century, already includes bush warblers in poems. The *Kokinshū*, compiled in the early tenth century as the first of the imperially sponsored collections of courtly poetry, contains any number of poems in which the bush warbler figures as a bird of spring. The preface of the *Kokinshū*, considered the first exposition of Japanese poetics, raises the rhetorical question "Is there anyone alive who hears the voice of the bush warbler singing among the flowers, or of the frog dwelling in the water, who is not himself inspired to poetry?" Such passages indicate how much this bird has stimulated the sense of beauty of the

TABLE 1

Variations of "The Bush Warbler's Home"

Transgressor	Prohibitor	Place	Forbidden Chamber
1 Young woodcutter	Beautiful woman	Forest	Next room
2 Clerk in a shop	Beautiful girl	Meadow	Twelve rooms
3 Man	Woman who proposes	Mountain	East and west storehouses
4 Traveler	Beautiful girl	Lost the way	One of two storehouses
5 Merchant	Girl who proposes	Street	Twelfth storehouse
6 Woodcutter	Woman	Lost the way	Fourth storehouse
7 Man	Young woman	Mountain	A storehouse
8 Two charcoal makers	Girl	Lost the way	Chest of drawers
9 Man	Woman	Meadow	Seventh storehouse
10 Sawyer	Woman who proposes	Mountain	Twelfth room
11 Man	Beautiful girl	Mountain	Second room
12 Traveler	Young woman	Meadow	Fourth storehouse
13 Young man	Woman	Lost the way	The back room
14 Young man who proposes	Beautiful girl	Mansion	Not to look at the girl for 3 years
15 Mother	Son	Own home	Guest room
16 Young traveling monk	Young woman	Inn	Twelfth storehouse
17 Woman	Woman	Mountain	Thirteenth room
18 Young woman	Man	Inn	Third storehouse

...side the Room	Results
...reasures; eggs	The woman becomes a bush warbler and disappears; the man left alone
...2 monthly events	Bush warbler's voice is heard; the man left alone
...ush warbler in plum tree	Bush warbler flies away; the man left alone
...ush warbler	The woman becomes a bush warbler; the man left alone
...ush warbler in plum tree	The woman chases the man away; the man left alone
...rowing stages of rice plant	The woman becomes a snowy heron; the man left alone
...sh in a tub	The woman becomes a bush warbler and disappears; the man left alone
...rowing stages of rice plant	The woman feels sorry; the man left alone
...ush warbler in plum tree	The woman becomes a bush warbler; the man left alone
...oom of the mountain deity	The woman becomes a bush warbler, the man an old man
...ush warbler in plum tree	The woman becomes a bush warbler; the man left alone
...ush warbler in plum tree	The woman becomes a bush warbler; the man left alone
...ggs	The woman becomes a bush warbler; the man left alone
...	The woman becomes a bush warbler; the man left alone
...on sleeping with wings spread out	The son disappears
...eavy snow	The woman flies away; the priest dies in a snowstorm
...en	Transgressor becomes a hen
...ragon (man's father)	The two marry

Japanese. The image of a bird so closely connected with the ideas of beauty and of spring would be transformed quite naturally into that of a beautiful maiden. Uguisu-hime, the Bush Warbler Princess who appears in *Kaidōki* and other medieval stories, is another of those images. The image of a maiden who lives in a village of bush warblers evidently has been strongly fixed to the psyche of the Japanese from ancient times.

Let us now consider what happened when the man and the woman met each other in a non-daily space in our tale. Their loci are shown in figure 1. The town where the woodcutter lived is clearly daily life space. A mansion suddenly appeared in an intermediate place between daily and non-daily spaces. No doubt the forbidden chamber belongs to a non-daily space. One can assume that those three areas are the conscious, intermediate, and unconscious spaces in the psyche.

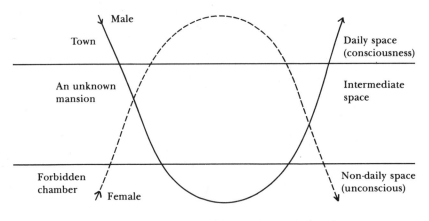

FIG. 1. *Loci of the Male and Female in "The Bush Warbler's Home"*

The man and woman who met at the intermediate place separated immediately. While she went off to town, he intruded into the forbidden room. When they met again, the catastrophe was at hand. They had to return to their own worlds separately, for, like two comets flying through the loci of two parabolas, they were destined never to come together again after the two momentary encounters. To be sure, some variants tell of the couple's marriage—namely, stories 3, 5, 10, 14, and 18. In stories 3, 5, and 10, the woman proposes marriage to the man as soon as they meet. In story 10, the young man becomes old in the last scene, suggesting the difference between the time experience in daily life space and non-daily space. This motif, as well as the motif of the woman's proposal, reminds us of the famous Japanese fairy tale "Urashima Tarō," which I will discuss in chapter five. If one may judge from the process of transformation that the tale of Urashima underwent through the ages, those variants of "The Bush Warbler's Home" which contain the motif of the woman's proposal are likely to be older than the others.

In most of the variants in which the couple marry, however, the union results in a tragic separation. The only exception is story 18, which ends with a happy marriage; moreover, here the man is the prohibitor and the woman the transgressor of the prohibition. For those reasons, I tend to share Keigo Seki's doubts about classifying this last version as a true variant of "The Bush Warbler's Home." In any event, we can conclude that the basic pattern of our tale is that a man and a woman separated forever after two momentary encounters while moving along their own parabolic paths.

What, however, will happen if the prohibition is not broken? Can we expect a resolution in a happy marriage? The variants of the forbidden chamber theme classified under 196B in CJFT include stories in which the men kept their promises to the women. Here the heroes are old men instead of young, and accordingly the marriage motif is absent.

One such story, from Aomori Prefecture, runs as follows. In a village lived a good old man and a bad one. The good old man met a beautiful princess on a mountain, and she asked him to watch over her home while she went to town to shop. As she left, she forbade him to look into one of the house's twelve rooms, the February Chamber, and the old man promised her not to do so. When the princess came back, she found that the old man had kept his promise, and she rewarded him with a magical spatula, telling him that its powers would enable him to obtain any kind of fine food he might wish for. The good old man took the spatula home with him and delighted in the fine food he and his wife made with it. When their greedy neighbor found out about their good fortune, however, he too went to the mountain to see the princess. This bad old man could not restrain himself from looking into the February Chamber. When he broke the prohibition, a bush warbler flew out of that room, and he was left alone on the wild mountainside.

There are a fair number of variants of this kind of tale, but not as many as of tale 196A. We have no concrete basis to judge which of the two types is older. Psychologically, however, we can assume that type 196A may have been changed into 196B with the intention of providing the tale with a happy ending. But even in that case, there is no resolution in a happy marriage. The change in the story brings happiness to the male hero, but not to the woman, who has to disappear at the end. Nobody could change the tragic fate of the female.

The Problem of Cultural Differences

I have already mentioned that fairy tales have two aspects: one universal to mankind and the other peculiar to the culture in which the story is told. How are both manifested in "The Bush Warbler's Home" and in comparable stories elsewhere in the world?

To find precisely corresponding stories in radically differing cultures is not always an easy task. On occasion one does come across a European fairy tale, such as "The Girl Without Hands" in the *Kinder- und Hausmärchen* (KHM) of the Brothers Grimm, which has a very close equivalent in Japan. When that close a correspondence cannot be found, however, we may choose stories of different types, depending on the motifs we wish to stress. Accordingly, Seki's types 196A and 196B of the forbidden chamber theme may be said to have affinities with Aarne and Thompson's AT 480 and AT 710, even if those affinities do not make for a perfect fit between the Japanese and European stories.[2]

AT 480 is the story of "The Kind and the Unkind Girls." The kind girl who entered the non-daily world obtained happiness, whereas the unkind girl became unhappy. Emphasizing the contrast between the two girls, this story is obviously similar to type 196B rather than 196A. AT 710, the story of "Our Lady's Child" (KHM 3), contains the motif of the "forbidden chamber"; but one who reads closely will feel that the plot differs considerably from the Japanese fairy tale's. To appreciate more fully that this universal motif manifests differently in different cultures, the reader may want to examine such Western fairy tales as the Grimm Brothers' "Faithful John" (KHM 6), on which I shall comment in the next section. In the strict sense, one cannot find in Aarne and Thompson's book a story precisely similar to "The Bush Warbler's Home." Indeed, this fairy tale seems peculiarly Japanese.

Let us look at how the motif of the forbidden chamber appears in some other countries. Classified as C 611 in Stith Thompson's *Motif-Index of Folk-Literature,* it occurs widely, but for our purposes a limited sample may suffice.[3] Five stories from a collection of the world's fairy tales prepared by Toshio Ozawa and two from the Grimms' KHM were chosen for comparison and are shown in table 2.

The differences between the stories in tables 1 and 2 appear at a glance. First, the relationship between the prohibitor and the enjoined person is different. In table 2, the prohibitor and the transgressor are a father and his son or daughter; a husband and his wife; a witch and a nine-year-old boy; and the Blessed Virgin Mary and a young girl. In the Western stories, the prohibitors are in general thought to be superior to the enjoined persons. In Japan, the prohibitors are women and the enjoined persons men, except for stories 15 and 18. Story 18, which comes closest to the Western pattern, we shall omit here as an exception (although the question of why we have this kind of tale in Japan deserves further investigation).

If we consider the places where the prohibitions were issued

TABLE 2

Stories of the "Forbidden Chamber" in the West

Title	Transgressor	Prohibitor	Place	Forbidden Chamber
1 Bluebeard (France)	Woman	Husband (Bluebeard)	Bluebeard's home	Secret room
2 Clever Maria (Portugal)	Daughter	Father	Home	Secret room
3 Three-Eyes (Cyprus)	Woman	Husband (Three-Eyes)	Husband's home	Secret room
4 Bellonick (France)	Boy (9 years old)	Princess (witch)	Witch's mansion	Secret room
5 Robber's Marriage (Croatia)	Three sisters	Husband (robber)	Hut in a forest	Secret room
6 Our Lady's Child (Germany)	Girl	Blessed Virgin Mary	Heaven	The thirteenth door
7 Faithful John (Germany)	Prince	King (father)	Castle	Secret room

Title	Inside the Room	Results
1 Bluebeard (France)	Corpses of the former wives	Heroine's brothers rescue her. She marries afterward.
2 Clever Maria (Portugal)	King's garden	The king nearly kills the heroine, but she marries afterward
3 Three-Eyes (Cyprus)	Husband as a man-eater	The husband is about to kill the heroine. The king rescues her and she marries the prince.
4 Bellonick (France)	Horse (prince)	The boy escapes from the witch's mansion and marries the princess.
5 Robber's Marriage (Croatia)	Corpses	The husband kills two sisters. The third one kills him with the help of others.
6 Our Lady's Child (Germany)	Trinity	The girl is driven from heaven and marries the king afterward.
7 Faithful John (Germany)	A picture of a princess	The prince visits the princess. They marry.

TABLE 3

Prohibitors and Transgressors in "Forbidden Chambers" in the West

	Prohibitor	Transgressor
Daily life space	Father	Daughter/son
Intermediate space	Husband	Wife
Non-daily space	Witch/Mary	Child (male/female)

in the Western stories, we find three different patterns, as shown in table 3. When the father is the prohibitor (stories 2 and 7), the locale is his own house—in other words, obvious daily life space. When the husband issues a prohibition to his wife (stories 1, 3, and 5), the place is their home. If we think of its binary character, such a place may be considered to be intermediate between daily and non-daily space. In stories 4 and 6, the prohibitions are issued in a witch's house and in heaven, which clearly belong to non-daily space, and the prohibitors are superhuman. If we correlate the divisions of daily, intermediate, and non-daily space with those of the conscious, intermediate, and unconscious in the human psyche, table 3 will delineate the structure of the Western psyche.

We have discovered an interesting set of relationships between the characters of the prohibitors and the places where the prohibition was issued in the Western stories. The Japanese fairy tale presents a different case: we still do not know who the prohibitors are in daily or in non-daily spaces. In the intermediate space, young women are the prohibitors, contrary to the Western rule. If we pay attention to the way the stories continue after the taboo is broken, the difference between the Japanese and the Western patterns becomes clearer. Keigo Seki pointed out that, in the Japanese fairy tale, the one who sets down the taboo becomes unhappier than the one who breaks it: the latter is not punished, whereas the former disappears sorrowfully. In the Western stories, one who breaks a taboo is punished, even though he may become happy at the end. Thompson's motif-index lists various punishments for breaking a taboo, but one cannot find the item "no punishment."

The Japanese story clearly belongs to the "no punishment" type. That the happiness which the hero might have obtained vanishes without a trace could possibly be interpreted as a kind of penalty, but if so, then surely not as punishment of a direct kind. In the Japanese fairy tales, such resolutions as "the woman chases the man away" (story 5) and "the priest dies in a snowstorm" (story 16) have connotations of retribution. Only in story 17, however, do we find a direct punishment: the heroine is turned into a hen. The fact that it is a woman who breaks the taboo does make this story somewhat of an exception to the tale's basic pattern.

Table 4 shows the many differences between the Japanese and Western stories after the taboo is broken in the intermediate space. Both the prohibitors and what is found in the forbidden chambers differ: in the Japanese stories, the chambers contain scenes of natural beauty, such as bush warblers, a plum tree, or rice plants showing their seasonal changes; in the Western stories, they contain corpses or the transgressor's husband eating a corpse. In the West, the punishment is the death penalty; in Japan, nothing. Actually, Bluebeard's former wives and the heroine's two sisters in "A Robber's Marriage" have already been killed. The results of the Japanese and Western stories diverge completely: the man who breaks the taboo remains untouched and the woman disappears sorrowfully in the former, whereas there is a happy marriage in the latter. In the Western stories, a man appears to save the woman by killing her monstrous husband. Except in the Croatian fairy tale, marriage happily ends the story.

TABLE 4

A Comparison between Japanese and Western Stories

	Prohibitor	Transgressor	Inside the room	Punishment	Results
Japan	Woman	Man	Beauty of nature	None	Woman disappears, man left alone
The West	Man (husband)	Woman (wife)	Corpses	Death sentence	Another man rescues woman

That type of happy ending is rare in Japanese fairy tales. Kiril Tchistov, a Russian scholar of fairy tales, has reported an anecdote which casts light upon the matter. While he was recounting the famous Japanese fairy tale "Urashima Tarō" and talking about the beauty of the Dragon Palace under the sea, he noticed that his grandson was not at all interested and seemed to be anticipating a different development. He asked the boy what he was thinking about, and the child answered, "When does he fight?" Evidently, he was expecting "the hero" Urashima Tarō to fight "the monster" dragon. The Russian child, according to Tchistov, "could not understand at all why the hero did not fight the dragon and why he did not marry the beautiful princess." Lerich, a West German professor of folklore, pointed out the same thing: in Japan, happy marriage is not a frequent motif in fairy tales, whereas in the typical European story the hero rescues the maiden from distress and marries her at the end.

To be sure, there *are* Japanese fairy tales in which marriage occurs. The famous Japanese folklorist Kunio Yanagita suggested that, when fairy tales came to be told only to children, adults would have omitted the motif—which was originally present— from some stories because they did not want to talk in front of children about the relations between men and women. This reluctance, we are told, was caused by the rigorous moral sensibilities imposed upon the Japanese by Confucianism. I cannot agree with Yanagita's suggestion because the Japanese still have quite a few stories in which sluggards, tricksters, and outright liars succeed; if the influence of Confucianism had indeed been so strong, those stories too would surely have vanished.

What do the striking differences between the Japanese and Western fairy tales indicate?

Consciousness

To a certain degree, human consciousness integrates even psychic contents which are conscious at a given moment and have the potential to be made conscious when necessary. It also has some autonomy, although it is influenced by others inwardly and outwardly. A person is recognized to have a personality insofar as he exhibits such integration and autonomy, which are afforded by the center of consciousness called the ego.

Rather than describing the ego function in detail, I would like to focus on the *peculiarity* of the ego which developed in modern Europe. It cannot be compared with others in its high degree of integration and autonomy, nor in its imperviousness. The Jungian analyst Erich Neumann described the process of the evolution of consciousness in Europe in his *The Origins and History of Consciousness.*[4] Neumann's description employs mythological images; hence his theory is quite useful for investigating the meaning of fairy tales, as they share many images with mythology. However, I am not going to interpret Japanese fairy tales by borrowing Neumann's method; they are so unlike those of the West that they must be analyzed according to a theory adapted particularly to them. One of the purposes of my research is to find such a method. Nevertheless, we Japanese have been strongly influenced by Western methodologies, and for that reason, if for no other, I must refer to Neumann's theory even while attempting to interpret Japanese fairy tales differently. The following summarizes his description of the evolution of consciousness.

As many creation myths tell us, the first stage begins with chaos, where the separation of the conscious and the unconscious has not yet occurred. The symbolic representation of this stage is the uroboros, a snake which bites its own tail, making a circle. "It is man and woman, begetting and conceiving, devouring and giving birth, active and passive, above and below, at once."

In the next stage, "the ego begins to emerge from its identity with the uroboros." The world experienced by the waking ego is that of the Great Mother. The figures of the Great Mother play important roles in the world's myths and religions. The Venus of Willendorf and Mary, the Virgin Mother in Christianity, are but two of the many variations of this image; the former emphasizes the physical aspect of the Great Mother, whereas the latter incarnates the spiritual. The Great Mother can be seen as positive or negative according to the way it appears to the ego: the positive mother nourishing children, the negative or terrible one devouring them. In Japan, Kannon, who accepts everything, is the positive Great Mother, and Yama-uba, who appears in fairy tales as an all-devouring mountain witch, is the negative image. Izanami, a great Goddess in Japanese mythology, gave birth to the land of Japan, but afterward she became the deity of the land of death; her image is that of the Great Mother who has two sides, positive and negative.

The ego raised by the Great Mother experiences in the next stage the separation of the opposites. Myths of the separation of the heavens from the earth and the bringing of light into darkness express this stage, in which the conscious and the unconscious are parted.

In the next stage of the evolution of consciousness, "a radical shift in the center of gravity has occurred." In contrast to the process so far, represented by the creation myth, the one that follows is symbolized by the hero myth. Here "man's consciousness has achieved independence," and "his total personality has detached itself from the natural context of the surrounding world and the unconscious." It is the phase of "humanization and personality formation." The cycles of the hero myth consist of the birth of the hero, his fight with the dragon, and his acquisition of a hard-to-obtain treasure.

Many myths and fairy tales describe the hero's birth as an extraordinary event. The heroes in Greek mythology were the children of Zeus and human mothers. In Japan, Momotarō (Peach Tarō), a famous fairy-tale hero, was born from a peach. Such stories are meant to express the unusual qualities of the heroes. Then comes the phase of the hero's slaying the dragon. Freudians interpret this event as the murder of a father by his son, thus reducing the myth to the Oedipus complex, to the context of personal relations in a family. In contrast, Jung understood that the dragon symbolizes The Father or The Mother instead of one's own parents. Slaying the dragon means, from a Jungian point of view, doing away with The Father and The Mother, archetypal beings in one's psyche. Slaying the dragon hence signifies the fight with the Great Mother who would devour the ego, the fight the ego wages against the strength of the unconscious in order to acquire its independence. The ego establishes its autonomy when this symbolic achievement occurs. After slaying The Mother, the hero must kill The Father, i.e., fight against cultural and social laws and rules, to achieve its full independence. The ego can reach its goal only insofar as it wins these dangerous battles.

As the result of his conquest, the hero obtains a treasure. In many Western stories, that treasure is a virgin who was imprisoned by the dragon and whom the hero eventually marries. This means, in short, that after attaining its independence and separating itself from the world by slaying its parents, the ego regains a relation with the world through the mediation of a woman. This result is not the uroboric, undifferentiated unity but a new relationship between the established ego and others.

In this summary of Neumann's thought, simplified as it is, there are two extremely significant points to notice. First, the ego is represented by a male figure. Second, marriage is the highly valued final goal. It is important to keep in mind that the masculine and the feminine are treated in Neumann's theory as symbols, different from real men and women. He stresses that "even in woman, consciousness has a masculine character" and that "the correlation 'conscious-light-day' and 'unconscious-darkness-night' holds true regardless of sex." He adds that "consciousness as such is masculine even in women, just as the unconscious is feminine in men." His use of the words *masculine* and *feminine* clearly differentiates these concepts from *man* and *woman*. The latter set means man and woman as human beings, and the former denotes male and female with symbolic connotations. When we speak about the problem of men and women, unnecessary confusion is apt to arise, because a clear distinction all too frequently is not made between the two terminological sets. Neumann's concern is with the ego in modern Europe, a type that is peculiar in the history of human consciousness. He calls it patriarchal consciousness—clearly separated from the unconscious and free of its influence. In contrast, in matriarchal consciousness the ego is still overwhelmed by the power of the unconscious and has not yet attained its full independence. According to Neumann, a real modern woman has patriarchal consciousness, and her ego is denoted by the masculine hero.

Neumann stresses again and again that in his usage the terms *masculine, feminine, patriarchal,* and *matriarchal* are meant symbolically, differing from the notions of man and woman as persons and paternal or maternal figures in the family or in social structures. Patriarchal consciousness and matriarchal consciousness do not accord with paternal and maternal familial or social structures, although some sort of relationship between them is not excluded. A Europe-centered attitude assumes rather easily the sequence of matriarchal to patriarchal consciousness in the process of ego-establishment. However, we should not apply the pattern directly to social structures in different cultures. While we may notice that agricultural peoples tend to be matriarchal and nomads patriarchal in their psychology, we would err were we to imagine on that basis that agricultural families are matriarchal and nomadic ones patriarchal. The structure of consciousness is not always identical with that of the society or the family.

Table 3 shows the relationship between the prohibitors and the transgressors in Western stories with the "forbidden chamber" theme. It assumes additional interest if we take into account the nature of the ego in modern Europe. First of all, in the daily space, which is supposed to denote consciousness, the prohibitors are fathers. This supports the notion that the patriarchal principle prevails in Western consciousness. In the non-daily—that is, the unconscious world—the prohibitors are Great Mother figures. Here the children who are the enjoined persons have no blood relationship with the prohibitors, contrary to the cases in daily space. Just in-between the two spaces exists the relationship of husband and wife, which is not a vertical relationship of superior and inferior but a horizontal one, although the prohibitors are always men. The union of man and woman provides a meaningful image of the integration of the conscious and the unconscious. As table 2 shows, almost all the Western stories end with happy marriages. Why is this important theme not found frequently in Japanese fairy tales? Perhaps a further look at the Japanese forbidden chamber will reveal at least part of the answer.

What Has Happened?

What are the essential characteristics of the Japanese version of the forbidden chamber motif? What does it really tell us? Let us first briefly compare the Japanese and Western versions.

In Grimm's "Faithful John," the enjoined person is a young male, just as in "The Bush Warbler's Home." His relationship with the heroine is schematized in figure 2. At the beginning of the story there are only the king and the prince, namely, the father and his son. Significantly, nothing is said about a queen or a princess at this point; here the patriarchal principle prevails. However, the dying king signifies that the principle is now losing its vitality and that a renewal is necessary. As he is dying, the old king forbids his son to enter a certain room in his castle. The prince breaks the taboo and finds there a picture of "the princess of the Golden Dwelling."

The old king has a dilemma. Consciously, he wants his son to follow his way, reigning over his country by the patriarchal principle. Unconsciously, however, he wishes that his son would achieve the task which he himself could never have accomplished—to bring a female principle to the country. The father knows so well the danger of that task that he has been obliged to behave in an entirely contradictory way: he took the trouble to hide a picture of the princess in a room and then forbid his son to see it.

If the problem is analyzed in this way, the psychological meaning of the "forbidden chamber" becomes clear. The young man who breaks the taboo falls in love with the princess. So that his wishes may be fulfilled, Faithful John, his servant, must

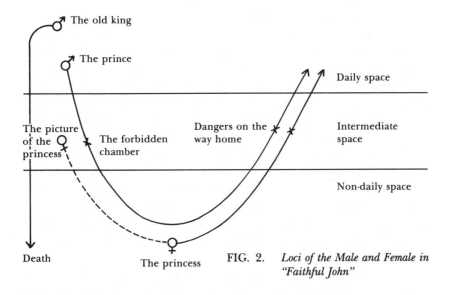

FIG. 2. *Loci of the Male and Female in "Faithful John"*

make strong efforts which need not be discussed here. Eventually, the prince succeeds in marrying the princess, after overcoming many dangers with Faithful John's help.

Although the story does not fit Neumann's theory completely, it clearly shows a process of ego-establishment in a culture where the patriarchal principle dominates. Signifying the ego, the prince acts against his father's will, overcomes the dangers, and finally marries the princess. The process can be seen, from a cultural point of view, as a way for the female principle to compensate for the prevailing male ethos. A higher unity comes about through the union of male and female, daily and non-daily.

"Faithful John" shows rather clearly what is meant by the "forbidden chamber" in the West. But what about the Japanese story? In "The Bush Warbler's Home," the hero had a rare chance to meet a woman beautiful beyond comparison, only to be left standing alone after everything precious has vanished. What has really happened?

The famous Swiss folklorist Max Luthi, in comparing Japanese with Western fairy tales, pointed out, "Breaking a taboo rarely provokes a hero's adventure which results in his promotion. It leads to the situation of nothing, where everything is lost." Indeed, in "The Bush Warbler's Home" the hero who broke the taboo went through no adventures and was led instead at the end to a "situation of nothing." One accustomed to analyzing Western fairy tales must have a good deal of difficulty with this type of Japanese story. Nothing significant will be said by simply relying on Neumann's theory and observing that Japanese fairy tales relate the regression into the uroboros or that they remain at a lower stage of ego development. If we adjust our standpoint properly, we can say that Japanese fairy tales have meaning in their own right. Insofar as we are able to develop that new perspective, we can say that we have arrived at a significant analysis of the Japanese stories—and perhaps of Japanese consciousness as well.

Let us start considering "The Bush Warbler's Home" by changing our attitude completely, putting a positive value on the fact that nothing happens instead of searching for that something which might have happened. In other words, "nothing has happened" can be interpreted as "The Nothingness has happened." The story may be assumed to be simply about "The Nothingness." Luthi's "the situation of nothing" has a negative connotation, but one can interpret it positively. Fundamentally, "The Nothingness" is beyond negative and positive values. When we change our standpoint in this way, a transformation occurs and the two intersecting parabolas in figure 1 converge into a circle (figure 3). The transformed circle contains everything beyond the difference between daily and non-daily, male and female. It is Nothing and, at the same time, Being.

A direct experience of "The Nothingness" is beyond human words. Positive and negative, subject and object are contained within the circle of nothingness beyond all differentiation, so that it becomes impossible to objectify it. Although we cannot verbalize it directly, we can do so with an interpretation of a part of its working, and a fairy tale may serve as that kind of interpretation. "The Bush Warbler's Home" is a Japanese folk expression of the primordial "Nothingness." The first and last

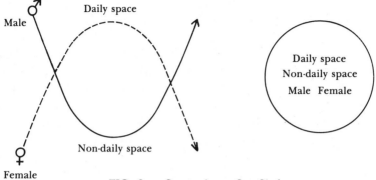

FIG. 3.   *Contraction to One Circle*

scenes of the story are identical: namely, nothing has happened. If there is any movement, the starting point and the goal are the same and can be anywhere on the circumference of the circle. Inside, the circle is empty; within it, there is nothing. But if one raises the question "What is The Nothingness," our tale provides an answer: "A plum tree; a bush warbler." In yet other variants, the answer is "The whole process of the growth of the rice plant through the seasons": that is, the most important thing in the life of the traditional Japanese community. This means the answer is "The Whole."

Or, if one may compact the process of the tale yet further, it runs as follows: "What has happened?" "Nothing." "What is this 'Nothing'?" "A plum tree; a bush warbler." This reminds me of *mondō* dialogues in Zen. Shizuteru Ueda, a Japanese philosopher with deep experience in Zen, has stated that "questions in Zen are fundamentally expressions of the question 'What is the Self?'" Rather than provide the answer to this question directly, the Japanese fairy tale gives an expression of what the Self is. Fairy tales express folk wisdom. Modern people are so far detached from this kind of wisdom that something which is essentially needless, the interpretation of fairy tales, becomes necessary.

Let us reread "The Bush Warbler's Home" and "Faithful John" after having recognized the superfluity of interpreting fairy tales. The two stories have a different impact: the Western one has a form of completeness which impresses the reader, whereas the Japanese seems to be incomplete. But if one considers the feelings apt to be induced in its audience, the story is complete. It cannot be discussed as a whole without appreciating the feeling of *aware* (softly despairing sorrow) which a Japanese would feel for the female figure who disappears in silence. We can interpret or analyze, without any other resources, the Western story's complete form; but if we treat a Japanese fairy tale as an object in itself, separate from the subjective feelings in the reader's mind, its structure will confound any analysis. This fact makes the interpretation of Japanese fairy tales difficult and puzzles Western investigators. Insofar as Japanese interpreters rely on Western theories, they too find their task quite difficult or decide in the end that, in comparison with Western stories, Japanese fairy tales are valueless.

The feeling of *aware* induced in the reader's psyche by "The Bush Warbler's Home" may be explained as a sense of beauty awakened by the sudden arrest of the story's process just before its completion. A young man meets a beautiful lady. The marvels of her residence are recounted one by one. When one feels that a completion is very near, tragedy happens through the man's mistake. The image of the bush warbler disappearing sorrowfully completes our sense of beauty.

A Woman Who Disappears

It is a Japanese cultural paradigm that a woman must disappear in order for sorrow to complete the sense of beauty. Many female figures of this type populate Japanese myths, legends, fairy tales, literary works, and dramas. A characteristic example is the famous fairy tale "Crane Wife": the heroine simply disappears when her husband violates the taboo she has set down. What pathos we find in this tale! The woman is far from angry with the man when her taboo is broken; she just vanishes.

In many Japanese stories the woman must disappear when a man looks into a forbidden chamber; among the obvious examples, the myth of Princess Toyotama and the Nō play *Kurozuka* (The Black Grave) immediately come to mind.³ The remarkable feature of both stories is the emphasis, not upon the guilt of breaking the taboo, but rather upon the shame of being seen in the forbidden room or having its contents discovered.

While we do not find an obvious theme of shame in "The Bush Warbler's Home," Akihiro Satake discovered when comparing that story with "The Cranes' Paradise" that the taboo in the latter is "not to go out" instead of "not to see." A man who was invited to the cranes' paradise was told "not to go out" by a woman there. When he observed this taboo, he was given precious cloths. Satake's conclusion is "The ages of the heroines might have a bearing on the difference between the 'not to see' and 'not to go out' taboos. 'Not to see' is a taboo connected with the sense of shame of a young woman, and 'not to go out' is a reflection of the painful wishes of an old woman." Although it is not directly mentioned, the sense of shame underlies "The Bush Warbler's Home" like a subcurrent.

The Nō play *Kurozuka* expresses in its extreme the sense of shame induced by a broken "not to see" taboo. A traveling monk comes to the moor of Adachi and asks a woman who lives there to give him shelter for the night. The woman departs to gather firewood in the mountain, leaving him alone in her home. As she goes out, she asks the monk not to look into her bedroom. He breaks the taboo, however, and looks: the room is full of blood and decayed flesh, with corpses piled up to the eaves. Terrified, the monk tries to escape, but the woman transforms herself into an ogre and pursues him; in the end, she is vanquished and made to disappear by the power of his prayers. Her parting words are highly significant: "Hide as I did in this black grave, how miserable I became! What misery! How shameful my figure!" The woman was trying to kill the man with the full force of her rancor, but the emphasis nevertheless is upon her feeling of shame.

Frightening as the scene of horror in the bedroom might be, one can see that the story of *Kurozuka* has almost the same essential structure as "The Bush Warbler's Home." The descriptions of the forbidden chambers' interiors differ completely: one was full of treasures, the other of decayed flesh. Nevertheless, these are in actuality two different aspects of the same thing: both chambers belong to a domain of shame, not to be seen. Viewed from the front, the domain of shame is a realm of beauty beyond description; but from the back, it is replete with ugliness. The woman has to disappear from this domain of shame as soon as it is discovered by anybody. One might assume that, since it is connected with the sense of shame, this realm would have been described as a dirty place, but folk wisdom preferred to depict it as a place of beauty.

Our recognition of these two sides of existence involves us in a consideration of the beauty of rancor *(urami)*, which backs up that of sorrow *(awaré)*. Akiko Baba, whose studies of Japanese demons and ogres (Oni) are remarkable for their insight, suggests in an interpretation of *Kurozuka* that the woman was not originally an ogre but "became an Oni because of the sudden womanly feeling of shame that overcame her when her bedroom, replete with pus and blood, was exposed to view." The monk broke his promise, and "by this cruel final betrayal, by the discovery of that most secret place where she had hidden the hoard of sacrificial offerings to her passions, she was driven to the depths of shame and turned into an Oni. But is that not almost too beautifully human?" This is the beauty of rancor, and it is something human par excellence. If *awaré* occurs at the sudden cessation of a process and is directed at something disappearing, then *urami* looks toward the continuation of a process and is born out of the spirit of resistance to the necessity of disappearing.

In "The Bush Warbler's Home," the vanishing woman left with the bitter words "No one is less trustworthy than a human! You broke your promise and killed my three daughters! How I miss them!" Could not this resentment be construed as showing the vitality of the Japanese common people? The sense of "nothingness" and the feeling of "sorrow" exist in the mainstream of Japanese culture. Indeed, females were sacrificed in order to establish that culture. The "disappearing women" resisted that process and left behind their bitterness as they faded from the scene. In *Kurozuka*, a drama for aristocratic society, that sense of rancor was made to vanish by the power of Buddhist prayer. In fairy tales, that sense is not dispelled so easily, because they are the finest expressions of the folk unconscious. Hence, in the world of fairy tales, we can even expect that the woman has disappeared only to return to this world with a newly gained strength. This woman symbolizes the urge to bring something new to Japanese culture. To pursue the woman who disappears sorrowfully from this world and then comes back again is therefore a worthwhile and a necessary task.

Neumann thought that the modern European ego is symbolized by a male hero who slays a dragon. We, however, think it valuable to pursue through Japanese fairy tales a female who disappears, leaving a grudge. In order to consider the difference further, we have to know more about the symbolism of male and female. Neumann symbolized a man's or a woman's ego by a male figure. But what connotations do male and female have in European symbolism? Sexual symbolism, which has a long history in Europe, is highly developed in alchemical thought. As Jung made clear, alchemy described the process of individuation as projected into the transformation of matter in which the symbolic union of male and female plays a great role. Regarding such symbolism, here I can give only a glimpse at Serge Hutin's schema, shown in table 5, which shows that many counterparts in this world are ordered in accord with the main axis of male and female. The combination of sulfur and quicksilver, highly important in the alchemical process, is nothing but the union of male and female, from which something new will be born.

One will notice immediately that Japanese symbolism does not fit table 5. For example, the sun is female and the moon male in Japanese mythology. Points that are emphasized in space symbolism in the West, such as the correlations of right–sun–consciousness and left–moon–unconscious, do not correspond with what is found in Japanese myths and legends. In symbolism, some areas are universal while others are influenced by cultural differences. One who fails to keep this in mind is apt to err seriously in interpreting Japanese fairy tales. Simply following Neumann's schema would oblige one to conclude that many Japanese fairy tales remain in the lower stage of ego development.

Considering all the above, it seems to me that the essence of Japanese fairy tales can be seen better through "female eyes" rather than "male eyes." The female in my expression "female eyes" is not the same as the one resulting after the clearcut division of male and female. To divide male and female clearly, as in table 5, is a categorization that is already based on the male principle. But if we look at table 5 with real "female eyes," there might be a different classification, or no clear classification at all. To look at things with female eyes means, in other words, that the ego of a Japanese is properly symbolized by a female and not by a male. The patriarchal social system that prevailed in Japan until the end of World War II obscured our eyes to this fact. In fairy tales, however, "female *heroes*" could freely take an active part. The investigation of those female figures will cast light on the psyche of the Japanese.

TABLE 5
Masculine/Feminine Dualism in Alchemy

Male	Female	Male	Female
Semen	Menstruation	Heat/Dry	Cold/Wet
Active	Receptive	Gold	Silver
Form	Substance	Sun	Moon
Spirit	Flesh	Yeast	Unleavened dough
Fire	Water		

Note: Redrawn from Serge Hutin, *L'Alchemie*

TWO
The Woman Who Eats Nothing

Another woman figure who plays an important role in Japanese fairy tales seems to be just the opposite of the woman in the bush warbler story of chapter one. This figure is the Yama-uba (*yama*: mountain; *uba*: old woman or crone). In her most common form, Yama-uba is a terrible woman who devours human beings. If investigated carefully, however, Yama-uba is not as simple a being as she might seem.

Stories about such Yama-uba are found all over Japan. Variations in their names are Yama-haha (Mountain-mother), Yama-onna (-woman), and Yama-hime (-princess), but they are all the same being. In his famous work *Tōnō Monogatari* (Tales of Tōnō), Kunio Yanagita says, "Yama-haha might well be Yama-uba." Then he introduces fairy tales of Yama-haha who come to devour girls. Among the many Yama-uba stories of Japan, we shall consider "The Woman Who Eats Nothing."

Yama-uba

The story so titled, listed as no. 244 in CJFT, is spread all over Japan and has many variants. What attracts us most about this version is that she appears at first as a woman who eats nothing, yet then eats everything. The polarity of "eats nothing–eats everything" contains unforeseen meanings.

The protagonist is a man who has been living alone for such a long time that his friends worry about it. We don't know how long he has remained single. In a version in Amakusa, Kumamoto Prefecture, in southern Japan, his age is distinctly mentioned as forty-five to forty-six years old. This situation is quite similar to that of Urashima Tarō, where the protagonist remains single and lives with his mother until he turns forty. The man in our story did not want to marry for a long time, if at all, but he finally answers, "If you find a maiden who eats nothing, please introduce me," when his friends press him to marry. Some versions explain that he was too poor or stingy. In our story, this is not explained. Quite possibly, he may have tried to say something unthinkable—as he had no intention to marry—in order not to be bothered by his friends. The reality of which this story gives us a brief glimpse seems to be that one must be careful when putting anything into words. Even when one says something while convinced of the impossibility of its occurrence, it can unexpectedly come to be.

Hence, the woman who eats nothing—and who is beautiful as well—does come to him. The woman asks him for lodging, but he tries to reject her request as he has nothing to eat. She enters the house saying, "I eat nothing." As she works well and eats nothing, the man lets her stay as she likes. Then in the next paragraph of the story we are told the man thinks there is no better wife than she. We are given to understand that they have married, but the situation is quite ambiguous as to when and how. This ambiguity may reflect the man's dubious attitude toward marriage and may be considered typical for Japanese fairy tales. In another version saying, "Please marry me as I eat nothing," the woman proposes to the man. In both versions, note that the man's attitude is passive. We should keep in mind also the theme of the woman's proposal.

Then, following his friend's advice, the man who was glad to get a nice wife peeps into her hidden aspect. Many versions mention this peeping. In fairy tales peeping is a favorite way of getting in touch with the truth in another dimension. "Double Faces," a North American fairy tale, has many similarities with "The Woman Who Eats Nothing." In "Double Faces" also, a man peeps at a woman eating the ears of human beings. Not only in fairy tales, but also in modern times, peeping has the same connotation of seeing the truth. In many cases today, one's way of life suddenly changes as one peeps at the truth in other dimensions.

The truth which the man in the story sees is indeed horrible. This beautiful woman who eats nothing has a big mouth on the top of her head which devours thirty-three rice balls and three mackerel. A woman who eats nothing is actually a woman who eats everything. In general, if a person strives to get something too extreme, he will be threatened by the opposite. So the man is surprised and runs away to his friend's. Disguising himself as a medicine man, the friend comes to the woman, who has become ill, to cure her. He says, "What sort of curse is on her? A curse with three-*sho* rice [which makes thirty-three rice balls]! A curse with three mackerel!"

While saying this, he must have stifled his laughter. Actually the story can end here as a humorous one. In CJFT, the editor classified this story as AT 1458, a humorous tale. In a parallel story from Turkey mentioned in CJFT, a wife promises her husband that she won't eat anything as he worries about his expenditures. Then he makes fun of her, finding that she is eating a lot of food in secret. In another parallel in Korea, a man who is very rich and stingy wants to get a wife who eats nothing. A wise woman becomes his wife and fools him. Realizing his wrongheadedness through his wife's wise help, he begins to treat her well. This is a moral story but is also considered humorous.

In our story, the friend who makes fun of the woman—saying, "A curse with three-*sho* rice!"—must be about to burst into laughter. But the situation changes here completely. The woman jumps on him and eats him up head first. Her original nature is fully revealed. The friend is about to laugh, but his face must become frozen stiff, changed into a fearful grimace. Here, laughter and fear unexpectedly press upon each other. We can laugh when we have proper distance, but the feeling changes to fear if the distance becomes too short. With this sudden change, our story, no longer humorous, is deepened into another dimension. The polarity of "eats nothing—eats everything" goes beyond humor or morality and into strange depths. This is a woman who eats even human beings. We just cannot laugh or make fun of her.

The husband is caught immediately, although he tries to run away from the horror, but he manages a narrow escape by grabbing a branch. At this point, we suddenly come across the word *Oni*, referring to the wife: "The-woman-who-eats-nothing-*oni* didn't notice this." As this story runs, the beautiful wife has changed into an Oni (demon). In another version, she is called Yama-uba or both Yama-uba and Oni. Finally, he manages her death with mugwort and iris. We may feel this ending is a bit abrupt, but it seems to be connected to the origin of the festival of May in Japan.

What is this Oni who appears in the story? Or, who is Yama-uba on earth? We shall think about such questions, taking into consideration other stories in which Yama-uba appear.

The first characteristic of a Yama-uba we have to take up is horrible: her devouring anything. In "Ushikata and Yama-uba" (The Carter and the Old Mountain Woman), the Yama-uba eats not only the salmon and codfish which are carried on the ox's back, but also the ox. And she tries to eat even the carter himself. In many versions of "The Woman Who Eats Nothing," the Yama-uba transforms herself into a spider. In one variant, the Yama-uba changes into a spider when her secret eating is revealed. In another, after a peeping man discovers her secret, she comes after him, transforming herself into a spider to eat him.

In a number of versions, the spider is killed, sometimes in connection with the saying "If a spider appears at night, kill it even
though it looks like your parents." The second half of this corresponds to another saying: "A child who does not look like his
parents is the child of Oni." Even if it looks like one's parents,
the spider must be killed since it is an Oni.

The dread of spiders is beautifully told in the fairy tale of
"Water-Spider," CJFT 34. A man is fishing at a deep pool in a
river. A spider comes out of the pool, attaches its thread to the
thong of the man's *zōri* (straw sandals). The spider comes out, attaches another thread and sinks back, again and again. Gradually, the strands become a strong rope. Noticing all this, the man
feels more and more uneasy. Then he takes the rope off his *zōri*
and attaches it to the roots of a tree beside him. Soon the rope is
pulled into the water, completely uprooting the tree and draw-
ing it into the pool as well. The man turns pale and runs away.
This story vividly describes the dreadful experience of seeing a
great object being pulled into the depths. Because the spider's
threads catch other beings, its image presents a horrible quality.
On the other hand, the image of weaving strands in the air is associated with fantasy-making. The contents of the fantasy can be
positive or negative. "The Woman Who Eats Nothing" begins
with the man's fantasy: a wife who would eat nothing. In other
words, the man is caught by the spider's threads from the beginning.

A spider's work is connected to spinning and weaving. In German, a spider is called *die Spinne*, obviously related to *spinnen*, 'to
spin.' Here we can readily see a possible association of spider
with the Goddess of fate who weaves the cloth of fortune. It
seems rather natural as well that Yama-uba have close relations
to spinning. In the story "Amanojaku," concerned with a being
similar to the Yama-uba, spinning plays a big role. In "Yama-uba
and the Spinning Wheel," CJFT 253C, Yama-uba is spinning in
the tree. According to Kunio Yanagita, there is another story in
which a woman picks up a *tsukune* of a Yama-uba on the road,
subsequently becomes rich, but also has an Oni's child. *Tsukune*
is a dialect word which means a ball of hemp string, thus further

connecting Yama-uba and spinning. Note that the one who got the Yama-uba's spinning ball becomes rich. Thus do we see how the Japanese acknowledge the positive side of the Yama-uba, hence also the positive side of weaving fantasy.

Greek mythology also includes a story connecting a spider and spinning. Athena is gifted at spinning; Arachne, a girl in Lydia, is also very able. She becomes so arrogant that she thinks she is better than Athena. Then the Goddess, transforming herself into an old woman—like Yama-uba!—advises Arachne to know herself, but the girl in her hubris neglects the caution. Athena reveals her original form and asks the girl to compete with her in spinning. When Arachne is defeated, in great shame she tries to hang herself. Athena feels pity for her and saves her life, but she changes Arachne into a spider who hangs in the air. Here also, the spider is associated with a negative female figure. Athena and Arachne have weaving in common, but the latter represents the shadow side of the former. Together they represent the positive and negative sides of the female.

Let us return to Yama-uba. She is not always terrible: in some versions of "Ubakawa," CJFT 209, she is kind to human beings. In that story, a girl who has lost her way asks the Yama-uba for lodging for a night. Yama-uba does not accept her, as the place is for man-eaters. Instead, she gives the girl a magic coat which can transform one into a child or an old woman. The girl has good fortune through its help. Also, in the legend of Kintaro, the hero was raised by a Yama-uba on Ashigara Mountain. These figures of Yama-uba show kindness and caring for children. In the next section, we shall consider this two-sidedness of Yama-uba.

The Mother

In Erich Neumann's formulation, "the world experienced by the waking ego is that of the Great Mother." As the images of the Yama-uba have become clearer for you, you might have noticed that they exemplify aspects of the Great Mother. We have seen, for instance, the connection between Yama-uba and spiders. A figure which catches insects in a net is just like the Great Mother who holds a tiny ego tightly to suppress its growth. The devouring quality of the Yama-uba is that of the Great Mother.

In general, a positive side of the Great Mother is expressed as embracing and being affectionate to a child. The Yama-uba's *tsukune* is said to be a string without end so that one can use it forever. There is a fine line between the earnest feeling to devote everything unlimitedly to one's own child and the negative quality which I have just described. A variant of "Yama-uba Go-Between," CJFT supplement 30, relates that a grandmother, while licking her dearly loved grandson, actually eats him up and becomes an Oni—a vivid demonstration that an excess of affection for one's child may deprive him of his life.

Whether the Yama-uba are good or bad, what their stories reveal is something beyond the experiences in an ordinary mother–child relation. Children feel their mothers' love is limitless, but it must have a limit insofar as they are human beings. We have in our own psyche, however, the archetype of the Mother which is beyond our personal experiences. When it becomes conscious, we grasp it as images of the Great Mother. This figure, from whom everything is born and to whom everything returns when it dies, is a container in which the process of death and rebirth occurs. She is especially important to agricultural peoples, becoming the object of worship quite naturally. We see how the Yama-uba could inspire reverence when the famous ethnologist Shinobu Origuchi says, "At first, [she is] in charge of raising and protecting a god and later she becomes the wife of the god."

While Origuchi has clarified the positive side of Yama-uba, why is the negative aspect generally expressed more frequently—especially in fairy tales? Perhaps they function to compensate the general trend in Japan to evaluate motherhood extraordinarily highly. It has been taboo to talk ill of or to neglect Mother. In contrast, fairy tales portray so vividly her dreadful devouring power. In "Two Kannons," a variant of CJFT 282, the Yama-uba transforms herself into Kannon (Kuan Yin) when she is chased and has nowhere to escape. Ultimately, her true nature comes out and she is killed. The story is especially interesting if we also sense that even Kannon—the positive Great Mother —has her shadow side.

Let us consider the relation between the Great Mother and food in "The Woman Who Eats Nothing." Food has strange meanings to human beings. Before one eats it, food exists as completely "other." It becomes, however, a part of one as one consumes it. Eating archetypally contains the function of as-similation or identification. The story in which the grand-mother ate her grandson shows the wish to become one, a unity. The witch's gingerbread house in "Hänsel and Gretel" (KHM 15)—or in "Mother Holle" (KHM 24) the oven full of bread and trees full of apples—reveals the strong connection between the Great Mother and food. While she eats humans as her nourish-ment, she also appears as a Goddess of fertility who gives them food.

In addition to identification, eating can mean transforma-tion: food changes into our own blood or flesh. Eating serves not only to maintain life but also to develop or change the in-dividual. The change from child to adult or from daughter to mother is qualitative and important for humans. One could almost say that one is equal to being dead when he makes no progress or change day by day. The transformation in connec-tion with motherhood has a strong tie to the body as is shown in eating, in conception, and in giving birth. Transformation in the male is sometimes too spiritual, tending to be cut off from the body. The male aspect of transformation is presented as flight, highly detached from the earth, and it always bears the danger of one's falling down. In stories of Yama-uba, she may eat a cow, "chomp, chomp" head first, or she may expose her big mouth when she unties her hair. When children hear these stories, they surely shudder. Characteristically, these stories create effects not only in the listeners' minds but also in their bodies. One must know the Great Mother through one's body if one would know her fully. We can therefore see that the transformation of the female mind is always accompanied by bodily change.

Then what does it mean not to eat anything but the rejection of transformation? One who rejects food is trying absolutely to reject transformation by the Great Mother. If one does so to an extreme, one must die. I would like briefly to discuss anorexia nervosa to show more concretely the meaning of rejecting food.

Anorexia nervosa is a neurosis characteristic of girls in puberty: they stubbornly reject food and become thin and worn-out. In some cases, they will die if no therapeutic measures are available. One of the syndrome's specific features is that the richer a country is, the higher its frequency of occurrence. Recently, anorexia nervosa has been increasing in Japan too. We feel it is really tragic when a girl who should be vivid and full of youth appears before us with features like a skeleton covered with skin. We cannot simplify here the psychological mechanism of anorexia nervosa, but anyone can at least recognize the wish "not to become an adult" or "not to become a woman," a wish revealed at the bodily level.

Many psychologists have pointed out problems between mother and daughter or in the marital relation of the patient's parents. If a girl is familiar with the bad relationship between her parents, she naturally does not want to become like them or to grow up. Here we must be careful in judging the mother-daughter relationship, which is not at the ordinary level but much deeper. Even if there seems to be no problem in the ordinary sense, a strong negative function of the Great Mother may still be at work at some depth. Since this archetypal negative power is strong, the mother herself in some cases has not accepted the fact of being a mother or a woman. The daughter rejects becoming a mother and so rejects food. The tight relation between the Great Mother and food influences the girl's symptoms.

A girl with anorexia nervosa can suddenly turn to the opposite extreme and eat too much food. She cannot stop eating and becomes fat quickly. Continuing to eat food which she can-

not digest, she may even die. The Goddess of death is functioning behind her both in rejecting food and in overeating. If we
look at this feature, "The Woman Who Eats Nothing" cannot be
as humorous a story as the parallels in other countries which I
have given. Revealing a much deeper level of the human psyche,
this story of a woman who eats nothing, who really eats thirty-
three rice balls at a time, is neither unrealistic nor humorous.
With collective value, it is directly connected to everyday
tragedies.

The Great Mother is often symbolized by containers, for she
holds everything and the process of transformation occurs
within her. There is a vase on which is painted eyes, a nose, and
a mouth, which is worshiped as a figure of the Great Mother. In
a variant of our story, the Yama-uba catches a man and brings
him back in a wooden bucket. This detail reflects the symbolic
quality of the Great Mother; the man is contained in her very
self. When he tries to escape, he jumps and catches the branch
of a tree—a symbolic escape by moving upward. Unfortunately,
he is found by the Yama-uba who immediately chases him. In
our version, the man kills the Oni (Yama-uba) with mugwort and
iris. Before considering this event, we shall discuss parallels in
other countries.

The Devouring Bottle-Gourd

The motif of eating and not eating appears in humorous
stories from other countries. If we emphasize the devouring
quality of Yama-uba, the parallels—both fairy tales and myths—
exist all over the world. A typical one is "Kishimo" in India who
carried off children and ate them. After she accepted the Bud-
dha's teaching, she became Kariteimo, a guardian for children.
Hence she represents both the positive and negative sides of the
Great Mother. An especially horrible tale of a devouring mother
figure is "The Devouring Bottle-Gourd" of Africa.

This is a story about a girl and a gourd. Fraila, daughter of the
mistress of a rich man, is being carried on her mother's back.

Fraila wants to get a small gourd, the last one attached to a big one. Her mother does not allow her to take it since it is the only one left there. Her father, however, permits it and she gets the gourd. From then on, the gourd walks along behind her, always saying, "I want to eat meat, Fraila. I want to eat meat." Then the gourd begins to eat everything: 150 goats and then 700 sheep. It eats up cows, camels and then slaves. Even while eating, it keeps saying, "I want to eat meat!" Finally it eats men, guinea fowls and chickens until only the girl's family is left. Fraila tries to escape from the gourd and runs to her father. Her father can find nothing other than himself and says to the gourd, "Go ahead and eat even me if you wish." So the gourd eats him too. Fraila runs to the sacrificial ram, and the gourd chases her. The ram gores it with his horns, and it breaks apart. Then every-thing—sheep, goats, cows and all—comes out of it. And here the story ends.

The devouring power of the gourd impresses everyone. Be-yond comparison with Yama-uba in Japan, the big scale seems beyond the scope of fairy tales. Atsuhiko Yoshida, a scholar of mythology, introduced a variant of this story as part of a crea-tion myth in Africa. It is really mythological that everything is devoured and then reborn.

When we think about it, it is interesting that the mother-daughter bond is told first of all. The mother's status as a mistress shows that the family consists of a mother and a daughter, while the father stands one step behind them. In an-cient times, people knew the importance of mothers who gave birth, but they did not know the role of men in conception. Thus females were highly valued. The mother–daughter unity was central; males were peripheral. Worship of the Great Mother and the strong tie between mother and daughter might be the beginning of human culture. Or, it might be better to say it is the situation from which culture emerged. It is a most "natural" state. Note, too, that the mother seems to disappear in the story when the daughter gets the gourd. Though eventually the gourd eats up the father, nothing is told about the mother, suggesting a secret connection between her and the gourd. The gourd wants to eat meat, and it eats up everything. Compared with its devouring power, the father is incredibly weak. The one thing he can do is to say, "Go ahead and eat even me if you wish." But then the gourd just goes ahead. Yoshida, after introducing variants of this story, pointed out that a gourd clearly means a woman in Africa. "Among many native tribes, a girl who has lost her virginity is called a 'broken gourd' in slang expressions. A gourd means a womb in the tribe of the Grumanche in Upper Volta."

When it seems that the gourd has eaten everything, there appears a sacrificial ram who breaks it with his horns. Clearly, the ram symbolizes an archetypal fatherhood in opposition to the Great Mother. Fraila's father was eaten up by the gourd, and the mother disappeared in the story. Beyond the personal dimension of father and mother occurred the clash between fatherhood and motherhood—and so the new world began.

Breaking the gourd reminds us of Erich Neumann's theory, though it is better to think of it as the stage of the separation of the world parents rather than that of the hero's slaying the mother. In the Moshi tribe myth which Yoshida introduced, when a gourd is broken one part becomes the land and the other the sea.

In connection with the motif of eat–not eat, let us look at a myth of the Pete tribe also introduced by Yoshida. In this story, a mother and her child come to see a gourd after it has eaten many things. The gourd immediately snatches and eats the child, so the mother sorrowfully goes to an old woman to ask for help. Having pity on her, the old woman teaches her how to cook a certain kind of soup. If she pours the soup on a rock in the west, the old woman says, the rock will open and she should go in and meet the God of the ram to ask for help. The old woman then adds the warning not to taste the soup when she makes it. Right away, the mother makes this soup. However, she also quite naturally tastes it as she is used to doing. But the soup is so delicious she eats it all. She returns to the old woman but lies to her, saying that her actions were not efficacious although she did everything the old woman had taught her. The old woman does not get angry but just asks her to make the soup right in front of her.

In this way, the mother finally does get into the underworld after pouring the soup onto the rock. Not one plant is there, although a river is flowing. It is a world of minerals. A stout white ram with splendid horns who lives there accompanies the mother to see the gourd. As soon as the ram gores the gourd, lightning strikes and thunder sounds. Then the gourd is broken, and blood from it floods the earth. From the gourd, human be-ings come out.

Two impressive points in the story are the appearance of the kind old woman and the motif of eat–not eat. A counterpart of the gourd's negative function, the old woman represents the positive aspect of the Great Mother. Her kindness is fully de-scribed when she not only forgives the mother who has trans-gressed the prohibition but also has the mother try again while she herself watches. Incidentally, this kind of deed of no punish-ment corresponds to the tendency in Japanese fairy tales which we have discussed, even though the situations are quite dif-ferent. Only with a Great Mother of that big a scale can one escape the gourd's harm. It is interesting that the old woman does not fight herself, but the ram appears to take the role of direct opponent. Rampant fatherhood may be the necessary counterpart here.

Even though the ram does fight the gourd, the mother first must exercise considerable patience in order to secure its help. She must suppress her desire to eat and continue to fast until she can meet the ram. The underworld, the world of minerals without plants, may be the womb of the Great Mother. This is the world, as Yoshida pointed out, which opposes the gourd's greediness. Only through this kind of strict abstinence can the mother meet the ram whose fatherhood element suffices to overcome the devouring gourd.

This story may show a drastic drama played in the depths of the psyche of a living mother. Or it may show how one needs strict abstinence and the experiences of the cool world of minerals in order to cope with the negative function of the

Great Mother. With this thought, we also sense that the story reveals the dreadful world which a girl of anorexia nervosa would experience. In the following section, we shall see how the Japanese cope with the horrible nature of Yama-uba, the negative Great Mother.

Subjugation of Yama-uba

In "The Woman Who Eats Nothing," the man escapes into a stand of mugwort and iris, and the Yama-uba is distressed not to be able to approach him. When he throws some of both plants at her, Oni though she is, she dies from the effects of the poison.

We perhaps feel that this killing of the Yama-uba is abrupt. In many variants, she runs away, being only annoyed by the mug-wort and iris. Though in some versions Yama-uba is killed, the basic theme for all is that she is driven away. The ritual of exor-cising Oni in many Japanese festivals corresponds to this theme. The preference for driving away rather than killing is based on the idea that we can at best escape from the harm of evil as we cannot eradicate it. We can escape as long as we continue our ef-forts, but the evil is never abolished. This idea is one of the unique characteristics of Japanese fairy tales when compared with European ones.

In some variants of this same story, the Yama-uba is killed when she transforms herself into a spider. In other stories, she has changed into a badger or a snake when she is killed. The animals reveal her original form. A Yama-uba is killed when the negative aspect of the Great Mother regresses to the stage which the animals represent. This may show that even Japanese cannot tolerate motherhood if it regresses too far.

One Yama-uba jumps into water and dies, misapprehending as her prey her own image reflected on the water. This is in line with the story that the witch thrusts her head into the oven and is burnt up when Gretel gives her a push. These stories show that, when a strong constellation of the negative Great Mother forms, we had better wait instead of becoming her victims when trying to do something. When the time comes, she annihilates herself.

The story of "Akuto-tarō" (CJFT 141) clearly indicates the subjugation of a Yama-uba. Once there was a young couple named Gon-no-suke and Okaku. When Gon-no-suke is preparing to go out for New Year purchases, he fears that Yama-uba will come while he is away. He asks his wife to get into a big wooden box *(nagamochi)* and locks it, hanging it high by a rope. When Yama-uba comes in, she finds Okaku, who is in her seventh month of pregnancy, and eats her up all except for the heels which are too hard. Leaving these, Yama-uba goes away. When Gon-no-suke returns and realizes what has happened, he puts the heels into a paper bag and hangs it up. He chants a Buddhist sutra for the heels. One day they crack open and a boy is born. Gon-no-suke is delighted and names the boy Akuto-tarō (Heel-tarō). When Akuto-tarō turns twenty, he goes out to conquer the Yama-uba. He eventually tricks her into eating stones, telling her they are rice cakes. He pours boiling oil on her. Since she is still alive, he binds a rope around her neck and pushes her down into a cold river covered with ice. Finally Yama-uba dies.

In this story a hero vanquishes a monster. It is noteworthy that there are few variants. In CJFT only one variant is mentioned, and the sentences are unusually elaborated. Given these considerations, the story is thought to have been transmitted to Japan in comparatively recent times. The story of Yama-uba's subjugation by a hero doesn't fit with Japanese mentality. Further, I cannot find a satisfactory interpretation for the strange motif of the child's birth from the heels.

On the other hand, the noteworthy motif of making the Yama-uba eat stones is worth our continued attention. This motif occurs in "Yama-uba and the Stone Rice-cake" (CJFT 267). In all the many variants, the Yama-uba is killed by being stoned or being made to eat stones. Stories about killing beings which devour call to mind "The Wolf and the Seven Little Kids" (KHM 5) or "Little Red-Cap" (KHM 26) in Grimm's fairy tales. In both East and West, negative Great Mother-like beings are killed when stones are put inside their stomachs. This motif is perhaps connected to sterility. In Japanese, "stone-woman" means a sterile woman. The West too can interpret stones as symbols of infertility. If the negative side of motherhood is emphasized too much, the mother becomes one-sided, denoting only death, losing the possibility of rebirth. The Great Mother-like being who has lost her fertility is killed by having stones put in her belly.

In Japan, however, we have to admit that confusion exists about killing a Yama-uba one-sidedly. This confusion is shown in variants in which Yama-uba says when she dies that the rice-cakes in the New Year will become stones—and they actually do. Another variant tells that the family of the man who killed a Yama-uba does not make rice-cakes for the New Year, as they fear her curse. Further, since people fear her curse after her death, they make a shrine dedicated to her which becomes a shrine for childbirth. In this case, Yama-uba becomes positive after death, reminding me of the change of Kishimo into Kariteimo in India. As Kunio Yanagita stressed, it is absolutely erroneous to judge one-sidedly that Yama-uba is merely a monster. The Japanese long ago saw both positive and negative sides in her and sometimes regarded her ambivalently.

We might also note that people have enshrined Yama-uba as the Goddess of birth although it is they themselves who killed her. To gain further insight into the Japanese psyche, I would like now to introduce briefly the story "Yama-uba Go-Between" which is in the CJFT supplement.

Once there is an old woman and her young son. This son wants to marry, but nobody wants to become his bride as he is extremely poor. One stormy night before New Year's Day, an old woman comes into the house and talks with the old mother and the son beside the fireplace. Some nights later, they hear the crash of something falling perhaps from the sky. Rushing out, they find a beautiful princess in a palanquin but she is nearly dead. They take care of her and ask who she is. She says she is the daughter of a big businessman in Osaka and was kidnapped while on her way to become someone's bride. The old woman who had visited earlier appears and says that she has done all this as she wants to be the go-between for the young man and the princess. She also warns the girl that she will eat her if she tries to escape. Then they marry.

Back in Osaka, everyone in the bride's home is upset. Finally, a clerk succeeds in finding the bride. She says, however, that now she loves her present husband even though he is poor. The clerk reports this to her parents in Osaka. They then build a house and storehouse for the young couple, who live happily together.

This is a happy story in the end. The most striking thing in it is Yama-uba's kindness which is so forceful, even capricious. Her kindness is most effective and may at the same time cause tragedy. For the princess and her family, her sudden abduction is a horrible experience, a terrible episode of "divine conceal-ment." However, the princess says, "My husband is the best one. I'll never go to another man." And her parents support her without any hesitation. If it were a story in the West, one of the two would have had to accomplish some difficult tasks in order to attain happiness. It is a specific feature of Japanese fairy tales that there is no strong conflict to develop the peripeteia of the story. This tale comes to a "harmonious" solution without any conflict at all.

The existence of conflict is a premise of becoming conscious. In order to resolve conflict, we confront the contents of the unconscious and make them conscious. A solution without the experience of conflict shows a harmony as a whole with an ambiguous demarcation between consciousness and the uncon-scious. This perhaps gives us a more balanced view of the "noth-ingness" discussed in the previous chapter. The happy marriage of the young couple is in a different dimension from the final stage described in Neumann's theory.

The marriage arranged by the Yama-uba go-between is com-pletely fated with no consideration of the couple's intentions. The story gives no clue as to why Yama-uba arranges it, and it oc-curs entirely unexpectedly. Of course, the desire to explain any event rationally exists in man's consciousness, and when we look at the many variants of "Yama-uba Go-Between," we see a number in which explanations are given for Yama-uba's deed.

For example, the man carries Yama-uba on his back, making her comfortable to avoid her eating him (from Hamana-gun, Shizuoka-ken); the man is dutiful to his mother (Kochiya-shi, Niigata-ken); the man has treated Yama-uba kindly (Joetsu-shi, Niigata-ken), etc. In other stories, duty to parents and kindness are often repaid. Though these explanations will be fully acceptable, I believe they might have been added later, while the older form is unembellished like the story I summarized. The function of the unconscious cannot be explained consciously when it works in the deeper dimension. Perhaps the older story tells about the workings of the unconscious as such by virtue of not rationalizing motives.

It is especially impressive how the Yama-uba and human beings can live together in peace as in this happy marriage arranged by the go-between. A peaceful co-existence such as this between Yama-uba—the potential destroyer—and human beings is another characteristic of Japanese fairy tales. While the Japanese do indeed know the fearful quality of the unconscious, they never try to reject it. Though they try to drive it away sometimes, they think that there must be the possibility of co-existence.

Now let us return to "The Woman Who Eats Nothing." Having come to know the two-sided nature of the Yama-uba, we will get a completely different idea about the Yama-uba who appears at first as a beautiful girl. Is there any other idea than that she transformed herself into a girl only to eat the man? Actually, Akiko Baba, a contemporary poet and essayist, says this about Yama-uba in this story:

> Perhaps she comes there to be a bride hoping to have relations with human beings, bearing the severe condition of not eating anything. The ridiculous idea of having a mouth in the top of the head may be a device to suggest in the mode of fairy tales that a Yama-uba is a person in a different world from that of ordinary people so that she cannot have relations with them. I feel pity for her, knowing the effort she made in order to have relations with ordinary people.

Let us fantasize a bit more, connecting this image of the pitiful Yama-uba to that of the woman in "The Bush Warbler's Home" who sorrowfully had to leave this world because the ordinary man broke his promise. My fantasy goes something like this: the woman in "The Bush Warbler's Home" who wanted relations with this world left for the other world because the woodcutter looked into the forbidden chamber in spite of the prohibition. Nevertheless, she returns to this world, on the condition of eating nothing, as she cannot shed her strong desire to have "relations with ordinary people." However, the man's peeping reveals that she is not a person of this world. Her resentment peaks. Being hurt twice as much—being looked at is the deepest wound for her—she can't do anything but kill him. She has to leave this world, as she is defeated by the limited understanding of the ordinary person.

As in the last chapter, my fantasy ends in a feeling of sorrow. How is this feeling connected with the feelings of laughter and fear which I discussed previously? We had best not think that the Yama-uba transformed herself into a maiden. Instead, we might realize that the same being can be seen as a beautiful maiden or a devouring old woman depending upon how we approach her. The man who married happily through Yama-uba's help would have to see his wife as a completely different being if he transgressed the prohibition of "not to look at." We can say that we feel sorrow if we approach such a being from the angle of seeing the girl-like side and we experience fear if we approach it from Yama-uba's side. And laughter occurs if we can take a proper distance from both sides. In the next chapter, however, we will hear the earthy laughter which may break open such a triangle of feelings.

THREE
The Laughter of Oni

Although an Oni may eat humans, it is a multi-faceted being, quite unlike the devil in Western culture. In this chapter we will discuss Oni through the analysis of the story "The Laughter of Oni." The Oni laughter presented in the tale is truly character-istic for Japanese, though it is connected to more collective layers. It would be hard to find a parallel story in any other country.

Recapture of the Beauty

The story is one of the variants recorded as "Oni's Child, Kozuna" in CJFT. Kunio Yanagita includes it in a group of stories in which a kidnapped beautiful female is regained through various devices. A beautiful girl is captured suddenly by others—bandits, Oni or other "negative" beings. The person who then tries to find and return her is the future husband, her mother, or some other intimate. And finally he or they succeed in rescuing her through much effort.

Let us look at "The Laughter of Oni." The only daughter of a rich man is abducted on the way to her own wedding by an unidentified being. As the bridegroom has nothing to do with the contents of the story, it develops around the central axis of mother and daughter. Journeying to seek the girl, the mother stays one night in a small shrine after searching for her daughter in the rain. A nun who lives there tells her that the girl is being kept in the Oni's house and also how to reach them. Thus, on the axis of the mother and daughter, another woman appears who is so kind and wise that she may be a Great Mother-like being.

Following the nun's advice, the mother succeeds in reaching the Oni's house. Her daughter is weaving there. Though this Oni is male, his enormous devouring power revealed in drinking the water of the river demonstrates a characteristic of the Great Mother as well. The editor of CJFT mentions "Hänsel and Gretel" as a parallel of "Oni's Child, Kozuna." There the witch plays a similar role to our Oni; a being which appears female in the Western story appears as male in the Japanese. If we focus on the motif of "somebody captured by an unusual being escapes from it," "Hänsel and Gretel" can parallel our story. But if we pursue the themes which I am going to discuss below, the parallel fails. While the motif of somebody's returning to this world from some unusual being's capture is universal, looking at it in detail we recognize the cultural differences.

The daughter is delighted by her mother's visit and prepares a dinner for her. The scene shows the strong bond between the two. The daughter hides her mother in a stone box before the Oni comes back. With his keen sense, the Oni suspects the presence of a human, and his suspicion is supported by his miraculous flowers there. The daughter wittily remarks that the flowers have become three as she has conceived a child. Notice here how the Oni expresses his joy: raising hell, shouting,

"Bring me drums! Bring me *saké*! Let's beat up the watch dogs!"
He even kills the watch dogs himself. When a man drinks
alcohol with joy, he tends to lose control. As the Oni goes so far
as killing his dogs, he must be good-natured. Here the point that
an Oni has a human-like nature—though it is different from
humans—is shown nicely.

While the Oni is drunk and sleeping, the mother and
daughter escape. The nun, appearing at the most opportune
moment, tries to rescue them and advises them to escape by
boat. The Oni awakens and, breaking the box in which he has
been put by the daughter, chases them with his followers. Then
the Oni and his fellows begin to drink all the water of the river
in order to catch the boat. The devouring power of the Oni is so
strong that the water ebbs and the boat begins to go backward.
Finally the Oni's hands are about to grasp it.

In similar stories in the West, water is drunk in order to catch
somebody. Take Grimm's fairy tale "Fundevogel," for example.
Chased by a witch, a boy changes into a pond and a girl into a
duck in order to escape. (Here the captured *are* children as in
"Hänsel and Gretel.") The witch tries to drink the water up, but
the duck catches her with its beak and kills her by pulling her
into the pond.

How can we cope with beings who try to drink up water and
stop the flow of the river? The solution in the Japanese fairy tale
completely differs from that of Grimm's. We are surprised at the
unexpected ending. Being driven into a corner, the mother and
daughter see the nun who says, "Both of you, hurry up and show
yourselves to the Oni!" The three of them then grasp the hems
of their kimonos and raise them. When the Oni and his helpers
see the women's display, they burst into laughter. In a moment
they vomit all the water. So, the mother and daughter have a
narrow escape and return to this world. The themes of the exposure of female genital organs and the laughter of Oni are
quite unique: one can hardly find parallels in fairy tales
elsewhere in the world. That terrible beings like Oni end in fail-
ure by bursting into laughter feels to me to be typically
Japanese.

In order to make Oni laugh, the sexual organs are exposed in this story. Other comical actions occur in the variants which are recorded in CJFT. Exposing hips and beating them with a spatula, the action most frequently found, can be considered as the exposure of sex organs in a wider sense. There is one story from Okayama City in which the Oni laugh when a woman lets out a fart. In Japanese fairy tales, one tells about a fart to make listeners laugh. I have not found this in modern collections of Western fairy tales so far (though parallels to "The Wife Who Lets a Fart" exist in Korea). Too vulgar to mention, it cannot be an object of polite laughter in the West.

We recall that the captured girl is rescued with the nun's help. In some variants, Oni or bandits are killed at the moment of rescuing the captured persons. In many versions, however, Oni are not killed. This story ends with a balance: the Oni return to live in the other world and humans remain in this one. In some variants, the woman, as the one who breaks the balance, gives birth to a child. Parented by an Oni and a human, the child is named "Katako" (one-side child) or "Kata" (one side). His other name "Kozuna" explains why a group of these variants are classified under the title of "Oni-no-ko-Kozuna" (Oni's Child, Kozuna). In the variants, the child, half-Oni and half-human, is always kind to human beings and devotes himself to rescue other humans from Oni's harm. He plays a role similar to that of the nun in our story. It is noteworthy, however, that the child becomes unhappy afterward. He cannot remain in the human world as he is half-Oni; he just vanishes or he returns to his *father's place*, or he asks to be killed as he feels an urge to eat humans. In one version, the Oni's child, Kozuna, builds a hut, enters into it, and kills himself by burning it, as he wishes to eat men now that he has grown up. This is not understandable, especially from the perspective of "As a man sows, so will he reap." The child who has rescued men becomes unhappy afterward. Interpretation of this point lies outside the scope of this book.

Gods in Japan and Gods in Greece

The exposure of female genitals and the laughter of Oni are motifs we find in the myth of the Sun Goddess Amaterasu's concealment, a central event in Japanese mythology. The highest Goddess in the pantheon, Amaterasu, concealed herself in the heavenly rock cave when her brother, Susa-no-wo, behaved violently. In the *Kojiki* (Record of Ancient Things) it is said:

> When Ama-terasu-opo-mi-kami was inside the sacred weaving hall seeing to the weaving of the divine garments, he [Susa-no-wo] opened a hole in the roof of the sacred weaving hall and dropped down into it the heavenly dappled pony which he had skinned with a backward skinning.
>
> The heavenly weaving maiden seeing this was alarmed and struck her genitals against the shuttle and died.
>
> At this time, Ama-terasu-opo-mi-kami, seeing this, was afraid and, opening the heavenly rock cave door, went in and shut herself inside.
>
> Then [heaven and earth] was entirely dark.
>
> Because of this, constant night reigned, and the cries of the myriad deities were everywhere abundant, like summer flies; and all manner of calamities arose.[1]

Many Gods assembled in front of the heavenly rock cave and contrived to lure the great Goddess out from it. One of the devices they tried was the Goddess Ame-no-uzume who,

> overturning a bucket before the heavenly rock cave door, stamped resoundingly upon it. Then she became divinely possessed, exposed her breasts and pushed her skirt-band down to her genitals.
>
> Then [heaven and earth] shook as the eight hundred myriad deities laughed at once.

Then Amaterasu the Sun Goddess, thinking it strange, came out from the cave. Here we recognize the two important themes: the dancing Goddess exposes her genitals and the Gods laugh. Moreover, close investigation shows other similarities in the Goddess myth, suggesting that the fairy tale of "The Laughter of Oni" may contain deep meaning. In order to make the meaning clearer, I would like to compare the Japanese myth —and our fairy tale also—with the Greek myth of Demeter (table 6).

TABLE 6

A Comparison of a Japanese Fairy Tale, a Japanese Myth, and a Greek Myth

	Japanese Fairy Tale	Japanese Myth	Greek Myth
Intruder	Oni	Susa-no-wo (horse)	Hades Poseidon (horse)
Victim/ invaded one	Daughter	Amaterasu Waka-hiru-me	Persephone (daughter) Demeter (mother)
Searcher	Mother	Deities	Demeter (mother)
The one who causes laughter/ exposer	Mother daughter nun	Ame-no-uzume	Baubo
The one who laughs	Oni's servants	Deities	Demeter

Many scholars of mythology in Japan and the West have pointed out the strong similarity between the two (I myself have discussed it elsewhere). In the myth, the great Goddess Demeter laughs when a woman called Baubo shows her genitals. Not only do the Greek and Japanese myths share this common motif— the laughing of Gods induced by the exposure of female organs —but also their basic structure is quite similar: the great Goddess conceals herself because of the male God's violence, and the world becomes sterile. Other Gods variously devise to console the great Goddess, and finally the world regains its fertility.

In the Greek myth, Hades rapes Persephone, the daughter of the great Goddess; hence, his deed tends toward the daughter. In the Japanese myth, however, Susa-no-wo's violence is done directly to the great Goddess. On this point they differ.

According to a variant of the myth told in Arcadia, it is Demeter herself whom Poseidon rapes while she is journeying to seek her beloved daughter. The Goddess tries to throw dust into Poseidon's eyes, transforming herself into a mare when she realizes that he pursues her with sexual desire. However, Poseidon sees through her transformation, changes into a horse, and unites with her. In this story, the great Goddess herself is raped, corresponding to the Japanese myth.

A horse appears in the Japanese myth too, as I showed in the quotation from the *Kojiki*. Although Susa-no-wo throws a horse into the house where the Sun Goddess is, the one who dies having "struck her genitals against the shuttle" is the heavenly weaving maiden. Susa-no-wo's deed suggests sexual violence, but his object seems not to be Amaterasu, according to the *Kojiki*. This indirect kind of expression is used frequently in order to avoid something too direct for the great Goddess. So, I can safely guess that the Sun Goddess herself has experienced the rape and death. The rebirth which occurs afterward is symbolically expressed in the story as her concealment in and reappearance from the rock cave. Her dark experiences are told as those of the heavenly weaving maiden, her other self.

My inference is supported by the description in the *Nihonshoki* (Chronicle of Japan), the other main source of Japanese mythology.[2] According to that text, when Susa-no-wo throws a pony, the Sun Goddess is astonished and hurt by a shuttle. Here Amaterasu herself is hurt, but it is not said that she has "struck her genitals against the shuttle." However, a variant recorded in *Nihonshoki* says: "Waka-hiru-me was startled and fell down from the loom, wounding herself with the shuttle which she held in her hand, and died."

Rather than deciding whether the victim is mother *or* daughter, we had better think in terms of a mother–daughter *unity*. That is, the stories may well be telling about one whole female being which appears as a "mother" or a "daughter" according to which side is being stressed in the story. The distinction between mother and daughter is unclear in the Japanese myth as we have just considered, so that the Sun Goddess carries both sides together; whereas, in the fairy tale, the distinction is so well-defined that the daughter as the captive of Oni and the mother who seeks her are treated separately. In this sense, the

Japanese fairy tale resembles the Greek myth. If we talk about the sterility caused by the retreat of the great Goddess, the Japanese myth parallels the Greek one. The larger difference between the two consists in the fact that the highest God, Zeus, orders and arranges the events going on in the world below, whereas the highest Goddess, Amaterasu, herself suffers, laments, and is consoled by other Gods.

Two common points of the three stories—our Oni fairy tale, the Amaterasu myth, and the Greek myth—are that the narrative begins with the male intrusion which breaks the mother-daughter unity and that the laughter induced by the exposed genitals plays the crucial role. There are, however, differences in detail. Although the existence of the male intruder is common for all three, the one intruded upon is the daughter and the seeker is the mother for both the Japanese fairy tale and the Greek myth. Here the Japanese myth differs from the others. All three vary in regard to the laughter. It is the Oni who laugh in the Japanese fairy tale, the Gods in the Japanese myth, and the great Goddess Demeter in the Greek myth. The ones who cause the laughter differ as well. Baubo (Iambe) and Ame-no-uzume may have similarities. In the fairy tale, however, those exposing genitals are the mother and the daughter and, interestingly enough, also the nun who has, in fact, initiated the ruse.

We shall return to the meaning of Oni, the exposure of genitals, and the laughter in the fairy tale in due course, taking further account of the similarities to and differences from the two myths.

The One Who Breaks the Mother-Daughter Unity

Who is the Oni who appears in "The Laughter of Oni"? asks Akiko Baba at the beginning of her excellent *A Study of Oni*. The Oni who appears in the festival of Setsubun in February is a grotesque, comic figure, the most familiar image that modern Japanese are likely to know. It has horns, wears pants of tiger's skin, and easily runs away when children throw beans at it. This is what we might call a "reduced Oni." Because of the extended difficulties which arise in any thorough investigation, I shall content myself with considering the image of Oni limited to "The Laughter of Oni," focusing on the meaning of that image as an inhabitant in our inner world.

The role of the Oni in the fairy tale and its similarity to the intruders in the two myths give us an important suggestion. Figures such as Hades–Poseidon or Susa-no-wo intrude as Gods into the world of the feminine. This recalls Shinobu Origuchi's famous theory: the Oni is a synonym of *Kami* (God).

In the Eleusinian mysteries, the theme of death and rebirth was most important. Regarding the special features of rebirth there, Akira Hisano says,

> If hunting is the means for living, men capture, kill and eat animals. If they eat up all the animals in one region, they travel to another place. The earth for them is the stage on which the fight for life occurs. If agriculture is the means for living, however, the preservation of seeds becomes necessary. The preserved seeds are sown and bring new lives through dying. A seed of wheat dies to produce many.

Even if we see the killing and eating of animals as a process of death and rebirth, we have to note that, when dead animals are reborn as life in the men who have eaten them, they are not the same beings. In the case of plants, however, a seed dying and a seed rebirthing are the same life. The same being appears repeatedly. A mother and a daughter are the same. A daughter becomes a mother when she becomes old. A mother, after her death, is reborn as a daughter. A mother and a daughter show only different aspects of the same life.

In the world where the primordial mother–daughter unity prevails, all events are repeated perpetually and no essential change occurs. A male intruder is necessary to destroy this perpetual repetition. Unless he is enormously strong, he will be deterred by the power of the unity. The image of Hades, who emerges abruptly from the split-open earth driving a chariot, is really fitting to his role, as is the violent character of Susa-no-wo described in Japanese mythology. The fact that horses are frequently associated with these Gods may be based on their rushing strength. In the Japanese myth, the unity of the mother and daughter is occluded by the prevalence of the mother, shown by the figure of the highest Goddess.

Although the intruders are violent males, their links to the mother are fairly tight. Hades is the king of the underworld, who comes up out of the earth—earth and mother are closely associated. If we think of his fetching Persephone into the underworld as swallowing her into the earth, this function can be connected with the Great Mother's devouring power. Susa-no-wo's link to his mother is clear in the Japanese myth. When his father orders, "You shall rule the ocean," he does not obey and weeps and howls that he would like to visit his mother's land (his link to the ocean associates him with Poseidon). Actually, he does finally live in the underworld—like Hades.

The Oni in the fairy tale also has devouring power, even though he is male. Hades, Susa-no-wo, and the Oni—who all break the mother–daughter unity—are manifestations of the uroboric father. They are fathers, not shining in heaven as Zeus, but gloomy, terrible and strong, though not authoritative, and they even fall into comical states. Though their rushing strength like a chariot is beyond comparison, they don't have the ability to orient it. An example of uroboric fathers would be the Japanese military in the Second World War: they simply repeated the same type of assaults regardless of the situation. Of course, the uroboric father itself is neither good nor evil. It tends to be labeled as evil because of its power of destruction and lack of orientation; but the mother–daughter unity is never broken without it.

The mother and daughter who have been separated by the intrusion of the uroboric father tend to recover their former state. The mother's rescue of her daughter is virtually the same as a rebirth ritual, but at the same time it brings the male intrusion to naught. Actually, the fairy tale ends as if nothing has happened;

the Oni come back to their world and the females to theirs. The nun reveals that she is a stone pagoda and asks the mother and daughter to build a pagoda each year. It is an impressive ending that the mother and daughter (whether she marries or not we are not told) build a stone pagoda annually, repaying the nun's kindness. The pagodas, increasing one by one, provide the image of repeating the same thing perpetually and peacefully —presenting peace and the gratitude of the mother and daughter. Nothing happens. (Peace or safety is *buji* in Japanese which means literally "no-thing.") We are forced to realize the strong function of nothingness in Japanese consciousness.

Now, let us think from the personal point of view rather than the cultural one. An infant lives naturally in the world of the mother–child unity. If it continues to live without any effort to proceed from there, the cycle of marriage, childbirth, child care, old age and death occurs *naturally*, contained in the lap of the Great Mother. In this case, the man's role as a man is not appreciated, or the males play only the role of the followers of the Mother. Some Japanese today still seem to live in this psychological condition. If the uroboric father breaks the mother-daughter unity and a woman accepts him, she changes from the state of mother–daughter unity to that of the father–daughter bond.

A woman confined by the father–daughter bond must then experience her acceptance of a man other than the father: this bond must be broken by the intrusion of a new male. If a woman's consciousness does not enter this condition, she will remain in a psychological incest between father and daughter. Though their lives can be seen from various angles, the majority of Japanese nowadays probably still live in this state. The male who destroys the father–daughter bond is at first recognized as a monster—or an Oni. Many stories of this kind exist all over the world as the so-called "Beauty and the Beast" stories, of which "Three-Eyes" is typical (see Appendix). The male who breaks the father–daughter bond appears as a monster with three eyes, and the heroine marries the prince after the monster is killed. The basic structure of the story is the same as the beast transforming itself into the prince in "Beauty and the Beast." First comes the acceptance of a male as a monster, and then the monster changes into a prince.

A transition from mother–daughter unity to father–daughter bond is depicted in a Japanese fairy tale, "The Oni Bridegroom." (A similar story is found as "The Monkey Bridegroom.") The following summarizes "The Oni Bridegroom" as found in Amami-Oshima, an island in Kagoshima Prefecture.

A widow has three daughters. The first is called Amewankashira and the third one, Otomadarukana. One day the mother has difficulty crossing a river because of a flood. An Oni appears and offers help to the mother who has to promise in return that one of her daughters will marry him. The first and second daughters vehemently reject becoming Oni's bride. The third, being completely obedient to her mother, accepts the proposal. The Oni delightedly carries her away with both hands. However, the Oni stumbles when he tries to cross a flooded river. The daughter succeeds in reaching the river bank while the Oni is drowned in the torrent.

When the daughter Otomadarukana survives, the lord called Ajiganashi comes to meet her and they marry, living happily. Hearing this, the first daughter, Amewankashira, envies her younger sister. Amewankashira pushes Otomadarukana into a well and she dies. Disguised as her sister, Amewankashira returns to the castle. Next morning when she goes to a well to fetch water, Otomadarukana appears in the water, transforming herself into an eel. The eel moves around violently, muddying the water so that her sister cannot draw any that is clear. Hearing his apparent wife's complaints, the lord goes to the well and catches the eel which he has somebody cook. When he is going to eat the eel, he complains because it is not boiled enough. At that moment, the cooked eel's head asks the lord why he cannot recognize his wife's change even though he can recognize whether or not the eel is boiled. The lord Ajiganashi comes to know the truth and laments. Amewankashira does not know how to behave and changes into a worm. Even today, undercooked food is called Ajiganashi (no taste) because of this story.

This appearance of the lord after the Oni's death may be in-terpreted as the transformation of the male intruder who breaks the father–daughter bond. That the happy heroine visits her parent and that her sister is envious are structurally quite similar to the Western "Beauty and the Beast." At the end of the story, however, the locus changes suddenly in a Japanese way; although the sister's evil comes out, she becomes a worm, and the story seems to dissipate into simple popular etymology: "undercooked food is called Ajiganashi (no taste)." Nothing is told about the sorrowful heroine. We only pity her.

We are compelled again to realize the strength of the mother–daughter bond in Japan. We feel nothing but pity for those women who die or leave this world to complete our sense of beauty. Of course, they do not remain in that state. But that is a more complex story. For now, let us return to the exposure of genitals.

The Exposure of Genitals

The profundity of the motif is shown by Baubo's deed in the myth of Demeter–Persephone. As far as I know, however, this motif appears in none of the world's fairy tales—one cannot find it in Thompson's motif-index. We may find some parallels, however, in the mythologies of the world, which may give us clues to its meaning.

A second exposure of genitals by Ame-no-uzume occurs when the Sun Goddess, Amaterasu, is sending her grandson to rule over the land of Japan. When the grandson is about to descend from the heavens, a forerunner comes back and reports that a monstrous God stands in the way. He is tall and has a long nose, a big mouth, and shining eyes. His face reminds us of Oni. No God can dare to ask him why he stands there. Then the Goddess Ame-no-uzume is sent to him. She exposes her breasts and pushes her skirt-band down to her genitals and laughs at him. Then the monstrous God begins to welcome the Sun Goddess's grandson.

Ame-no-uzume's deed in front of the heavenly rock cave door is similar to Baubo's behavior in the Greek myth. What does it mean when she repeats the exposure to the monstrous God? Atsuhiko Yoshida, from the standpoint of comparative mythology, gives us an excellent answer: "Ame-no-uzume's deeds told in Japanese mythology are in almost all cases interpreted as having the function of opening up closed mouths, entrances, passages." The exposure of genitals is a deed of "opening." In the case of the myth of the heavenly rock cave, the Goddess's exposure makes the Gods' mouths open by laughter and even the Sun Goddess's mouth which she has closed because of her rage. And, hence, the heavenly rock cave door opens.

Yoshida also suggests that Ame-no-uzume, who has the function of opening closed mouths and bringing light to the world, may be thought of as "the goddess of dawn like Ushyas in India." Ushyas in the *Rig-Veda* laughs, dances, and exposes her breasts and her body. This figure of the Goddess of dawn reminds me of an Ainu legend introduced by Nobuhiro Matsumoto in which, it is told, the exposure brings light to the world. The story begins with the following impressive words:

> Spring is the season of women. When spring comes, green grasses burst into bloom and the branches of the trees are in bud. Winter is the season of men. When winter comes, green grasses lie down on the land and the branches of trees become bare. White snow covers the land.

The words "Spring is the season of women" evoke the Eleusinian mysteries which are a rite of spring, connected with the death and rebirth of wheat. In the Ainu story, a bad God (devil) of famine comes to a village. Wanting to cause a famine in the village, the devil asks a young man passing by to work with him. The man, named Okikurumi, is a cultural hero there. He tries to find a way somehow to hinder the devil's action. He asks the devil to drink *saké* but the devil is not tricked at all, saying, "Only good Gods like *saké*. How could bad Gods want to drink it!" At that moment, a sister of Okikurumi "unties the string of her cloth and exposes her breast. Then it becomes light in the east and dark in the west." Seeing this, the bad God changes his mind. He is subjugated as he is tricked by Okikurumi to drink poisonous *saké*.

After introducing this Ainu story, Matsumoto says that the deed of Okikurumi's sister "makes the devil of famine smile. A smile releases his tense will. The rage and ferocity of the devil vanish in the smile." It is not clear whether the devil smiled or not in the text, but it is certain that the exposure of the woman's body "releases his tense will." There is a liberation from tension, a kind of opening. The exposure of genitals has a common aim in Greek and Japanese myths—to break the silence of the great Goddesses—whereas in the Ainu legend it is done with the intention of releasing the tension of the devil.

Yoshida offers further parallels as in the following Oset epic. A Nalt hero named Pshi-Padinoko was born in a Nalt village but raised in a different place as his own mother had put him into a box and thrown him into the sea. He comes to know that a brave man named Soslan lives in a village of Nalt. Pshi-Padinoko visits the village as he wants to fight with Soslan. Soslan's "mother" (actually their relation is complicated, but I skip it), Satana, comes to know through her maid that the proud knight, Pshi-Padinoko, is coming to her village. She thinks that he will kill Soslan. She orders her maids to make him come into her house as they provide plenty of wine and meat as well as many beautiful women. Pshi-Padinoko says that he has no interest in such things and that "I am a free knight who wants to distinguish himself seeking the one Nalt who would become my friend and fight with me." Then Satana herself, making herself up, tries to seduce him. As she realizes that no words have any effect, she shows her white neck, taking the veil off her head, but in vain. Satana then "exposes her breasts before his eyes. Finally she exposes her private parts, untying the silk strings of her cloth."

Satana's exposure, however, has no effect: Pshi-Padinoko continues his ride to confront Soslan. The story ends with the friendship between the two heroes. Although Satana's deed resembles Ame-no-uzume's behavior, it is mainly a sexual seduction of the male hero who is intent only on male combat and friendship, and so Pshi-Padinoko ignores it.

A Celtic legend provides another parallel. Kufrain, a nephew of the King of Alster, Conbrobal, is a demigod hero. He defeats one after another the enemies of Alster and comes back to his capital city. The King Conbrobal thinks his capital is in danger as the hero's body is incandescent with the heat of wars. Then the king orders the queen Mugain and one hundred and fifty ladies to become naked and go out from the castle, exposing their bodies and private parts before Kufrain, who makes every effort to turn away his face in order not to see them. Taking advantage of this, the people immerse his heated body into three buckets of cold water, one after another, and succeed in cooling it. The king then has Kufrain come to his palace, and there he praises him.

In the Celtic legend, exposure of the private parts helps calm the incandescent hero. The reason the hero turns his face away is, we guess, the magical power of the exposure rather than his feeling of shame. We are not quite sure whether the exposure has the power to overwhelm the hero or to calm him.

An old legend in Ryukyu (Okinawa) shows the power of sexual organs directly. Once upon a time there is a man-eating Oni. The people are worrying about it. A sister of somebody shows her genitals. The Oni asks her for what purpose the mouth is used. She replies that the upper mouth eats rice cakes and the lower mouth eats Oni. In terror the Oni falls down from the cliff to die.

The Laughter of Oni

There are so many discussions of laughter that it is beyond my ability to take account of them all. Hobbes and many in accord with him consider the feeling of dominance to be the essence of laughing. The Oni's laughter makes us fearful rather than cheerful; Oni is a horrible being. For a typical example, a laughing Oni is shown in the painting *Jigoku-zōshi* (Book of

Hell), and he laughs while tormenting humans, thus displaying absolute dominance over them.

Oni's behavior is similar here with Tengu laughter (Tengu is a monster in Japan), which Kunio Yanagita discusses in "The Origin of the Literature of Laughter," where he writes:

> We hear sometimes in the dense forest in mountains suddenly a great laugh echoing throughout heaven and earth called "Tengu laughter." Then people are terrified more than if they heard, "I shall catch and eat you."

And he adds,

> The laughing is a mode of aggression. It is an active behavior (without using hands) toward other persons. We might think it a mode of pursuit as well. By laughing, one imposes further upon those who are weak and already in inferior positions. In other words, it is the privilege of one who is about to win.

Yanagita's insight reveals that both the anger and the accompanying fear, which is supposed to be the opposite of laughing, are unexpectedly connected with laughing.

How about the laughter in our fairy tale? In this story, the dominance of Oni over humans is almost absolute. The Oni captures human beings and even can "catch and eat." It swallows the water on which a boat is sailing and carrying human beings, trying to escape from Oni who nearly catches them. However, the Oni *must not* laugh, and this "imposes further upon those who are weak and already in inferior positions." (This is the most interesting part in the story.) Yet, the Oni laughs and laughs, rolling all over the place, and his dominance vanishes in a moment. The laughing reverses completely the superior and inferior positions. With these considerations, we understand that the laughter of Oni is not so simple. The laughter has different connotations from the laughter of Oni in *Jigoku-zōshi* or the devil's laughter in stories in the West.

You may have noticed, through comparison of the fairy tales with myths of Japan and Greece, that the laughter we are dealing with has to do with the laughter of Gods. The common element in all three stories is that one makes others laugh by exposing genitals. The one who laughs is different: the Oni, the Gods, or the great Goddess. Their ways of laughing differ also: Demeter's laugh seems a reluctant smile; Oni and Gods in Japanese stories laugh uproariously. The Oni's laughter, in particular, may be called earthy laughter.

Behind Demeter's laugh are rage and sorrow; she keeps silent and does not open her mouth. Then, in response to an unexpected deed by Baubo, the Goddess in spite of herself laughs. Here one can see the phenomenon of "opening," as if she is ending her mourning over the daughter's death. This is the dawn after the night and spring after winter. "The princess who does not laugh" who appears sometimes in fairy tales implies, perhaps, a woman whose "spring time" comes later. And a male who can "open" the bud of the flower is suitable to be her husband. For example, in Grimm's fairy tale "The Golden Goose," the *dummling* who makes the serious princess laugh marries her and becomes king.

The laughter of the Japanese Gods in front of the heavenly rock cave may have a meaning similar to Demeter's laughter. The main difference between the Greek and Japanese myths is the gender of the highest deity. Accordingly, one can talk about the rape by Poseidon or the laughing induced by Baubo *directly* as Demeter's behavior, but in the Japanese myth, insofar as we want to protect the Sun Goddess's highest dignity, it is hard to talk about these acts directly as the Goddess's. Therefore, a kind of alter-self like Waka-hiru-me is necessary for the construction of the myth. Those who laugh in front of the rock cave are the Gods. Their reply to the Goddess, who asks suspiciously why they laugh, is quite suggestive here: "We rejoice and dance because there is here a deity superior to you." Symbolically speaking, the Gods say that a God who laughs is "superior" to a God who does not. The fact that the great Goddess joins the Gods, leaving the rock cave, means that she becomes the Goddess who laughs. This contains the paradox that the highest Goddess who does not laugh comes nearer to the Gods (or the human beings if we go further) by laughing, and she becomes more "superior" than before because of her deed.

Hideo Takahashi's superb comment about "the laughter of the gods" is this: "Laughter draws gods nearer to human beings, and at the same time, it draws monsters also from the opposite direction.... the laughter humanizes other beings." Here the phenomenon of relativization occurs by laughter.

I have said previously that it is hard to find real parallels with "The Laughter of Oni." A legend which Yanagita introduces from an island in the South Pacific has some parts which resemble our story. According to it, in an ancient time a great frog devours all the water in the world and leaves not even a single drop. Many wise men try to make the frog laugh. Finally, still trying to squeeze his lips together, the frog bursts into laughter. Hence the water returns to the world, and the humans avoid suffering from a great drought.

Here, the intention to make the frog laugh is clear and the listener can understand it, while in "The Laughter of Oni" the exposure of genitals occurs quite suddenly as does the laughter. It would be difficult for the listener to guess such an ending. Even the women who expose their private parts would not have expected it. In the Naltic and Celtic myths, we saw that the exposure of genitals had the power of consoling or calming down the terrible beings or seducing them; and the women who exposed their genitals might have had such intentions. Yet, there occurs the outbreak of Oni laughter; hence the relativization takes place abruptly. Akiko Baba, in her *A Study of Oni*, makes a remarkable parallel between woman and Oni: "It is better that an Oni and a woman cannot be seen by others" (a quotation from "Mushi-mezuru-hime" [a princess who likes worms]). However, at the end of the fairy tale, the woman and the Oni reveal something which they should conceal. There is an absolute reversal of the value.

We have considered that one of the important functions of the Goddess Ame-no-uzume is "to open." The laughter we have dealt with so far is also concerned with "opening" in the wider sense of a religious meaning. While we generally recognize a certain limited space as the only world of existence, all of a sudden we are compelled to experience the existence of the other world. What brings us this opening is not only laughter but also rage, which Hideo Takahashi discusses in regard to the wrath of the Judaic God. He says that the wrath of that God does not occasion any relativization as does the laughter of Greek and Japanese Gods, and "the God exists always in a vertical relation to human beings." He points out that the God of Judea is the one and only one, whereas in Greece or Japan even the highest God is not the only one and has "horizontal" relations with other Gods. In Judea, the difference between God and human beings is *absolute*, while in our fairy tale "The Laughter of Oni" the earthy laughter of Oni causes absolute relativization in a horizontal direction. The wrath of God in Judea brings opening in a vertical direction, whereas the laughter of Gods (Oni) in Japan creates opening in a horizontal direction. This thought corresponds to the words of Japanese philosophers when they talk about Japanese culture and language as follows:

Miyakawa: "The absence of the ultimate being [in Japan] does not have to mean the absence of the absoluteness as Sakabe put it."

Sakabe: "Yes, I think there are various kinds of absoluteness, not vertical, something like horizontal...."

Yujiro Nakamura, agreeing with them, says that the absence of the idea of absolute being and the absence of science in Japan result from too limited a point of view. He adds, "There have been the absoluteness in various forms and scientific thinking in various forms." It is necessary for Japanese, he stresses, to endeavor to realize that "absoluteness in various forms."

Takahashi's indication that the highest God in Greece or Japan is not the supreme one is very important. In addition, I would like to stress the difference of the highest God's being male in Greece and female in Japan. Hence, in Greece, under the sovereignty of Zeus, the intrusion into the world of mother–daughter unity occurs to Demeter–Persephone; whereas in Japan, the disruption affects Amaterasu, the highest Goddess. Accordingly, the relativization goes further in Japan, and it tends to show in its extreme form in "The Laughter of Oni." The end of the fairy tale tells us that the women set up a stone pagoda every year. We are forced to recognize the strength of the absolute nothingness which relativizes everything. Analyzing the laughter of Japanese, Takeshi Umehara says, "The highest laughter in the Orient is—unlike the one which Jean Paul describes as the result of the contrast between limited reality and unlimited idea—the laughter which results from the comparison of every relative being with the absolute nothingness." This is, I think, in line with our thoughts.

In the variants of "Oni's Child, Kozuna," in order to make Oni laugh the women beat their buttocks with a spatula, show themselves naked, or let a fart. This might seem "vulgar," but only if we imagine that something spiritual has value while something to do with the body has none. The "opening" may occur through psyche or body: that which may come from above tends to be connected with the spirit, whereas the opening which may come from horizontal directions occurs through the body. The fact that one cannot find *elsewhere* the same type of fairy tales as "The Wife Who Lets a Fart," which may induce earthy laughter, may be based on the point discussed above.

FOUR
The Death of a Sister

Oni's intrusion into the world of the mother–daughter unity ends up, after all, with every being returning to his original place. Even though "The Laughter of Oni" gives us a positive feeling, we are compelled to realize the strength of the nothingness shown in chapter one. Or, as I have shown in "The Oni Bridegroom," the monster who intruded into the female world just dies instead of marrying her and transforming itself into a human being. Few Japanese fairy tales end in a happy marriage, as Lerich, a West German professor of folklore, has concluded after investigating some tales translated into German by Toshio Ozawa. These stories contrast with Western ones which relate the success of the proposal or the success of the accompanying adventures. Of Japanese stories he says, "The level of aspiration is different from that in German tales although a transformation occurs often in Japanese tales. The word or the concept of 'redemption' is never found in Ozawa's Japanese fairy tales."

Though I agree with his conclusion, what interests me most is that we can find in almost any case exceptions breaking the general rule. Investigating the exceptions carefully can clarify the meaning of the general rule. Hence I am going to take up a story which involves "marriage" and "redemption."

The Sister, the White Bird

What sort of impressions do you have after reading "White Bird Sister"? Since it tells about marriage and redemption —presumably rare in Japanese fairy tales—one might even feel that it may not be a Japanese tale. In fact, this story is found in Oki-no-erabu Island (a southern island) and has few parallels. On the other hand, the figure of the sister, who is so faithful and so sorrowful, does present a typical Japanese feeling. I have chosen this story because of her. The tale reminds us of the story of Anju and Zushi-wo, familiar to most Japanese.

We shall first just look through the story. The Lord of Sashu loses his wife after they have had a girl and a boy. As many scholars of various countries have pointed out, Japanese fairy tales are close to legends, hence lords, princes and princesses seldom appear in them. The beginning thus seems quite similar to stories in the West. Unlike the story of Cinderella, the children are a girl and a boy—which is rather rare in the case of Grimm's fairy tales. The lord gets a second wife as Cinderella's father does, but he has waited for ten years. As far as I know, it may be rare that ten years of waiting occurs in such stories about a stepmother and children. The Japanese story shows that the bond between the father and his children is strong.

It is a rather familiar pattern from "Cinderella" that the second wife comes with her own child whom she prefers to her stepchildren. At this point we might consider the meaning of stepmothers. Those in "Hänsel and Gretel" and "Little Snow-White" are the real mothers in the original stories. Even if a mother is not a stepmother, through her negative side she has the power to kill her child. Because of the general tendency to stress only the positive side as the essence of motherhood, the negative is driven to the unconscious. If we look at the mother's unconscious elements, it is not strange that she kills or gives up her own children. If we stand for the collective conscious attitude approved by society, a mother becomes completely positive and all her negative sides are imposed on the image of a stepmother. The stepmothers in fairy tales show, therefore, far worse traits than stepmothers in reality.

Looking through the stories which are classified as "Stories of Stepchildren" in CJFT, one notices immediately that all except one are about stepmothers and daughters. The exception, "Ash Boy," is itself a very interesting story. However, Seki (the collection's editor) suggests that it might be classified under another category. So I will skip "Ash Boy" as an exception and think about why the stepmother–daughter relation is important in Japanese fairy tales. "Stepmother" here denotes the negative side of motherhood, and the character is not necessarily an actual stepmother. If we look at the relation from the daughter's angle, we see that she is conscious of her mother's negative side.

Given her awareness, the relation of stepmother–daughter shows symbolically that the mother–daughter unity is no longer as tight as before. When a human being wants to be independent and break identification with others, he must become conscious of their faults. This is seen in many girls who in puberty begin to be too critical of or to underestimate—or even hate —their mothers. They go so far as doubting whether their mothers are their real ones. Only by passing through this period can a girl become independent from her mother. This may explain why the heroines, the stepdaughters, succeed in marrying happily in many fairy tales.

Our story goes a bit differently from this pattern. A more typical one in Japanese fairy tales is "The Handless Maiden." Although stories in which the *male* hero marries after accomplishing some task (like a dragon fight) are quite rare in Japan, there are many tales in which *heroines* marry after overcoming their stepmothers' persecutions. We shall discuss this further in chapter seven. Here I content myself only with pointing out the importance and meaning of the relation between stepmothers and daughters in fairy tales.

The typical relationship occurs in "Cinderella." Our story tells, unlike "Cinderella," nothing about the heroine's trials before her engagement, and her fiancé is easily found. In other Japanese stories about stepmothers and daughters, however, all sorts of persecutions by stepmothers take place. Additionally, everything goes smoothly before the engagement is settled in our story, because it focuses elsewhere. Although marriage occurs, the important relationship is not the conjugal union but that between sister and brother. The end of the story, for instance, says the siblings each marry other persons, and "sister and brother, helping each other even now, continue to lead happy lives." The ending is the same as that of "The Elder Sister and the Younger Brother," which will be related in a later section of this chapter. The most important goal is that the siblings live happily and cooperatively; in the course of reaching this goal, their marriages also take place.

Let us pick up the story at the point where the stepmother kills her daughter by throwing her into boiling water in a big pot. In other variants, she is killed by being thrown into some big container such as a big iron pot or bath. This may symbolize returning to the mother's womb. Generally, in initiation ceremonies for reaching female adulthood, such a symbolic return is important. When a daughter becomes a wife, she must experience death inwardly.

The sister Chu dies, and the stepmother succeeds in having her own daughter, Kana, marry. This is the stepmother's own plot. On the other hand, we can look at it symbolically as follows: a daughter can become independent and marry when she becomes aware of the negative sides of motherhood. When she marries, however, she is not always protected by her husband initially and has to be sheltered, for the time being, by the positive sides of motherhood which she also accepts. Her body is in her new house, but her soul is protected still by the blood tie. The story shows this when Kana, instead of Chu, marries. She is accompanied by Kaniharu who symbolizes the familial bond. When the time comes for her to be convinced of her husband's love, she can separate from the world of the mother-daughter unity so definitely that she will be united with him. This process is reflected in the change of Chu–Kana–Chu from the engagement through the death and rebirth of Chu to the last happy marriage.

The brother's accompanying his sister when a bride is quite unusual, even though it is psychologically understandable. The sister Chu's devotion to her brother emphasizes the unity of sister and brother. If we look at the developmental stages in the depths of the human psyche, the stage of mother–daughter incest is followed by that of sibling incest: witness the strong bond between Chu and Kaniharu. We shall consider the important theme of sibling incest in the next section. Here we would like to pay attention to Kaniharu's extreme passivity. In "The Elder Sister and the Younger Brother," the boy takes a more passive role than in stories about older brothers and younger sisters. More than Westerners, Japanese prefer the stories of older sisters and younger brothers to those with the relationships reversed. In our story, Kaniharu obeys his stepmother's order to stay with his stepsister as a servant. When his sister is killed, he is not able to fight against it nor to tell anybody about it. Obeying others always, he cannot tell the truth until the lord speaks to him gently. If we reflect further, however, we can say that his sister Chu can deepen her relation to her husband, the lord, only through this passive man.

After the lord learns the truth, there occurs the redemption which is said to be rare in Japanese fairy tales. One might have worried that the ending would be in the Japanese mode, knowing that "all that remained of her in his hand were three little flies" when he touched his wife in spite of the prohibition. In "The Elder Sister and the Younger Brother" and its variants, introduced later in this chapter, the sister's marriage is seldom mentioned. We can infer that the story of her marriage was added at a later time or the death and rebirth motif in "The

Elder Sister and the Younger Brother" "contaminated" the sister's story in our "White Bird Sister." We are still not quite sure about this.

Ending happily, the story develops against the power of nothingness. The bird's redemptive bathing in the water corresponds to Chu's earlier involuntary immersion in hot water. Since immersion is characteristic of many initiation ceremonies, immersion here in hot water and cold may symbolize the agony and the joy in the process of death and rebirth. The contrast between heat and cold reminds us of the fire and water often used in initiation ceremonies as the means of trial and purification. In the variants of "White Bird Sister," the sister who has transformed herself into a white bird asks the lord to prepare the water in a basin and the fire in a furnace. "As he prepares what she has requested, the white bird comes flying and enters into the fire and then into the water; then it changes to the wife." The reborn beautiful lady marries the lord. The evil wife is killed and her mother dies too.

Fully separated from the mother–daughter bond, Chu is happily joined with the man by her brother's help. Nevertheless, we think the story focuses on the unity of sister and brother, as the ending stresses their good relation.

Sisters and Brothers

In primitive ages, the father–child relation was not understood as a blood bond. For that reason, the mother–daughter unity is the primordial blood relation. The bond between siblings of the opposite sex comes as the next stage. As a counterpart to the bond by blood is marriage as a union by sex. We noted in chapter one that the process of ego development in the West may be summarized as the process to establish the relation between the sexes separated from the mother–child unity. Namely, the bond by blood is to be transferred to a bond by sex or, better said, a bond by contract. At this point, the sibling relation exists as a transitional situation. Having both the relation

by blood and by sex, a marriage between siblings can be interpreted as either a transitional stage or possibly as an extremely
high stage. An example of the latter are the marriages in ancient
Egypt of kings and queens who had to be siblings.

This may explain the frequent occurrence of sibling marriages in the world's mythologies. Sibling marriage occurs as a
sacred marriage, being suitable to the myths of the beginning of
the world, or it takes place as the transitional stage from the
culture of mother–daughter unity to the paternal culture. In
Japanese mythology, Izanagi and Izanami—who gave birth to
the land of Japan—are both a couple and siblings. Amaterasu,
the Sun Goddess, and Susa-no-wo, whom we discussed in the last
chapter, are siblings. Although their marriage is not expressed
distinctly in the myth, symbolically speaking one of their
children becomes the ancestor of the imperial family. Here,
Izanagi and Izanami's sibling marriage occurs in the beginning
of the world, whereas the sibling relation between Amaterasu
and Susa-no-wo is the next stage after the mother–daughter
unity. Poseidon and Demeter are siblings. His raping her has
the same meaning as Susa-no-wo's disruptive relation to
Amaterasu.

Many stories told in the *Kojiki* and the *Nihonshoki* concerning
the events after the age of the Gods show how important was the
relation between sisters and brothers. It has been a controver-
sial problem for historians whether the marriages and incests
between siblings were factual or not in the early history of
Japan. A sibling marriage as a *psychological* reality may have been
the general situation at that time. The *Kojiki* and *Nihonshoki*
often mix inner and outer reality. Therefore, it may be difficult
to find evidence acceptable to a historian of the existence or
non-existence of sibling marriage or incest. Since I am concerned with sibling marriage and incest in the psychological
dimension, I will just ignore the problem in outer reality.

Many activities of sisters related in the *Kojiki* and the *Nihonshoki* remind me of Yanagita's famous *The Power of Women*. He
makes it clear how women play a large role in their families,
pointing out the importance of Onari Gods in Okinawa and a

pair of Gods who are brother and sister in Ainu myths. He says, "Originally [in Japan], women controlled the religious acts concerning ceremonies and prayers. The shamans were women in this country as a rule." He states that sisters (or women in general) have been recognized as having spiritual powers in Japan from ancient times. Sisters have been the guardian Gods for their brothers, as shown in Onari Gods. Although Yanagita is concerned exclusively with Japanese culture, he points out that the sister's role may be found in cultures all over the world as is evident in their fairy tales.

Sisters rescuing their brothers—this is also considered a type of fairy tale. One of them, classified as AT 451 by Aarne and Thompson, is titled "The Maiden Who Seeks the Brother." The story is concerned with sisters who try to find their brothers who have disappeared. "The Twelve Brothers" (KHM 9), "The Seven Ravens" (KHM 25), and "The Six Swans" (KHM 49) from Grimm's are three others like this. In each story, by dissolving a magic spell the sister rescues her brothers who have been transformed into ravens or swans. The interesting point here is that the sister's birth directly or indirectly causes her brothers' transformations. In "The Twelve Brothers," when the queen conceives her thirteenth child, the king provides twelve coffins for the twelve brothers so that in case a girl is born she can inherit a fortune. Although the sister will rescue her brothers, her birth itself has threatened their lives without her knowing it. The story shows that the spiritual power of sisters can work either positively or negatively.

We can find the same point in Japanese fairy tales. In "The Oni and the Betting" (CJFT 248), for example, the elder sister helps her brother bet against the Oni. He finally wins through the aid of his sister's wisdom. "The Seven Swans" (CJFT 214) is a story about a younger sister who rescues her brothers transformed into swans. The story completely resembles Grimm's "The Six Swans." Its variants are found only in two places: Kikai Island and Oki-no-erabu Island in southern Japan. We must await further investigation to know whether the story was transmitted to Japan rather recently. Unlike these liberators, a sister can appear as a terrible being as we see in "The Sister Is an Oni" (CJFT 249). In this story, the sister-Oni devours her parents but is finally overcome by her elder brother. Yanagita, who introduces this story in *The Power of Women*, concludes, "The position of sisters has been especially important throughout [Japanese] history."

If sisters have such power and the bonds between sisters and brothers are too strong, the development of the psyche is fixed at that stage, as we have seen in the case of the mother–daughter unity. A woman for the brother and a man for the sister must appear, more alluring than their siblings, to break their strong tie. When persons with enough attraction to break the sibling alliance appear, the relation will move to the next stage. According to the mode of speech in fairy tales, the appealing woman is described as the one who has some magical powers.

In his "The Psychology of the Transference," Jung introduced typical fairy tales in which sibling relations moved into opposite-sex relations. Although he presented two fairy tales, one from Iceland and one from Russia, since they are almost the same type I shall summarize only the Russian tale. At first I quote from Jung:

> Another example is the Russian fairytale "Prince Danila Govorila." There is a young prince who is given a lucky ring by a witch. But its magic will work only on one condition: he must marry none but the girl whose finger the ring fits. When he grows up he goes in search of a bride, but all in vain, because the ring fits none of them. So he laments his fate to his sister, who asks to try on the ring. It fits perfectly. Thereupon her brother wants to marry her, but she thinks it would be a sin and sits at the door of the house weeping.[1]

When she is weeping, some old beggars come and give advice through which some magical powers work. After the wedding ceremony, the earth opens and swallows her up. She falls into the hut of Baba Yaga but returns to her brother prince with the witch's daughter who has helped her escape. As the magic ring also fits the daughter's finger, the prince marries her and gives his sister a suitable husband.

Jung presents the structure of the story in a diagram like figure 4.[2] The Icelandic fairy tale has the same structure: the siblings' incestuous relation yields to the appearance of another woman with magical power. The brother marries her, while his sister marries another man—a happy ending with two pairs of marriages. When we apply this diagram to "White Bird Sister," we get the interesting result shown in figure 5. The two stories have quite similar patterns: the sibling relation at the beginning, two pairs of marriages at the end. In the Russian story, the plot develops around the prince as the central figure, whereas the Japanese story centers on the sibling relation. The incestuous relation, clearly told in the Russian tale, remains latent in the Japanese.

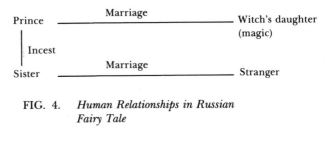

FIG. 4. *Human Relationships in Russian Fairy Tale*

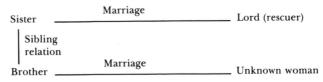

FIG. 5. *Human Relationships in "White Bird Sister"*

Here the contrast between the two tales becomes very interesting. In the Russian story the incestuous relation is explicit, but its resolution is also clearly presented in the course of the story's development. The sibling relation in the Japanese story is carried through until the end but only vaguely suggested. The former presents the magic power of the woman who dissolves the sibling tie; the latter doesn't make this power explicit. The sibling relation is disrupted by a lord, a man of high rank, but it is the sister who seems to have magic power. As the incestuous tie dissolves, the Russian girl plays a passive role as a younger sister; while in the Japanese story, the woman plays a central role as the elder sister. This reminds me that, in the Japanese pantheon, the female, Amaterasu, is the highest deity.

If we look at "White Bird Sister" in the light of the Western diagram, the development from mother–daughter unity to brother–sister unity to union of man and woman is a suitable description—but not completely. One of the reasons is that in Japanese stories elder sisters figure prominently, whereas in stories of the West younger sisters appear more often. We shall now consider in more detail the role of the elder sisters in Japanese stories.

The Elder Sister and the Younger Brother

In *The Power of Women,* Yanagita shows the importance of Japanese women in their families. As we discussed in chapter one, the process of ego establishment in the West requires a strong rejection of the blood bond, symbolized by killing the mother, followed by the bond between opposite sexes. There, also, the role of women becomes important, carrying the leadership in the spiritual world. Women's roles differ in East and West, depending upon whether they act as mothers or as the opposite sex. Here the sisters play an intermediate role. Yet, elder sisters are nearer to being mothers, whereas younger ones approach being sexual companions. Although younger sisters occasionally appear in Japanese fairy tales, the elder ones seem to act more frequently—probably because the power of motherhood is strong in Japan.

Since we have been looking at these stories from a Western developmental point of view, we now need to look for something characteristic of Japanese fairy tales. To do so, we shall go into "The Elder Sister and the Younger Brother" (CJFT 180), which has much to do with "White Bird Sister."

The story, found in Oki-no-erabu Island, may be summarized as follows. When the brother Ijo is three years old, the mother dies and after three more years the father dies too. Hito-musume, the sister, raises Ijo without relying on their relatives. She sends him to a school (*Terakoya*). As Ijo gets the highest grade, his classmates become jealous. They challenge him to a fan contest; everybody is to bring a fan and participate. Hitomusume, going out to buy a fan for her brother, meets an old man with white hair who gives her a splendid fan. The brother wins the contest. His classmates challenge him con-tinuously: a ship contest, a bow contest. Each time his sister gets help from the old man; thus, the brother always wins.

The classmates finally decide to have a party with Ijo. The deceased parents tell the sister in her dream that the classmates will try to put poison in the party food. She advises Ijo not to eat anything at the party and to escape by riding on a horse. Although Ijo declines to eat, his classmates force him by stuffing food into his mouth. On the way home Ijo dies on his horse. Only his corpse arrives. The sister places Ijo's body in the wooden *saké* bucket in order to preserve it. And she, disguised as Ijo, sings. Thinking that the food was not poisoned after all, every classmate dies after eating it. Then Hitomusume, dis-guised as a man, journeys to the castle of Hana-no-mōshin. When she/he is asked to become a bridegroom in the castle, she agrees on the condition that she can get "the flower of life" there. Returning home with the flower, she restores Ijo to life and arranges to have him become the bridegroom. In this way Ijo becomes a rich man. Later, "when the sister becomes poor, things are brought to her from the castle of Hana-no-mōshin. When the castle of Hana-no-mōshin becomes poor, the sister takes some things there; thus, they have lived richly even until now."

In this story the elder sister plays a big role like that in "White Bird Sister." Her actions aim at her brother's happiness rather than her own. We felt this already in "White Bird Sister," but this tendency is more pronounced here. The sister raises her brother, assuming the role of guardian after their parents die. She sends him to school. Relying on the old man's help, she always enables her brother to win the contests to which his classmates challenge him. The figure of the old man who appears here is important (discussion of him will be found in chapter eight). Through her dream she realizes her brother's life is in danger, but she cannot prevent his death. It may be necessary for the sister to experience separation once in order to break the sister–brother unity. In "White Bird Sister," the sister and brother are separated by her death and reunited only by her rebirth. In this story, separation begins with the death and ends with the rebirth of the brother. In both stories, the sister does everything, while the brother is always passive.

It is notable that the sister disguises herself as a man when her brother dies. With her disguise, she kills three birds with one stone: she retaliates against her brother's classmates, she gets the flower of life for her brother, and she finds a proper place where her brother can become a bridegroom. Does her disguise as a man becoming a bridegroom also show a homosexual tendency? In the developmental process of a man in the West in which the stage of mother–child unity changes into that of getting a woman for marriage, there is the intermediate stage of the sibling marriage. Jung pointed out that the stage of homosexuality follows that. The person who separates from the blood tie wants a bond with the same sex before attaining union with the opposite sex.

The sister who maintains her sibling relation after losing her parents goes a step further toward the homosexual stage. Since the parents have died, this story focuses on the situation after the stage of mother–child unity. Accordingly, this is not a story about persecution by a stepmother as in "White Bird Sister." Note that the group of male classmates breaks the sister–brother bond by poisoning the brother. Not nearly as terrible as Hades who intrudes from the underworld, they are ordinary boys, living in this world. They act as a group, namely, as a non-personal, non-individualistic being, and do not accept Ijo's peculiarity: being the top of the class. The group, in which peer pressure pushes expressions of individuality back into the norm, has a uroboric character. Like the mother–daughter unity, the sister–brother tie, too, needs some uroboric male entity to disrupt it. If the persons who are attached are weak, there occurs the danger of death. If they are strong, they can go a step further, experiencing symbolic death and rebirth. All this is the same as in the case of mother–daughter unity.

The sister's disguise as a boy has a connection with the initiation ceremony of adulthood for women in which a novice, in her isolation period, is regarded temporarily as a not-male, not-female being, i.e., as androgynous and asexual. During this period, the sister succeeds in arranging her brother's marriage. The story does not, however, mention her own marriage, stressing instead the strong tie between sister and brother at the end. "White Bird Sister" focuses on the sister–brother relation even though the sister marries. This tendency is clearly seen in "The Elder Sister and the Younger Brother" as well. In order to discuss the union between man and woman, we will rely on the other stories reviewed in later chapters.

We can look at the story from a different standpoint. The sister maneuvers a great deal for her brother's marriage, even disguising herself and tricking others. Yet she herself does not marry. Her role resembles that of John in "Faithful John." In chapter one, focusing on the behavior of the prince, we did not note that John plays a typical trickster role in the story. He is a simple prankster, but he is also close to being the savior in his highest form. The sister, like Faithful John, is both tricksterish and savior-like. She reminds me of the God Onari (who is the sister of the family chief and becomes the family's guardian deity). A trickster usually is a male figure, though he is androgynous or asexual. The sister is especially interesting if we look at her as a female trickster. Probably a trickster who is almost a savior is female in Japan because the Goddess is the supreme deity.

In "The Elder Sister and the Younger Brother," the sister as a trickster brings some cheer. Here, if the figure of the sister changes into what is nearly a self-sacrificing mother image, and if the story is pulled toward outer reality where death and re-birth do not occur so easily, the story becomes a sentimental/ tragic one—which Japanese are certainly fond of. A typical story of this kind is "Sanshō-daiu," in which the sister, Anju, and the brother, Zushi-wo, are the protagonists. "Sanshō-daiu" is one of the stories which were generated at the end of the medi-eval age in Japan. Buddhist priests told the stories when they preached, for the narratives presented religious ideas in an at-tractive form. Compared with fairy tales which contain much unconscious material, the stories reflect a lot from the con-scious states of the people at that time, although we cannot deny that these stories have some connection with the unconscious. Many Japanese have come to know "Sanshō-daiu" through its recreation in a modernized form by the famous novelist Ogai Mori. The following summarizes its older version.

The father of Anju and Zushi-wo is the chief of a big rural clan. When the children are still very young, their father is sent to a far island because of a false accusation. Their mother travels with her children to Kyoto, the capital at that time, to bring a suit. On the way, they are captured by a group of ban-dits. Anju and Zushi-wo are sold to Sanshō-daiu who is also the head of a clan in a different district. Sanshō-daiu and his son Saburo treat them very badly and torment them. Finally they try to run away. Zushi-wo succeeds in a narrow escape, while Anju sacrifices her life in helping him flee. After that, Zushi-wo secures a high position in Kyoto. When he makes the long trip to the far island, he is delighted to find his mother, though she is completely blind and engaged in a job to drive away sparrows coming to eat kernels of grain. Meanwhile, Zushi-wo very bit-terly takes his revenge on Sanshō-daiu.

In this story, Sanshō-daiu fully reveals the negative side of the uroboric father. In Japan one can hardly find a father figure behind whom a unique male God stands, though there are many uroboric father figures in outer reality as well as in stories. The feeling of fatherhood is carried by the qualities of strength and fearfulness. Yet we feel a mixture of the maternal element in it insofar as it is wet and cold rather than dry and hot. The father is a tremendously fearful being who leads many persons into death. If we compare this story with "Hänsel and Gretel" (KHM 151), the difference between the West and Japan becomes distinct through the ways in which the elder sister and younger brother cope with a terrible being. The Western version tells of the siblings' fight against the witch who tries to devour them. In the Japanese story, however, the sister and brother escape from the uroboric father who has persecuted them, scaring them to death. In "Hänsel and Gretel," the children kill the witch. In "Sanshō-daiu" we find the brother's escape and his revenge on the terrible chief, along with the sacrifice of his sister's life.

After Zushi-wo attains his high position, the story focuses on his meeting his mother (Japanese people are deeply touched by the sentimental descriptions of their reunion) and his revenge: he orders Sanshō-daiu's son to saw his father's neck slowly, over three days, with a saw made of bamboo. Ogai Mori cut this scene in his Sanshō-daiu as he perhaps felt it was too cruel. For the medieval age, however, one of the key aspects of the story was revealed here as "the expression of the closed, nowhere-to-go emotion of the people," as Takeo Iwasaki once put it. The punishment given to Sanshō-daiu must not be done cleanly and swiftly, but rather in the uroboric, slow manner. The resentment which executes the deed is very deep. Here is the vitality, though negative, of the Japanese people of that time.

The story is supported by two main poles: the sorrowful feeling caused by Anju's death and the resentment which Zushi-wo sustains for so long, both discussed in chapter one. There I mentioned that the feeling of resentment in fairy tales might be construed as showing the feelings of the Japanese common people. "Sanshō-daiu" shows this resentment vividly. Its expressions are exaggerated in order to win the people's applause, but going so far that Ogai Mori's aesthetic sense cannot tolerate them. Taking all of "Sanshō-daiu" into account, let us think about "White Bird Sister" and "The Elder Sister and the Younger Brother" again. These two stories contain something which is deeper than the consciousness of the medieval age as shown in "Sanshō-daiu."

In "Sanshō-daiu," Anju is tortured and killed by fire and water. In "White Bird Sister," the sister is restored in the initiation ceremony or the mystery of rebirth by fire and water. When the brother who dies by the uroboric male group's trick in "The Elder Sister and the Younger Brother" is reborn by his sister's help, he gets up as if nothing has happened, saying, "I slept in the morning or in the evening. How strange!" His sister explains, "You did not sleep in the morning or evening. You were killed by the poison!" This humorous scene evokes our smiles. The smile is, I think, connected to the earthy laughter in the last chapter. Underneath the story telling of fearful persecution or death, subliminally there exists laughter, which takes a cheerful view of life. This strong affirmative feeling for life does exist in the depths underneath the vitality of resentment shared by common people. The figure of the sister who prays only for her brother's happiness and dies as its victim is especially fitted to Japanese culture where the maternal principle prevails.

We must always, however, pay attention to the female figures in fairy tales whose activity surpasses the tragic sister figure. They really show the vitality within the depth of the Japanese psyche, though they still remain at the stage of sister–brother unity. These refreshing women who are far beyond the Japanese sentimental feeling of resentment will be associated with the figure of "The Woman of Will" which I shall present in the ninth chapter.

FIVE
Two Feminine Figures

The portrait of a self-sacrificing elder sister given in "White Bird Sister" presents a truly Japanese image. Although her marriage was mentioned, our focus on its psychological structure reveals that the story is talking about a stage of sister–brother union. Only after this stage do we proceed to a fully masculine–feminine marriage. I have pointed out repeatedly that a surprisingly small number of Japanese fairy tales end with "happily ever after" marriage. For instance, in our well-known story "Urashima Tarō," although the hero encounters the beautiful Otohime, he returns home without marrying her.

We must investigate the feminine figure appearing in Japanese fairy tales and its relation to marriage or, in other words, the feminine figure in the Japanese psyche in terms of marriage. Practically speaking, the Urashima story (whose many variations I will discuss later) is quite appropriate for this purpose. Some variants which are not commonly known have the marriage theme of Otohime or Kamehime (turtle princess) and Urashima. By cross-examining images from several variants of women who marry and who do not marry, I think we might get closer to our question.

Urashima Tarō

Hardly anyone born in Japan does not know this story. The hero, Urashima Tarō, goes to the Dragon Palace under the sea escorted by the turtle which he has rescued.[1] There he is welcomed by the beautiful Otohime. But he eventually gets homesick and goes home. As he returns to his village, those three years in the Dragon Palace turn out to have been three hundred years in our world. So, finding himself lonely and troubled, Urashima opens the jeweled casket which Otohime has given him with the stipulation that he never open it. Immediately he becomes an old man. This is a commonly known version of Urashima today.

Its original form, however, was recorded as a legend in the Nara period in *Tango no Kuni Fudoki*, a volume of the *Nihonshoki*. In the ninth volume of the *Man'yōshū* (760 A.D.) is a poem by Mushimaro Takahashi referring to the legend about "a man of Urashima at Mizu-no-e." With the passing of time, the story gradually changed to the present story pattern (form), but with numbers of variations. A great deal of research has been done, too, because this may be Japan's favorite story. Indeed, writers of the current generation have produced a number of literary works using Urashima as material.

I would like now briefly to introduce some versions which I've come across, since giving a bird's-eye view of all the works is impossible. Chronologically, the two documents I introduced above were formulated in the Nara period (710–784 A.D.). Then, another three documents followed in the Heian period (794–1200 A.D.): *Urashima ko den; Urashima ko den*, second series; and *Mizukagami*. In the Kamakura period (1200–1392 A.D.) came

Mumei sho, Koji-dan and *Uji Shūi Monogatari,* and in the Muromachi period (1392–1573 A.D.) "Urashima Taro" in *Otogi zōshi* and "Urashima" in the Nō drama lyrics, etc. The prototype of the present Urashima Tarō is believed to be from the *Otogi zōshi* (Book of Fairy Tales). From the Edo period (1600–1867 A.D.) come many works, including the plays "Urashima Ichidaiki," "Urashima Shu Shussei Ki" and especially "Urashima Nendai Ki" by Monzaemon Chikamatsu. As I will discuss later, I believe the material for these was based on the Urashima legend.

Something about the story of Urashima Tarō must indeed appeal to the Japanese psyche. In current modern literature, many works deal with the Urashima legend: *Shin Urashima* by Rohan Koda, the poem "Urashima" by Tōson Shimazaki and *Tamakushige Futari Urashima* by Ogai Mori are prime examples. Fujimoto has comprehensively discussed the above works and others in his *Urashima Legend and Modern Literature.* I will examine a few of the impressive ones. Related to the Urashima story are extensive studies in the fields of ethnology, anthropology, and Japanese literature. Changes in the story down through time are described in great detail in *Urashima Setsuwa no Kenkyu* (Studies of the Urashima Legend) by Tamotsu Sakaguchi and in *Kodai Shakai to Urashima Densetsu* (Ancient Society and the Urashima Legend) by Yu Mizuno.

Sakaguchi's discussion of the historical transformation of the legend—including current works—closely parallels my own idea on the subject. Mizuno's theory, briefly, is that the story reflects important cultural characteristics from each era. In the Nara period it still retains elements of an ancient legend which described a divine marriage. Then, in the Heian period, it emphasized Taoist ideas of longevity and immortality, while in the Muromachi period the story inclined toward the theme of repayment of kindness, colored by the values of common people.

Among the studies of myths and legends is the long influential work by Toshio Takagi called *Urashima Densetsu no Kenkyu* (Study of the Urashima Legend). He researched parallel stories in East and West, comparing them with the main motif in

Urashima. Ideishi, in his investigation of Chinese myths and legends, has studied Urashima's Chinese parallels. He paid special attention to the motif of the sequence of supernatural time and discussed its significance. Following such pioneering work in this field, Keigo Seki's catalogue to his CJFT contains numerous Urashima stories gathered throughout Japan. Kunio Yanagita seemed to think that because the Urashima story has "too simple a plot with a poor ending, it has no universality as a fairy tale except on the point of 'swift passage of time.'" Due as well perhaps to already existing studies such as those mentioned, he wrote no essays dealing exclusively with Urashima, although he did touch upon the story in various publications. (His *Kai zin gū kō*, for example, is well-known.) Sekiyo Shimode discussed the world of Urashima as a facet of the development of Taoist ideas in Japan and investigated thoroughly an image of a certain *sennyo* (Taoist fairy) which suggests quite obvious similarities to images of Otohime in "Urashima Tarō," of *tennyo* (heavenly maiden) in the Hagoromo (feather cloak) legend, and of Kaguya-hime in *Taketori Monogatari*. Nakata has done a similar study in *Urashima and Hagoromo*. There is also an unusual work by Mitsutomo Doi comparing Urashima and the Scottish folk song "Thomas the Rhymer." Lastly, I would like to mention Hisako Kimishima who presents material which might be of considerable importance for our future comparative research in Chinese and Japanese cultures. In her commentary on her modern Chinese folklore collection, she pointed out a story remarkably similar to "Urashima Tarō" called "The Dragon Princess Legend of Tung Ting Lake."

The particular version of "Urashima Tarō" given in the Appendix was collected in Kagawa Prefecture (of course, many similar versions are presented in CJFT). The main theme is that a young hero goes to the Dragon Palace in the other world and is welcomed by the princess, Otohime; but since the passage of time at the Dragon Palace greatly differs from that in this world, Urashima is shocked upon returning home. In his consternation, he opens the jeweled casket which makes him an old man and brings on his death. The only story which clearly mentions

Otohime's marriage was collected in Gushikawa City, Okinawa. That version states that "I returned home with two boxes given by my wife of the Dragon Palace." In another similar story recorded in Saga Prefecture is the phrase "asked to be Otohime's husband but returned home." Generally, the reason Urashima goes to the Dragon Palace in the first place is as a reciprocation of his kindness in rescuing a turtle.

Among these stories is one in which the turtle and Otohime are identical. I think this is worth paying attention to. Once in a hundred years, Otohime transforms herself into a turtle and pays a visit to Sumiyoshi Shrine to pray. While there this time, she is caught by children but then rescued by Urashima Tarō. I will refer to these stories in my later discussion of the Turtle Princess (Kamehime) legends. Now we will proceed to investigate the noteworthy version given in the Appendix.

Mother and Son

As our story indicates at its beginning, Urashima Tarō comes from a family composed of a single mother and an only child. The mother is eighty years old, the son in his fortieth year. Remarkably, he feels "while mother is still around" there is no compulsion to marry. Other versions hardly mention the mother–son relationship. This seems to bring up a most appropriate image in terms of considering his masculine identity which I will discuss shortly. First, let us think about this mother–son relationship.

Eiichiro Ishida has already fully discussed the significance of the mother and son constellation in fairy tales. In his book on Momotaro's mother he pointed out the appearances of "a mother-like feminine figure" in the background of a little boy who often enters upon the stage of our folklore tradition. Also, he points out that such a mother–child union is recognized widely in world mythologies: Isis and Horus in Egypt, Ashtoreth and Tammuz of Phoenicia, Cybele and Attis of Asia Minor, and Rhea and the divine child Zeus of Crete are given as examples of the pairing of the Great Mother Goddess with her son God. Such widespread myths of mother-child would, undoubtedly, be considered by Freud to reflect the Oedipus complex. In fact, frequently in these myths the Great Mother Goddess causes her own child God to become her subordinate husband by whom she procreates all living beings—obviously a mother-son incest motif. Freud's theory of the Oedipus complex, a psychology based on a patriarchal principle, evolved on the father-son axis. But Freud tried to understand father-son conflict, mother-son incestuous union, etc., only on the strictly personal dimension. Jung, while not denying Freud's idea, went beyond the personal dimension to discover a more collective psychic phenomenon.

Instead of reducing to personal family relationships these myths which indicate a mother-son relation, Jung broadened them. For him they represented especially the relationship between the ego and the unconscious. Following Jung, Neumann enunciated the theory of ego development mentioned in chapter one. Since his theory is patriarchal, it is not suitable for the study of Japanese consciousness and I have not incorporated it into my overall discussion. But in this section I will look at the image of Urashima Tarō with his theory in mind. Seeing it from a different standpoint may help clarify the Japanese psyche.

The unity of single mother and only son at the beginning of the Urashima story probably indicates that the son has not separated from the mother—psychologically, the ego has not established independence from the unconscious. Since a father figure does not enter the scene, our hero lacks a model for establishing masculine identity and understandably remains single at forty. A description in one of the oldest documents, *Tango no Kuni Fudoki* (written in the Nara period), reads "a man of beautiful appearance, his elegance beyond any comparison." This gives us a handsome male figure with a somewhat fragile quality, not at all with masculine strength. The *Mizukagami* of the Heian period describes his return as he opens the jeweled casket: "his youthful figure changed in an instant to an old man." The later *Koji-dan* even uses the expression "like a young child" here. Both describe Urashima as a youth. This might be the result of the Taoist conception which has Urashima visiting Peng Lai Shan (see Turtle Princess section below), gradually becoming young again. In any case, it is remarkable to find the image of a young boy here.

Here the image of the young boy reminds us of Jung's archetype of the puer aeternus. I understand that the words *puer aeternus* come from Ovid who speaks of the child God Iacchos playing a very important role in the Eleusinian mysteries as a leader of the procession of initiates. Also, he is said to be Persephone's son or sometimes Demeter's. Literally an eternal youth, a God of constant rejuvenation who does not reach adulthood, he is also a God of cereal and rebirth, as in the Eleusinian mysteries. With the power of the Great Mother behind him, he maintains eternal youth through repeated death and rebirth.

The eternal youth archetype, as described in myth, exists in each of our psyches. According to descriptions by Jungian analysts, persons living in modern society who identify with eternal youth are not necessarily chronologically young. A puer aeternus type experiences difficulty in adapting to society. He tends to think it would be a great loss to bend his special talent, justifying himself by saying that it's not necessary to adjust to society or that society is wrong not to give him a perfectly fitting place. Always keeping himself in a state of "not yet" in space and time, he can't find the real thing and so forth. But suddenly one day we see this youth attempting an abrupt ascent, trying to exhibit his great art work or set himself up to save the whole world. His flash of sharpness and forceful strength at the moment might elicit the wonder and admiration of many people, but unfortunately he lacks durability and tenacity, a characteristic weakness of this type. Since he does not fear danger at such a time, he is often thought to be a brave man. Actually, working behind his bravery is the wish to return to the Great Mother's womb, and sometimes he meets his death in accord with this wish.

If he is smart enough, he may avoid death, but the subsequent sudden descent leads to an aimless life for a while. Then one day, suddenly, he will make a move toward ascent in a totally new form. He exhibits dazzling activities, chasing after the interest of the moment—today Marx, tomorrow Freud—but without consistency (figure 6).

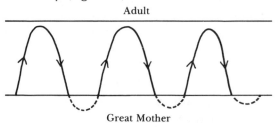

FIG. 6.   *Pattern of Eternal Youth*

This eternal youth is bound with a strong psychological tie to the mother. This "mother," however, does not necessarily have to be his personal mother, but rather "motherness." This compelling connection to this being who is "mother"—i.e., a mother complex—commonly results in his becoming a so-called Don Juan type or a homosexual type. Seeking the Great Mother in a woman, he finds that woman to be only ordinary and has to start all over again. Or, if his masculinity is not so well-developed, he may settle with activities among a group of the same sex or be satisfied by getting a homosexual partner. I have discussed this eternal youth at length (maybe too much), but for studying the Japanese psyche, you will see how important an archetype this is. Now to continue our discussion of the story.

It seems reasonable, then, to consider Urashima Tarō as an eternal youth who has a strong tie with his mother. According to the fairy tale, he was a boy of forty years. This forty-year-old boy went to sea alone to fish, and he caught nothing. The *Fudoki* says, "rowing out into the sea, he spent three days and three nights, not catching even one fish." The ocean of unfathomable depth and width contains immeasurable things within, thus symbolizing the unconscious itself. Urashima's being all by himself, isolated on such an ocean and catching nothing—all these together present a suitable image of "regression."

According to Jung, regression is a phenomenon in which psychic energy flows from the ego toward the unconscious. At this moment, because the ego is losing the energy at its disposal, it manifests various regressive symptoms such as daydreaming, unrealistic fantasy, or outrageous emotional behavior and sometimes even delusions. Indeed, an extremely pathological state could ensue. Jung pointed out that such regression is not always pathological; rather, it is necessary for the creative psyche's process. In regression, the ego can gain a great deal through contact with the unconscious. Of course, there may be some pathological or evil things, but regression could seed future development or generate a sprout of new life. Therefore, it is quite understandable why fairy tales—which reflect human psychic development—often begin by describing a regressive phenomenon.

For instance, the main characters in fairy tales are abandoned by their parents or get lost in a forest and fall into a deep hole chasing after a rice ball. A typical example would be the young woodcutter in "The Bush Warbler's Home." In order for the regression to be creative, a new element must emerge and the ego has to make an effort to assimilate it. What about our hero? He fishes up a turtle or, according to the most commonly known version, he rescues and releases a turtle tormented by children. In some versions, a beautiful woman appears at the beginning, but no turtle. Most forms of this story have a turtle appear which directly or indirectly relates to the princess, Otohime.

Turtle and Turtle Princess

The Hungarian classicist and mythologist Karl Kerényi describes the tortoise as "one of the oldest animals known to mythology." Japan is not excluded from the turtle's appearances in myth and legend. In the CJFT there is a story related to

"Urashima Tarō" under the name of "Ryūgū dōji" (no. 223, Dragon Palace Boy). There the turtle appears as Otohime's messenger. A similar story, "Umisachi-Yamasachi" (in the *Nihonshoki*), has a passage in which Toyotama-hime appears riding on a large turtle. These tales suggest that the turtle has a strong connection with the ocean or a woman who lives under the sea.

In one of the important pairings in Japanese mythology, the God of Land (Okuni-nushi) is characteristically described in the *Kojiki* as riding on a turtle's back, unlike the Goddess of Heaven (Amaterasu) who has no vehicle. We should also note that the crest of Izumo Taisha, the great shrine of Izumo which serves the God of the Land, has a hexagon design perhaps inspired by the tortoise shell, although it is not certain there is any relation between them.

Incidentally, I might add that according to Tamotsu Saka-guchi, since there are no ancient stories which include Urashima's riding to the Dragon Palace on the turtle's back, this theme must have been added near the end of the eighteenth century. Although the available documents point to such a date, it is interesting to see that the turtle appears in the ancient era as the vehicle of the God of Land.

If we shift our attention to China and India, the symbolic meaning of the turtle becomes clear. According to the Taoist sage Lieh Tzu, there are five mountains (Tai, Yuan Ch'iao, Fan Kun, Ying Chou, Peng Lai) constituting a world of immortality several million Chinese miles east of the Gulf of Chihli. In early times, these mountains were floating on the ocean, never ceas-ing to move about, so sages suffering from the disequilibrium appealed to the heavenly emperor. In response, the emperor gathered fifteen gigantic turtles and formed them into three teams. Then he had them support these five mountains in three shifts, each shift said to be sixty thousand years.

This is indeed a story with Chinese grandeur. There is significance not only in the turtles' appearance, but also in the name of one of the mountains: Peng Lai Shan. In the *Nihonshoki* there is a passage in which Urashima goes to Tokoyonokuni (the other world). However, the Chinese ideographs for Peng Lai Mountain were used, although they were to be pronounced as "Tokoyo no Kuni." Another work, the *Tango no Kuni Fudoki,* also used these same ideographs. When a woman-turtle who is transformed invites Urashima saying, "Let's go to Tokoyo" (using "Peng" and "Mountain" only), we are not certain whether the ideographs used in this name were influenced by the Taoist idea or were simply an abbreviated form of Tokoyo no Kuni. We have to be satisfied with finding that there already existed the image of the turtle as a support for the "other world" which Urashima visited.

The turtle as a "base of the world" can be found in native American myths and in the mythology of India. When the "churning of the Milky Ocean" was going on under Vishnu's guidance, it was so violent that the world was almost destroyed. Vishnu turned himself into a gigantic turtle which became a bearing to the churning axis, thereby stabilizing the world.

When we consider elemental opposites such as heaven and earth, father and mother, or spirit and body, we find that the turtle represents a constellation of images of earth, mother, body, etc. In other words, the turtle indicates *primordial* states before heaven–earth, mother–father, etc., separate. In this sense it seems suitable that Jung compared the symbolism of the tortoise with the alchemical *massa confusa*—primal material as yet unrefined.

The *Tango no Kuni Fudoki* has a remarkable description of such a turtle making a dramatic transformation. The hero Shimako has no success in fishing for three days and three nights. At last he catches a five-colored turtle. "How strange," he thinks as he pulls it up in his boat. While he briefly dozes off, the turtle rapidly changes into a woman of whom it is said, "She is an unparalleled beauty." But she says suddenly to him, "My decision is firm; how about you? Please, make up your mind quickly."

This turtle's transformation is impressive, but I have a question here. Why did this turtle's metamorphosis theme disappear from "Urashima Tarō," and why was another theme which was not there originally (that of reciprocating kindness) then added? Before I discuss this curious problem of substituted themes, I will briefly touch upon the theme of repayment of kindness by a turtle.

Other than "Urashima Tarō," stories which include this theme appear in the *Nihon Reiki,* the *Konjyaku Monogatari,* in the *Uji Shūi Monogatari,* and in the *Uchigiki shu.* Although the plots vary somewhat, essentially they are stories of an animal reciprocating kindness for having been rescued. The hero is later saved in return, or the tortoise comes to repay with some money. Chitose Nakata seeks the origin of this theme in the *Ming Bao Ji* in China. Yen Gung of Chen was rescued by a turtle because he had saved a turtle. This is probably a Buddhist story which originated from India as a way of teaching about retribution or the karma of a good deed. Psychologically speaking, however, this theme indicates that progressive state of energy flow which follows after regression. Energy which was flowing toward the unconscious now starts to flow back toward the ego, becoming available to it. But in order to become a creative kind of regression, this has to be more than the ordinary repetition of energy exchange, regression and progression. Some new elements have to emerge.

In the original Urashima story a new element did emerge: a beautiful woman—the turtle transformed. But when replaced—under the influence of Buddhism—by the theme of an animal's repayment of kindness, this important subject dropped out. Indeed, a proposition by a woman transformed into a turtle is a very important problem. I have said the story starts with the regression of a man who has a strong bond to his mother. If he is to succeed in cutting this bond, he must meet a woman who possesses a different attractiveness from his mother. We might say that the ego, after gaining a certain degree of autonomy, again penetrates deeply into the unconscious and seeks out a feminine image unlike the mother figure. Then it has to be able to establish a relationship with the feminine.

In an important process in Western ego development, the male figure tries to separate from Mother (symbolically by killing her) and then to gain a new woman. However, in the *Fudoki* version of "Urashima Tarō," there is no sign of an incident which might symbolize killing the mother. Instead, suddenly, the turtle princess appears and proposes to him. Urashima, not knowing anything about this woman, follows after her. In short, rather than getting a woman after a heroic battle, this hero was captured by her!

This man's passive attitude reminds us of the man in "The Woman Who Eats Nothing" in chapter two. Urashima Tarō's isolation upon the ocean indicates a regressive condition, like that of the man in the other story with his self-seeking ideas of taking a hard-working wife who does not eat meals. At such a point, there emerges a woman who will devour everything —including a man. Furthermore, we cannot forget that the proposition was the woman's. Thus, we find that, although the turtle princess is beautiful, basically she too has a strong element of the Great Mother. Urashima is innocently pulled into her world. The feminine figures in "Thomas the Rhymer" and in the Irish legend of Oisin also take active roles similar to that of the turtle princess. In the former case, a woman who is an astonishing beauty appears in front of Thomas. "Now ye maun go wi' me," she said. "True Thomas, ye maun go wi' me; and ye maun serve me seven years, thro' weal or woe as many chance to be." This, as Mitsutomo Doi points out, is a service for the Goddess, not a love life for the man—like the relationship between the Great Mother and a small, subordinate male God. A similar psychic nature exists in the background of the Urashima story.

According to the *Fudoki* version, Shimako (Urashima), lured by a turtle princess, marries her and lives far apart from this world for many years; then he, an eternal youth, suddenly has to meet his tragic end, becoming an old man in an instant. The *Man'yōshū* version intensified this tragic ending. As Urashima opened the jeweled casket, "He ran around, screaming and waving his sleeves. Then he fell all about and, while stamping his feet, lost his strength. His youthful skin wrinkled, black hair turned to white; even his breath ceased so at last he died." This might be a rather natural outcome for a youth who was attracted to a woman similar to his mother. Then, what else might he have done in this case?

While it may not answer the question directly, the story of another youth who met a turtle might be worth relating. That youth is Hermes, who has a unique position among Greek Gods because of his manifold and paradoxical nature. Let's listen to a story Karl Kerényi told (according to the *Homeric Hymns*) about how Hermes met a tortoise feeding on rich grass. Kerényi declares that "Meeting and finding are revelations of Hermes' essence."[2]

> ... at sight whereof the luck-bringing son
> of Zeus laughed, and straightway spoke, saying:
> "Lo, a lucky omen for me, not by me to be
> mocked! Hail, darling and dancer, friend of
> the feast, welcome art thou! Whence gatst thou
> thy gay garment, a speckled shell, thou, a
> mountain-dwelling tortoise? Nay, I will
> carry thee within, and a boon shalt thou be
> to me, not by me to be scorned, nay, thou
> shalt first serve my turn. Best it is to
> bide at home, since danger is abroad. Living
> shalt thou be a spell against ill witchery,
> and dead, then a right sweet music-maker."
> So spoke he, and raising in both hands the
> tortoise, went back within the dwelling,
> bearing the glad treasure. Then he choked
> the creature, and with a gouge of grey iron
> he scooped out the marrow of the hill
> tortoise.

In short he made a lyre of the turtle. As described here, Hermes' attitude toward the turtle is totally opposed to that of our hero Urashima. Of course, like Hermes, Urashima has a sudden "meeting and finding" as the turtle appears in front of him, but—lured by a woman, a turtle transformed—he follows after her, not knowing who she is. Hermes, on the other hand, immediately "sees through" the tortoise the moment he en-counters it. Kerényi writes that he "sees already the glorious in-strument while the poor tortoise is still alive. For the tortoise, that glory means a painful death.... This is what Hermes does, not naively, but roguishly and without compassion." As soon as Hermes sees the tortoise he immediately thinks of making an in-strument. Regarding the proverb "Best it is to bide at home, since danger is abroad," Kerényi comments, "The irony of his words springs from his divinity and is as merciless as Being itself."[3] Indeed, it is suitable for a guide of souls.

Our Urashima never succeeded in becoming a Hermes who sees through the turtle's nature. However, as the eras changed so did the story. As we will see clearly in the following section, the character of the image of the turtle princess is especially changed.

Otohime—Eternal Girl

The *Fudoki* clearly describes Shimako and Otohime's mar-riage. In our Urashima version, however, they are not con-sidered to be married. And the fairy tale "Urashima" also does not mention their marriage, only noting that there are "Oto-hime and many beautiful women, . . . and they help me change clothes."

Why did Otohime come to be considered not a mate? The theme of Urashima's marriage carried into such Heian period documents as the *Urashima ko den,* but in these documents the word *Kamehime* (turtle princess)—which does appear in the *Fudoki* (713 A.D.)—was already lost. Instead, the terms *sennyo* (Taoist fairy) or *shinnyo* (priestess) were used, feminine refer-ences obviously showing strong Chinese influence. I am espe-cially interested in these changes in the image of Kamehime. It seems to me that, as Kamehime's image gets closer to that of a *sennyo,* the theme of marriage starts to drop out. In short, when a physical aspect of the feminine—which may be represented by a turtle—is cut off, the princess becomes more and more *sennyo-*

like. As a result, an image of Otohime emerges which is no longer that of a marriage partner. The turtle princess is divided or separated into a turtle and a princess.

When they hear of a beauty who denies physicality and who is not considered as a marriage partner, Japanese naturally think of the image of Kaguya-hime. In contrast to Kamehime who forcefully proposed to Urashima, this beautiful woman was proposed to by five noble men. Even so she ascended to the moon, refusing all of them. Kamehime lives under the sea, while Kaguya-hime lives in heaven. Therefore, I would say that Oto-hime is commonly perceived by us as this image of a Kaguya-hime-like Kamehime from which the turtle has separated.

Parallel to stories about Kaguya-hime are Hagoromo (feather cloak) legends about *tennyo* (angel) wives in the fairy tale category, with many variations widely spread in Japan. Stories about a woman who originally lives in the heavenly realm but appears in this one are found all over the world. In the West it is not a woman from a heavenly world, but often a princess who gets changed into a swan by a magic spell. These legends of the swan maiden, as Emma Jung pointed out, have quite a long history; the story in the *Rig-Veda* is probably the oldest of all.[4] Now let us look at an unusual example of the Hagoromo story, a legend which I think will reflect a Japanese feminine image.

Called "Shrine of Nagu," this story is again from the *Fudoki* of the Tango area. Eight heavenly maidens are bathing at Manai. A certain old couple sees them and hides one of their flying cloaks, thus causing the heavenly maiden who now cannot fly to become their foster child. Through her hard work, the couple becomes rich. Once rich, they kick this heavenly maiden out. Sobbing, she wanders about here and there, for she no longer is able to return to heaven. At last her heart settles down at the Nagu village. She decides to stay there saying, "I am the Toyouka-no-me-no-mikoto residing in the Nagu shrine in Takeno." Here the story ends.

This story is unusual because there is neither romance nor marriage for this heavenly maiden. No prince is coming to rescue a poor abused woman. The female figure instead somehow calms herself, and at the end she simply settles down as a local deity. I have continued to focus on the theme of marriage because it was lost completely in the Urashima story. The Japanese feminine figure characteristically is divided in two. One is a Kamehime living under the sea who strongly empha-sizes the physical aspect; the other lives in the heavenly realm as an eternal girl who would not be a marriage partner. It seems to be quite daunting to develop a feminine figure who becomes a lover on an equal basis or on the same continuum with a man.

The example I've given of the second type, Kaguya-hime, refuses all proposals and ascends to heaven. We may say that, as an eternal girl, she would be a perfect match for our Japanese eternal youth. I will add an association regarding Kaguya-hime: there are many stories explaining her birth as hatching from a bush warbler's egg. For instance, the *Kaidoki* of the early Kamakura period says that a girl was born from a bush warbler's egg in a bamboo forest. The old man who found her in the nest made her his own child, and she was called Kaguya-hime or Uguisu (bush warbler)-hime.

Uguisu-hime reminds us of the story we discussed in chapter one which evokes a similar association. Now, is the Uguisu-hime/Kaguya-hime actually a child left by a woman who la-mented the untrustworthiness of men and left this world? As beautiful as her mother, this child has learned a lot about men's unreliable nature from her own mother's experience. Did she come back to this world in order to satisfy her mother's rancor? When we speculate along these lines, it seems indeed under-standable that Kaguya-hime made these high-ranking officials suffer by forcing each of them into a mission impossible. Leav-ing men's confusion behind, she left this world, and maybe she even saw her mother in the other one. Laughing hand-in-hand, they both have watched men's continuous failures one after another. It may be such bottomless laughter as that of Oni, but it may be "Oh, it's funny" laughter, pulling each other's sleeves. Behind the "sorrowful" beauty of one who disappears, there is also the laughter of amusement. Those conditions men get into —toiling and moiling over her impossible tasks, even losing their lives at the end—begin to get comical instead of sorrowful. Japanese women do not live only in the meekness of disappearance.

I have pointed out the feminine image which Japanese have split in two: first, the "earthy" Kamehime is in an earlier version of Urashima, and, second, Otohime—who, like Kaguya-hime, is not a marriage partner—appears in a later period. They seem to be typical cases. One reason Otohime's image changes may be influenced by Confucius's teaching: "Boys and girls must be clearly distinguished at age seven." Then, with the added influence of Buddhist stories, more emphasis is placed on the repayment of kindness, and so Kamehime becomes a Kaguya-hime-like Otohime. Thus, the turtle—which can no longer coexist —becomes separated from her.

Inner World and Outer World

According to the *Fudoki,* Shimako (Urashima) stayed in the other world for three years after marrying Kamehime. This three years corresponds to three hundred years in this world, so Urashima was totally lost after returning home. His sense of time was altered from the moment he stepped into the unconscious world and met a woman. That timelessness in the unconscious has been emphasized by analytical psychologists. We always experience it in our dreams. Past and present get mixed up, and it is not unusual to experience a long span of time within a moment.

In a story called "Saka Betto no Jōdo" (in CJFT), the time relation is reversed from that of Urashima. That is, a fisherman asked a villager to change the thatch roofing. During that time, the fisherman visited underwater the Pure Land of Saka Betto. There he married and had three generations of offspring. But when he got worried about his home he returned. Then he found that the villager was still in the middle of the roofing job. Such a long time spent in the other world was not even long enough to change a thatched roof in this one. This reminds us of the famous Chinese Taoist story "Dream at Hantan." The *Otogi zōshi* of the Muromachi period contains another description of the Dragon Palace: there is a spring scene in the east window, summer in the south, autumn in the west and a winter scene in the north window. This presents a vivid indication of the Dragon Palace being outside the law of time.

The puer aeternus figure such as Urashima indicates the timelessness of the unconscious. Often an eternal youth spends his time in the unconscious world, and therefore you might say he does not age.

Urashima literally "forgets time passing," but he does become homesick. According to the *Fudoki*, Kamehime grieves his departure but finally does say, "If you would not forget me and would like to visit me again, please never open the casket." She lets him go, but three hundred years have passed, totally changing his village. "He could not find his relatives of the past seven generations." Almost all versions of Urashima include the themes of the great passage of time and the jeweled casket in connection with his return.

It is extremely difficult for one who once has been to "another world" to return and live the same life as before (even for Japanese students and businessmen today who return from foreign countries!). To us psychologists "another world" means the unconscious. It is important for the clinician not to lose a connection to the outer world once he enters the other one with a patient. Unless this difficulty is conquered, we may make the same mistake as Urashima. In the Yamashiro *Fudoki*, there is a beautiful instance in which the hero did not relinquish a connection to this world. Briefly, the story "Hashihime in Uji" goes like this: there was a man whom the Dragon King asked to become a son-in-law. While at the Dragon Palace, he tried not to eat anything. He managed not to eat until, finally, he was able to return home.

The idea that when one eats in the other world one cannot return to this one is widely known. Two primary examples are the story of a Japanese Goddess, Izanami—"Eating in the Underworld"—and the Greek myth of Persephone. Remarkably, the man in this Hashihime story does not lose his connection to this world. Maintaining the relationship, never eating a meal in the other world, requires more sustained will power than an eternal youth usually commands.

Urashima was too unprepared, marrying Kamehime as she seduced him, then getting homesick and coming back—all without much thought. Therefore, it must be significant that it was at such a time that Kamehime gave him a jeweled casket which "You must never open." I consider this situation a last chance for Urashima's will power. To deal with the emergence of a new element—when regression is creative—a hero has to involve himself energetically. Urashima made too little effort.

One of the characteristics of the Japanese people is the absence of a clear distinction between exterior and interior world, conscious and unconscious. Reflecting this, Urashima's return was officially documented in Japanese history in the *Nihon-Kōki* (825 A.D.), more than three hundred years after the *Nihonshoki* (478 A.D.) was written. Why 347 years later is, of course, unknown. Another reflection of this trait is the extreme simplicity of the descriptions of the journey to the other world, e.g., when Urashima goes undersea to the Dragon Palace. In Japanese mythology, when Izanagi visited the underworld to try to bring back Izanami, his deceased wife, his journey was accomplished without difficulty. By contrast, "Thomas the Rhymer" relates that "for forty days and forty nights, he wade thro blud to the knee, and he saw neither sun nor moon. But he heard the roaring of the sea." With several parallels to our story, a Babylonian myth describes the Goddess Ishtar's descent into the underworld to rescue her husband. In short, for Japanese the wall between this world and the other world is, by comparison, a surprisingly thin one.

That the membrane between inner and outer or this and that world is paper-thin—like a *fusuma* (sliding room-divider) or *shoji* (a paper door-window)—reflects the nature of the Japanese ego. Established by successfully "killing the mother," the Western ego clearly distinguishes between conscious and unconscious and between I and thou—grasping things objectively. In comparison, Japanese consciousness tries to grasp the whole as an undifferentiated state by always making borders vague. This permeability may explain why Japanese fairy tales are closer to legends (a kinship Western folklorists often point out).

The theme of "prohibition" relating to the jeweled casket resembles that of "Don't look" discussed in chapter one. The person who breaks the prohibition can reach a higher stage of individuation only when he has the strength to conquer various hardships occasioned by the break. Urashima was too weak. So the consequence that the *Man'yo*-poet gave him—suddenly becoming an old man—seems unavoidable. However, we have the more recent "Urashima Nendai Ki" by Chikamatsu (1653–1724), who gave a new interpretation, quite different from the original story. At the end Urashima opens the jeweled casket, fully aware that it contains his 8,000 years of life, in order to show that he himself is Urashima. Thus he is able to overcome some criminals who threatened him by purposefully opening the casket. Sakaguchi called this the "Willed Urashima." This version by Chikamatsu is a noteworthy experiment to overcome the image of Urashima as an eternal youth, but even here it did not result in the happy marriage of Urashima and Otohime.

Unless one changes the story at least as much as Chikamatsu did, giving it a happy ending would be very difficult. The story's conclusion shown in the Appendix is interesting, but we will discuss it in the next chapter.

The legend of Urashima has in the course of time become a fairy tale which modern Japanese know well. In the changes of the Otohime figure since earliest times, we can find both of the female images characteristic of the Japanese psyche. The two images are standing on lower and higher planes than the Japanese male. We will try to find a female image on the same plane as the male in the following chapters.

SIX
Non-Human Females

In a group of stories classified as "Non-Human Wives," non-human beings appear, transform themselves into women and then marry. Considering the paucity of marriages in Japanese stories, this seems peculiar. However, in many cases those marriages suffer catastrophes, so the stories go quite differently from Western stories which end with happy marriages.

Various non-human wives appear in Japanese fairy tales, such as snakes, fish, birds, foxes, and cats. Toshio Ozawa, a Japanese scholar, points out that fairy tales of the non-human wife are peculiar to Japan and the countries near it. Their uniqueness makes them very important in considering the psychology of the Japanese, especially since we are focusing on marriage in fairy tales. Let's take up "Crane Wife" whose many variants are widespread in Japan.

Crane Wife

Karoku, the hero, lives with his mother, as in "Urashima Tarō." Since his mother is seventy, he must have stayed celibate for years. He goes to buy a *futon* (folding mattress). Perhaps he needs some warmth in his home. He spends his money, however, to rescue a crane and comes back empty-handed. Though it may be cold at night, he thinks, "It can't be helped." And his mother says, "What you have done is just fine" and does not blame him. The mother and son are poor but good-hearted. The story tells it all in short sentences quite vividly.

It is common to many of the story's variations that the poor hero pays a fair amount of money to rescue the crane. The story strongly tends toward becoming like a Buddhist story in which the poor man would become rich because of the crane's repaying his kindness. Some versions stress the theme of repayment, losing the story about marriage (as happened with "Urashima Tarō"). The fact that these variations are rather few indicates the importance here of the theme of marriage.

Transforming itself into a woman, the crane visits Karoku. Here the transformation from the crane to human is told rather naturally, and no magical element comes in like the tales in the West. (This point holds in the cases of other non-human wives.) Regarded as a spiritual bird in Japan because of its beautiful form when flying, the crane in this story presents the lovely female figure by association with its elegant form in flight. A crane is also considered a bird of good omen based on a legend in which a crane brought rice the first time to the land or on the Chinese proverb "A crane lives a thousand years, a turtle lives ten thousand years."

The crane Karoku has rescued becomes a human being and wants to be his wife—another clear proposal by a woman. The man's attitude toward it, however, differs from Urashima's attitude to Kamehime described in the last chapter. Urashima behaves extremely passively and just submits to the woman's initiative. Karoku, on the other hand, is quite aware of the reality of his life, so he declines the proposal because he thinks that such a beautiful and splendid woman cannot be his. The man's conscious resistance creates a different plot development from that of "Urashima Tarō."

Sometime after their marriage, the wife asks him not to open the door of the closet while she stays in it for three days. Here appears the prohibition of "Don't look at." And he keeps his promise this first time. The wife weaves a beautiful cloth. (Its meaning as the women's task I mentioned in the second and third chapters.)

The appearance of weaving here connects the image of the crane wife to the image of Yama-uba in my own fantasy, given in the last part of chapter two. The woman who leaves this world through distrust of the man in "The Bush Warbler's Home" wants to have relations with common people again. She tries to do so even bearing the condition of "eating nothing." However, she gets angry at the man's peeking and reveals her dark side. Then she is driven away by the narrowness of ordinary people. Her anger and revenge against men are paid by her alter-self, Kaguya-hime. Then she wants to return to this world. Transformed into a crane, she can find a kind and reliable man, one gentle and steady. Thus, she tries to devote herself to help him. The prohibition which she gives him because of her own suspicion is not violated and the cloth is woven. Finally, the time may come when her fate will be beautifully woven. She is delighted: the happy marriage will be achieved.

Here occurs an unexpected pitfall. The man becomes desirous of more. They should have lived happily the rest of their lives when the cloth was sold for two thousand pieces of gold. But when the lord says, "Can you make another bolt of it?" the husband replies that "I must ask my wife." However, he may already have made up his mind when the lord says, "You don't need to ask her. If you agree, that will do." A variant found in Ryotsu City states distinctly that the man "becomes more desirous and asks her to weave one more bolt." When the wife hears about it, she neither gets angry nor feels sad. Instead, she decides to continue her devotion.

When he is poor, he tries to save the crane, even enduring the cold. He devotes himself to her. When he becomes rich after the marriage, however, his attitude completely reverses. A man who becomes rich tends to be greedy, and a greedy man is always restless. He cannot wait for a long time to keep a promise. Thus, the husband finally breaks the taboo. This peripeteia may seem to reduce the story into too ordinary a dimension: the husband shows the typical behavior of a Japanese man of today. Poor, he devoted himself to a woman before marriage. When he later becomes rich, he presumes his wife's devotion, yet does not keep his promise to her. Here we could say that the contemporary Japanese man lives his life as a negative manifestation of the basic structure of the Japanese psyche revealed through the study of fairy tales.

The man transgresses the prohibition again. I say "again" as I am thinking of the man in "The Bush Warbler's Home." The woman this time, too, does not get angry. She just departs saying, "Since you have seen my true body you are surely disgusted with me, so I must leave this place." She does not blame the man who breaks his promise, but leaves him as she is ashamed of being seen naked. Is that simply because of her naked body? Many variants tell us that the woman departs as her true nature, that of a crane, is revealed. These statements may denote the same thing symbolically: the woman cannot live with the man who comes to know her true nature, the naked truth. In order for them to live together as a couple, she must perfect hiding her identity. In all variants of "Crane Wife," the man does not know that the woman who proposes marriage to him is actually a crane. He is utterly surprised to learn his wife's identity when he transgresses the prohibition. Taking the fact as the undeniable condition for the divorce, he who would have loved her so much never prevents her going away.

For comparison, we shall take up a Grimm's tale, "The Raven" (KHM 93), as an example of stories in the West in which a woman transforms herself into a bird. Here, a princess is changed into a raven by her mother's spell. The raven lives in a wood where she meets a man. She reveals her true nature and asks him to accomplish some tasks for her redemption. Though he makes mistakes and fails to heed some of her admonitions, he attains the goal with her help. The raven changes back to the princess, and they marry in the end.

We are impressed with the strong contrast with "Crane Wife." Table 7 compares the plots of the two stories from the point where the man and woman meet (after the man has saved the crane in "Crane Wife" and the princess has been metamorphosed into the raven by her mother's spell in "The Raven"). Table 7 shows the heroines' true nature: one is originally a crane, the other transformed into a raven. In the Japanese story, the marriage is contingent on "hiding the true nature," and in the Western tale the raven expects the man's redemption by "revealing the true nature." Accordingly, the climactic task is the woman's for the Japanese tale and the man's for the other. "Crane Wife" ends in tragic divorce when the heroine's true nature is disclosed, whereas the Western story ends in happy marriage. These stories differ in every detail, reversing the order of the events of marriage and revelation of identity.

In table 7, one may wonder whether "Crane Wife" is a typical Japanese tale of non-human wives or not. So, we shall investigate other stories of non-human wives in the next section.

Non-Human Wife

All the differences between the Japanese tale and Grimm's seem to stem from the basic fact that the woman is originally the crane in "Crane Wife," whereas the raven is originally the woman in "The Raven." So far, I have not been able to find any story from another country with the same pattern as "Crane Wife." Toshio Ozawa, who has studied the world's fairy tales thoroughly, could find only "Dragon Wife" in Korea as a similar type. Acknowledging that "we cannot predict how the situation will be if the investigation of fairy tales in the world makes much further progress," he concludes, "So far, these stories are found only in Japan and in its neighboring countries."

Let us look at the story of the non-human wife according to

TABLE 7
A Comparison between "Crane Wife" and "The Raven"

	Exposition	Development	Culmination	Result
Crane Wife	The woman visits the man	Marriage when the woman proposes	The woman's task (blocked by the man)	Divorce because the woman reveals her nature
The Raven	The man meets the Raven	The Raven reveals her nature, asks the man to redeem her	The man's task (helped by the woman)	Marriage because the man accomplishes his tasks

TABLE 8
The Stories of Non-Human Wives

Story	Proposal by the Woman	Prohibition by the Woman	Revelation of the Woman's Nature	Divorce	Children
Snake Wife (110)	x	Don't look at me while I'm giving birth	x (by peeking)	x	A child (The woman leaves her eyes)
Frog Wife (111)	x	—	x (by following)	x	None
Clam Wife (112)	x	—	x (by peeking)	x	None
Fish Wife (113A)	—	Don't look at me while I'm bathing	x (by peeking)	x	Three (Two are left. They disappear when the man re-marries)
Fish Wife (113B)	x	—	x (by peeking)	x	None
Crane Wife (115)	x	—	x (by asking her origin)	x	None
Fox Wife (116A)	x	Don't look at me while I'm giving birth	x (The woman confesses)	x	One (becomes a great person)
Fox Wife (116B)	x	—	x (The child discovers)	x	One (becomes a *Chōjya*)
Fox Wife (116C)	x	—	x (The fox's tail is seen by the man)	x	One (who never cries)

Note: The number denotes the classification number in CJFT.

the CJFT. Stories classified there from 100 to 119 are "Snake Wife," "Frog Wife," "Clam Wife," "Fish Wife" (A, B), "Dragon Palace Wife," "Crane Wife," "Fox Wife" (Magic Ear Type, One Wife Type, Two Wives Type), "Cat Wife," "Heavenly Wife," and "Flutist Bridegroom." The women who appear in "Dragon Palace Wife," "Heavenly Wife," and "Flutist Bridegroom" are not animals. As one can see easily enough, the number of animals which can transform themselves into women is quite limited. The "Crane Wife" variations include a few exceptions such as a pheasant or copper pheasant wife instead of a crane wife. In another group of stories, an animal transforms itself into a man and marries a woman. The snake and frog can become non-human bridegrooms, as well as human females. These two animals can get projections of both the male and female images from human beings.

As it is too complicated to check all the many variants of non-human wife stories, I am going to give an overview based on those which are taken as typical in CJFT. I think it enough to get an overview, especially since a statistical approach is not feasible. I shall refer to some variants when necessary. Looking through all these stories, we find that, except for "Cat Wife," "Dragon Palace Wife," "Heavenly Wife," and "Flutist Bridegroom," all the tales have the same characteristics and patterns as "Crane Wife." In order to make the common elements clear, I have arranged them as table 8. I shall discuss the four exceptions later.

As table 8 shows, the man and woman marry under the condition of the woman's "hiding her true nature." After a while (though some have children), they divorce because the woman's identity is revealed. This is the central pattern of Japanese non-human wife stories.

Next we have the theme of marriage as a result of the woman's proposal. It is also typical that the marriage does not occur at the end but rather the beginning of the story. All stories except "Fish Wife A" include this theme, and in almost all these stories, the man first saves the animal, and the woman (the animal) comes to marry him to repay his kindness. In

"Snake Wife," however, the man rescues no animal: the woman just appears suddenly and proposes marriage. In "Clam Wife," also, the woman unexpectedly visits the man and says, "I came here to marry you." But, when she is going to separate from him, she confides that he had saved her before the marriage. The sudden proposal occurs in some variants of "The Bush Warbler's Home" and "Urashima Tarō." Perhaps this simple form is the oldest one, and the story about repaying kindness was added later under Buddhist influence. We can cite the evidence from the case of "Urashima Tarō."

The types of prohibitions that the woman imposes on the man are rather few in number. An especially noteworthy one occurs in "Fox Wife" (Magic Ear Type). Even though the man does not break the taboo of "Don't look when I'm giving birth," the woman herself confesses that she was originally a fox when nine months pass after the child's birth. The man laughs it off as a silly thing. The woman goes so far as to show her original figure as a fox, turning her body around (this is the way by which a fox can transform itself into anything). This story, however, ends differently from others: her child becomes a great person. So the whole situation may be a bit different. At any rate, the man's transgression of the woman's prohibition does not play a big role in the non-human wife stories, which emphasize instead the revelation of the woman's true nature.

Let us look at the taboos. "Don't see my delivery" in "Snake Wife" and "Fox Wife" (Magic Ear Type) reminds me of the myth of Toyotama-hime, who also forbids her husband to see her delivering a child. The prohibition "Don't see me while bathing" in "Fish Wife A" means she rejects his knowing her naked truth, as in the case of "Crane Wife." (There is no story of prohibition in "Crane Wife" which is recorded as the typical one in CJFT 115.) In a variant of "Frog Wife," when the wife goes to her parents' house to have her baby, she says to her husband, "Don't ask where I am going. We will become unhappy if you do." In some stories the man's "peeking" reveals the woman's true nature though her prohibition is not explicit. It is not a sin of transgression, but it is still a shady act.

We touched upon the meaning of "peeking" in chapter two. The man's looking at the woman in spite of her admonition goes back to the Japanese myth of the world parents. When the mother Goddess Izanami dies, her husband Izanagi visits her in the underworld where she forbids him to look at her for a while. The God cannot wait and makes a fire in the darkness. He then sees his wife in a terrible state of decomposition. Awestruck, he runs away. The Goddess pursues him saying, "He has shamed me!" Dragging a tremendous rock to the pass between the world and the underworld, the God blocks it off. Thus they separate. In "Clam Wife" and "Fish Wife B," when the man peeks at his wife cooking, he is surprised to see her urinating into a cooking pot. This indicates the same idea as the myth of Izanagi and Izanami: the man sees the dark or unclean side of the "other" which he should not discover.

Though in Japanese folk tales peeking is the common means of discovering the woman's true nature, "Frog Wife" shows a different pattern. The wife visits her parents when the family has a Buddhist ceremony, and the husband follows her secretly. She enters the pond and the frogs croak. Upon seeing this, he throws a stone into the pond and comes home. When the wife returns, she tells him that her family had trouble during the ceremony as somebody threw a stone. She leaves home the next day. This story mentions nothing about her being a frog, but she leaves home, presuming that her true nature is now known. In another variant, the man turns the wife out saying, "I cannot live with a frog." Even though they have lived nicely as a couple, he rejects her because a frog is, after all, a frog.

When the couple separates after the wife's identity is disclosed in these stories, it is almost always the woman who claims there is no alternative to permanent separation. Rarely does the man ask his wife to leave as in the variant of "Frog Wife" mentioned above. It is the woman who is active in the marriage, the work and the divorce. The man is always passive. If one compares these stories with Grimm's "The Raven," it becomes clearer that they are stories of women. "The Raven," in contrast, is a man's story.

Regarding children, the stories form two groups: in one, the woman leaves them when she departs; the other tells nothing about them. In the former group the children become happy or unhappy. An example of the latter group is "Snake Wife": the snake leaves her eyes, which have magical power to raise her child, when she leaves the house. The people in the village steal the treasured eyes. In a rage, the snake causes a flood which destroys the whole village. In "Fish Wife A," when the man remarries, the child "is lost and cannot be found anymore." The resentment of the woman who left may have worked in some way here.

The most interesting of these stories is "Fox Wife." In "Fox Wife" (Magic Ear Type), the child is raised by a flute from which milk flows, and the conclusion records that "he became a big man." In "Fox Wife" (One Wife Type), the child becomes a *chō-jya* because of the precious ball which the mother fox left for him.[1] These stories are saying that a child who has the blood of the fox flowing in his veins is great even though a husband can-not continue to be married to one. Here the fox is highly valued. The same idea occurs in the myth of Toyotama-hime, who asks her husband not to look into the parturition hut. When he looks and sees she is a crocodile, she goes back to her palace under the sea, leaving her baby behind. The baby becomes the father of the first emperor of Japan. Hence Toyotama-hime's (i.e., a crocodile's) lineage is highly esteemed. The Japanese have an ambivalent attitude toward non-human beings in these stories, treating them both as something below humans and as something beyond them. The former is evident in the stories of animal wives—except "Fox Wife"; the latter attitude is stressed in "Heavenly Wife" and "Dragon Palace Wife," which I discuss below.

Before doing that, however, I would like briefly to comment on "Cat Wife," which I've excluded from table 8. A peculiar fairy tale, it ends happily in marriage. Though a farmer is over forty, he does not marry because he is very poor. He keeps and loves a cat which was thrown out by the *chōjya* living next door. He says often to the cat, "I wish you were a human being."

Meanwhile, the cat, waiting to help him, thinks that it cannot fully repay him for his kindness insofar as it is still an animal. The cat goes to Ise Shrine and returns "transformed into a woman by the Goddess's power."[2] Then they marry and work so hard the husband becomes a *chōjya*.

Though this is an extremely rare story in Japan, its pattern differs from stories in the West in which a human being is transformed into an animal and then recovers its original form through marriage. I question how far we can treat the story as an original Japanese fairy tale, because it is only found in Tono City in Iwate Prefecture with no variant anywhere else in the country. I suspect that it was created recently. We need further research regarding this.

Now we will consider "Dragon Palace Wife," "Flutist Bridegroom" and "Heavenly Wife." Although all three are interesting, I shall touch upon them only enough to relate them to the pattern of the animal wife story which we have just discussed. The women in these stories are, respectively, the princess of the Dragon Palace, the daughter of the Bodhisattva king, and the heavenly maiden. Each one gives us the feeling she is higher than human beings. In the former two, after the splendid woman has married, the local lord plots to get her. He imposes many difficult problems on the young couple, but the wife's wisdom solves all of them, and the story ends happily. While these are also stories about non-human wives, their pattern differs completely from that of the animal wife stories. The stress here is laid, not on the difficulty of continuing marriage with the non-human wife, but on her wisdom. Between these two extremes we have "Fox Wife." We need to bear in mind that stories of non-human wives do not have to end in catastrophe: some have happy endings.

Marriage takes place in "Dragon Palace Wife" and "Flutist Bridegroom." We should note that the theme of "hiding the true nature" does not play any role in them. In contrast, the animal wives who marry while disguised must separate when their identities are revealed even though they are very nice or talented women. In "Dragon Palace Wife," the man visits the

Dragon Palace and says to the God there, "I would like to have your daughter." He proposes, knowing the woman's true nature. This is diametrically opposed to the animal wife stories where the man marries after the woman's proposal without knowing who she is. In "Flutist Bridegroom," the daughter of the Bodhisattva king in India falls in love with the man who is the greatest flute player in Japan when she hears his music. In this case, her true nature is evident to the man from the beginning.

"Dragon Palace Wife" and "Flutist Bridegroom" end happily. They differ, however, from Western stories as marriage occurs in the beginning and the couple becomes happy at the end due to the woman's activity. Stories of women rather than men, these are useful in considering the psychology of Japanese, especially since they have happy endings. We must not forget, however, that the stories with this pattern are much fewer in number than the stories ending in separation. According to CJFT, the "Flutist Bridegroom" stories are spread only in the eastern part of Japan. This interesting fact awaits further investigation to clarify its implications.

Not all these stories focus on the woman's activity. The man in "Heavenly Wife" performs a man's task. In this sense, the story is the one nearest to Western stories. The young man called Mikeran marries a heavenly maiden through the trick of getting her clothes while she is bathing. Of course, her true nature is exposed in the marriage. They have three children. The wife, however, returns to heaven when she retrieves her clothes which enable her to fly. Mikeran chases her up to heaven where her father imposes many difficult tasks on him. With the help of his wife, he accomplishes them one after another. This part resembles the stories in the West. In the last task, however, he fails, disregarding his wife's advice. He follows her father and is carried away by a flood. Then Mikeran and his wife become stars. Here the story parts company with Western stories which end happily. "Heavenly Wife" stands between the animal wife stories of Japan and the Western stories. Since this story is found throughout Japan, one cannot easily conclude that it was transmitted from outside.

So far we have discussed the characteristics of non-human wife stories in Japan. What happens if we compare them with the world's fairy tales? In the next section, we shall make some comparisons taking account of non-human bridegroom stories as well.

Human, Non-Human Marriage Stories in the World

When we contrast Japanese stories like "The Monkey Bridegroom" or "The Snake Bridegroom" with "Beauty and the Beast" in the West, we reach the same conclusion as in the non-human wife stories: in Japan, animals transformed into human figures (or remaining as animals) try to marry humans and cannot achieve a happy union. In the West, on the other hand, human beings are transformed into animals by magic, and they succeed in marrying women when love overcomes the power of magic. Before comparing specific stories, I would like to point out that, in Japanese non-human marriage stories, many non-human bridegrooms are killed whereas non-human wives never are. They just leave their homes. We shall discuss the meaning of such a distinct difference in the next section.

Toshio Ozawa focuses on the stories of marriage between human beings and animals, as he thinks this focus will clarify the cultural differences in fairy tales. I have been studying Japanese fairy tales from a psychological perspective, focusing on the marriage stories in general. Though Ozawa's standpoint is literary, our foci meet at the same point. As he investigates stories not only in Japan and Europe, but also in Africa, New Guinea and northern Canada, his discussion is based on a wide view. I will briefly introduce his theory after summarizing an Eskimo non-human bridegroom story he takes up.

A hunter has a beautiful daughter. Rejecting the proposals of young men, she marries a big crab without her parents' knowledge. The crab, ashamed to appear in front of people, hides himself always in his wife's pelt tent. When their family makes a poor catch in winter, the father complains about the bridegroom's inability in hunting. One day during a snow storm, three seals are thrown into their house. Transformed into a human figure, the crab hunts them. Meanwhile, the young couple has twin babies. Still the crab does not show himself to others. The mother-in-law, out of curiosity, peeks into her daughter's bedroom through a hole in the tent. The bridegroom is "a small man with a wrinkled face and his eyes are big, big ones hung down from his head." The mother-in-law falls down in surprise and dies. At the end, the story says, "After that, nobody tried to peek through the hole of the tent at the crab sleeping with his young wife. The crab lives happily with his wife and children. He brings in a good catch for his family."

The most notable aspect of this fairy tale is, as Ozawa points out, that the demarcation between human beings and animals is quite thin, almost non-existent. The parents do not seem to be surprised to know that the crab is their daughter's bridegroom. Unlike those in Japanese stories, this couple does not separate, nor is the bridegroom killed when the parents come to know his true nature. The only complaint is his inadequacy in hunting, and this problem is resolved afterward. The mother, however, is surprised to death—not because the bridegroom is a crab but rather because he looks so strange. After the mother's death, nobody peeks at the crab and he lives happily with his family. This differs from the Japanese stories in which peeking causes catastrophe. In the Eskimo story, humans and animals are thought to be of the same species.

In "The Monkey Bridegroom" (CJFT 103) in Japan, a man and a monkey talk as equals before the marriage. There one can say that a human and an animal are treated as the same being. The Japanese and Eskimo stories diverge when the marriage comes in. The daughter born to the couple hates the monkey and kills it, having become aware that a human being and a monkey are different. In the West, marriage between different species essentially never occurs. Monsters or animals can marry humans only when they have been transformed by some magic. The demarcation between human and animal is distinct in the West. Japanese stories are located between the Eskimo and the European type.

A detailed discussion of marriage stories between different species is found in Ozawa's book. I content myself with showing in figure 7 a somewhat modified version of the diagram resulting from Ozawa's investigation.

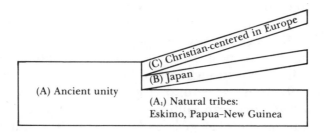

FIG. 7.   *Diagram of the Non-Human Marriage Story (modified from Toshio Ozawa)*

In figure 7, (A) denotes the stories people might have had in ancient times when men felt no difference between themselves and other beings: a feeling of unity prevailed. Then (A₁) denotes the stories of national tribes such as Eskimo, Papua–New Guinea, which succeed (A). "The transformations between human beings and animals occur as natural phenomena. The marriages between humans and animals are regarded as marriage between the same species rather than different species." On the other hand, (C) represents the stories found among Christians centered in Europe. "The transformation is possible only through magic. Apparent marriages between human beings and non-human beings are actually marriages between human beings. One of them has been transformed into a non-human being by some magic. The magic is resolved by human love, and the human male and female marry." Here the demarcation between humans and other beings is very strict. No one can ever actually cross over it. Then (B) refers to Japanese stories which fall between (A) and (C). In (B), metamorphoses occur without magic, and marriages between humans and animals are told as a matter of course. In this sense, (B) shares the same view toward animals as (A). However, in the case of a non-human bridegroom, the bridegroom is rejected or killed because it is an animal. And if a wife reveals her non-human nature, the marriage never continues. In this sense, the distinction between humans and animals is quite firm.

Japanese fairy tales are peculiar among all those considered, located in-between the stories among Christians centered in Europe and the natural tribes such as Eskimo and Papua–New Guinea. This seems to suggest that Japan as a culture has never cut itself off from its "natural" roots. At the same time, Japan has absorbed European culture far more quickly than other similar cultures. This fact gives us support for the validity of this study, namely, the investigation of the psyche of Japanese through the analysis of their fairy tales.

Man and Nature

How can we interpret the peculiarity of Japanese fairy tales? First, let us consider the ending of "Urashima Tarō" which we left untouched in the last chapter. The conclusion in the Appendix of this book differs from many other variants in which Urashima becomes an old man or dies. When Otohime gives him the *Tama-tebako* (jewel casket) she says, "Open this if you are completely at a loss." When he opens the casket in his desperation, he becomes a crane. While he is flying around above his mother's tomb, the princess comes onto shore transformed into a turtle. And the ending states that an Ise folk song about a crane and a turtle dancing together comes from this story. The scene of this ending is worth noticing. Reversing the sequence in the West, the human being becomes the animal and the story ends happily—at least for Japanese it seems a happy ending.

Here is the idea that man's returning to nature is happy. We cannot, however, deny the influence from China, namely, the idea that "a crane lives a thousand years, and a turtle lives ten thousand years." Similarly, the idea of returning to nature appears in the ending of "Crane Wife," though it is not so distinct: Karoku tries to seek his crane wife who has left their home. He visits the land of cranes through the guidance of an old man. Though Karoku meets his wife there, he neither lives there with her nor brings her back home. A Western reader must be amazed at the ending: Karoku enjoys the entertainment for a while and comes home in the old man's boat. One can understand that some Western scholars say they would not notice when Japanese stories end if there were no words like "This is the end." However, for Japanese the story has a fine ending. The man and crane have their deep but temporary relation, and in the end the man lives in his world and the crane lives also in its own land. They can coexist by "living in divided territory." There is no sense of controlling each other.

The animal wife stories in which a wife just disappears as soon as her true nature surfaces are peculiar to Japan. Toshio Ozawa, however, points out a related story from Germanic legend. Heine, a German poet, says in "Stories of Spirits": "When a nix falls in love with a human being, he asks not only to keep the love secret, but also not to raise questions about his origins, his birthplace and his tribe. They never tell their true names but instead give falsified names." And he introduces the following legend.

In the year 711, Beatrix, the only daughter of Duke von Klewe, becomes Duchess at her father's death. One day, a swan comes along the Rhine River towing a small boat. A handsome man is sitting on the boat with a golden sword, a golden horn and a golden ring. Beatrix falls in love with him and they marry. The man asks her not to raise questions about his origin and his tribe; otherwise he has to separate from her. He tells her his name is Helias. After they have some children, the wife finally asks him where he comes from. As soon as that happens, Helias departs by the swan boat. The wife dies after a year of worry and repentance. However, he has left the three treasures—the sword, the horn and the ring—for his three children. His off-spring are still alive. On the top of the tower of Klewe castle is an ornament of a swan. People call this structure "Tower of the Swan."

A legend and not a fairy tale, the story does not start "once upon a time." It mentions the specific time and place and gives individual names. Luthi says, "The events in legends do not stir from the place where they occur. They are likened to specific places as if they were at rest." The man who appears here —Helias may be an artificial name—is a being from a different dimension, presumably a nix. He simply leaves his family as soon as his origin is asked about and, further, does not reveal it. This nix is a spirit of nature. If animals which appear in Japanese non-human marriage stories symbolize nature, the Germanic legend becomes quite similar to the Japanese fairy tales—almost the same as the well-known Japanese legend "Ogata Saburo," especially when we note the prosperity of Helias's offspring. In "Ogata Saburo," after the snake bride-groom left, his son (Ogata Saburo) became a great hero.

Now we are facing a difficult problem. Why do Japanese have fairy tales with tragic endings, whereas European tales end hap-pily although their legends are quite similar? We need further investigation and reflection to answer this. My tentative response is as follows. If we accept Luthi's words—"The beings of the other world appearing in fairy tales have in general good, balanced figures, whereas the beings of the other world appear-ing in legends have distorted faces"—we may say that fairy tales in the West have "balanced figures" of happy marriages and stories in Japan have "balanced figures" of sorrowful beauty. Thus, I would not agree with some Western scholars who have concluded that Japanese fairy tales are close to legends as they do not end happily.

Let us go back to the general interpretation of non-human marriage stories. As we have already used the expression "re-turning to nature" in commenting about the end of "Urashima

Tarō," what if we imagine non-human beings appeared in the stories as representatives of nature? Of course, human beings themselves are part of nature. However, as Jung once put it, humans have a "nature against nature." The relation between humans and nature becomes sometimes very difficult, even tricky. We shall consider the problem with figure 7 in mind. In the (A) group, human beings live as a part of nature, in unity. On the other hand, in the (C) group, humans and nature are separated. The (B) group, Japan, stands in a delicately mediate position. At first, human beings and nature seem to be at one, but at some point the humans try to see themselves as beings different from nature who know what nature is. Nature, however, does not like *to be known*. Thus, humans and nature coexist in a vague, harmonious whole. On the other hand, in group (C), human beings who are radically separated from nature try to recover a relation to it through "nature" in themselves (that is, their animal transformations). The transformation of animals into humans who marry expresses the recovery of a relationship to nature—or reintegration.

What I have said about the relation between human beings and animals can be understood to apply, in man's psyche, to the relation between the conscious and the unconscious. Let us try to see the structure of the psyche through analyzing the pattern of "Crane Wife" and Grimm's "The Raven." Following Erich Neumann's theory, the hero of "The Raven" expresses beautifully the process of Western ego development. The princess is transformed into the raven by her mother's spell. This distinct separation of mother and daughter clearly distinguishes this story from those focused on the mother–daughter unity (chapter three). The male hero must accomplish his tasks for the redemption of the cursed woman. A man is cut apart from nature, a child is separated from the mother, consciousness is severed from the unconscious—these are the same phenomenon. It is a great and, at the same time, cursed event. Thus, only he who can accomplish the task for redemption is able to establish an independent ego.

This is, of course, the Western model, whereas a female figure more suitably symbolizes the Japanese ego. The crane wife tries to establish her position in the human world, preserving her tie with nature in its secrecy. Unlike the Westerner's ego, the Japanese ego is not apart from nature. The crane wife creates her position by proposing marriage and by working. However, by its nature, the developed ego itself must *know*. Thus, the ego *knows* that it is a part of nature. When its function of knowing becomes too discriminating, the ego must detach itself from nature. The man's figure in the story denotes this function of separating. As the wife cannot fight against it, she leaves: there is no alternative but to return to nature.

If we imagine that the ending of "Crane Wife" shown in the Appendix is happy, we can look at what I have said above in a different manner. In the West, a man tries to recover his totality after severing the unity of man and nature, to reintegrate an aspect of nature which differs from the original wholeness. "Nature," for Japanese, here also is not based on a naive unity of man and nature but on the recognition of nature as nature and man as man. Thus, the pain in "knowing" which exists behind the ego's establishment is experienced as "original sin" in the West but in Japan as the sorrowful feeling called *awaré*. These are the foundation stones of their respective cultures.

It is a pity that the woman who appears in this world after so much trouble goes back to the world of "nature" again. We have interpreted it as a kind of happy ending, but we expect her to return. In order to understand the significance of this feminine image, we have to know the structure of the world to which she returned and her strength of endurance so necessary to come back and stay in this world. The former we will take up again in chapter eight; the latter we will discuss next.

SEVEN
The Woman of Endurance

Happy marriages do exist in Japanese fairy tales even though they are small in number. In the last chapter, we discussed women who sorrowfully leave though happy marriage was nearly in their grasp. I would like now to discuss women who achieve this state. From a group of such stories, I'll take up "The Handless Maiden" (CJFT 208) as a useful example.

This fairy tale is especially useful because it exists in Europe in almost the same form. If one reads "The Girl Without Hands" (KHM 31) after having read "The Handless Maiden" given in the Appendix of this book, one will be struck by their similarity. We have already shown how some stories in various countries share some motifs with Japanese tales. But in the case of "The Handless Maiden," the similarity is far closer than that: it and Grimm's tale resemble each other even in most details. When the likeness is so great, everybody tends to think about the possibility of the story's transmigration. Kunio Yanagita points out that some of Grimm's fairy tales, in addition to "The Girl Without Hands," resemble some Japanese fairy tales to quite a high degree. However, he advises us to be cautious in talking about "transmigration." From my standpoint, rather than dwell on this problem, I would like to appreciate that these similar stories are accepted in countries with different cultures. Some of the many variants of "The Handless Maiden" are told all over Japan and Europe. However, if we compare the versions of Grimm and of Japan carefully, interesting cultural differences emerge.

The Handless Maiden

Because we need to bear the European version in mind when considering the Japanese one, I shall give the list of European variants for "The Girl Without Hands" compiled by Bolte and Polivka.[1] It goes as follows: (A) the heroine's hands are cut off because (A-1) she does not accept her father's proposal, (A-2) her father sold her to the devil, (A-3) her father wants to prohibit her prayer, (A-4) her mother is jealous of her, (A-5) her sister-in-law slanders her to her brother; (B), a king finds her in a wood (a garden, a hut, a lake) and marries her in spite of her crippled body; (C), the heroine is driven away again with her newly born child because (C-1) her mother-in-law, (C-2) her father, (C-3) her mother, (C-4) her sister-in-law, (C-5) a devil falsified the letter from the king; (D) the heroine gets her hands again by a miracle in a wood; and (E) the king finds her again.

We shall now examine the Japanese story. The one presented in the Appendix is found in Hinuki-gun, Iwate Prefecture, though its variants are found all over Japan. Most of them consist of the combination of (A-4), (B), (C-3), (D) and (E) according to the list of Bolte and Polivka. At the beginning, the heroine's mother dies when she is four years old and the stepmother comes. The stepmother keeps plotting how she can drive away her stepdaughter because she dislikes her. In a variant in

Europe, the heroine's mother cuts off her daughter's hands because of jealousy, but this is the real mother. In Japanese stories, the stepmother cuts off the daughter's hands. As we saw in chapter four, the stories classified as "Stories of Step-children" in CJFT, including "The Handless Maiden," feature the stepmother's persecution of her daughter and the daughter's happy marriage. Almost all the variants of "The Handless Maiden" in Japan go into the stepmother's persecution whereas, interestingly enough, this is not always necessary in Europe.

As mentioned in chapter four, the stepmother's role in the story is to emphasize the negative sides of motherhood. Here we have to pay attention to the difference in symbolic meaning of what the stepmother does in "White Bird Sister" and in "The Handless Maiden." Both stepmothers wish for their daughters' deaths, showing their power to draw them into the world of The Mother (in this case the world of death). However, the step-mother in "White Bird Sister" puts her daughter into a large pot, whereas the stepmother in this story cuts off her daughter's hands. The former act is "containing," the latter "cutting." In many variants, the mother herself cuts off her daughter's hands. In our story, the father does it, thus underlining the meaning. In driving the daughter to death, the negative mother sets in motion an action out of her innermost depth, but it is a paternal act. "Cutting" belongs to the paternal function.

The story says, "the father listened to what the stepmother said." He obeys his wife completely, following her order to expel his own daughter. Here fatherhood is absolutely subordinate to motherhood. As an example of the cruelty of fatherhood controlled by motherhood, we have mentioned some acts of the Japanese military in the Second World War. In the story, the father mercilessly cuts off his crying daughter's hands. The phrase "cutting off hands" in Japanese means to sever relations. Thus, the daughter has to set out on a lonely journey as a person whose relation to her parents has been sundered.

Here I would like to think about the meaning of the step-mother in this story, who shows, not only the negative side of the mother, but also of the paternal side under the mother's control. Thus the mother figure herself, in some variants, cuts off her daughter's hands. Using a paternal function under her influence, the mother tries to kill her child by cutting. This is quite unlike mothers who love their children too much, whose power works destructively to kill them. In the former case, the child's suffering and loneliness are naturally deepened. This kind of child often cannot have any contact with others.

"Cutting off hands" means severing relations, but its meaning is much wider. Once, when I had a chance to talk about "The Handless Maiden," I asked three women in the audience, "What can't you do if your hands are cut off?" I thought their answers —"can't embrace children," "can't cook," and "can't turn the pages of a book"—reflected their individualities. Moreover, note that the heroine gets back her hands when she tries to embrace the child. In a variant in Brittany, the handless maiden cannot turn the pages of a book of prayer on her lap, so then the wind does that for her. As these associations demonstrate, a person who has lost his or her hands lacks a relation to the outer world and cannot work upon it.

The heroine is driven to cruel loneliness, her hands being cut off as well as her relation to her parents. If she were a heroine in the previously discussed stories, she would have "left the world" for the land of The Mother, but she is cut off from The Mother. She can do nothing but endure. It is true suffering to live apart from The Mother, and the suffering is doubled in a country like Japan where the maternal principle prevails. In a variant, the stepmother first kills a rat in her husband's absence. She shows the dead rat to him, saying it is their daughter's illegitimate child. The father angrily blames the daughter, then cuts off her hands. If we take this version symbolically, we may say her mother feels that the heroine has conceived a new, illegitimate possibility: the decision to live apart from The Mother in Japan. She who intends to live this kind of new life is driven to the world of severe loneliness. Only in front of such a person does "a splendid-looking young man on horseback"—a quite rare figure in Japanese fairy tales—arrive on the scene.

The splendid young man helps her to go back to his home. As his mother is a warmhearted person, she accepts the heroine kindly and agrees to their marriage. The one cut off from The Mother meets here "a graceful mother." Inasmuch as she is a woman, she cannot live completely unrelated to The Mother. If she does not experience this kind of reconnection to mother-hood, she might die. Fortunately, the heroine regains a relation with motherhood, as her loneliness ends. She marries happily and has a child. But her happiness does not last long.

Delighted to have a baby, she writes a letter to her husband. Their communications are, however, disturbed by the interven-tion of the stepmother. Miscommunication between a couple due to a negative mother's intervention occurs often in Japan today. In the many European variants, it is the mother-in-law who rewrites the letters. It happens often that a couple's rela-tionship becomes bad because the mother-in-law tells the wife's words to the husband and vice versa, "changing" the words a bit. Apart from this kind of concrete interpretation, we can think about this situation in a more abstract way. A woman who has experienced marriage and childbirth, finally accepting motherhood, faces difficulty in her relationship with the man by experiencing again the negative side of motherhood. This heroine had a positive experience with the mother before she became four years old, namely, before her mother's death. The changes and the repetition of positive and negative mother ex-periences give important suggestions in considering the psy-chological development of women.

Once again, the heroine has to leave her home—this time with her child—because of the stepmother's plot. On this occa-sion also, the only thing she can do, or what she must do, is en-dure. She does not say a word against her husband or the mother-in-law. She leaves the house with her child, though she has no hands to hold him, saying to her mother-in-law, "It is so sad to leave without reciprocating your kindness to me, a poor crippled one, but if this is my husband's wish there is nothing I can do so I will leave home." If we compare this figure with the women who just leave and return to the land of The Mother, her way of endurance will be understood more vividly. She has to suffer from much deeper distress and loneliness than when she was driven away by her parents.

Repetition of a motif, which occurs often in fairy tales, is always significant—and especially in this story. Not *mere* repetition, it deepens. After having relations with her husband and the graceful mother in a deeper dimension, the woman experiences again, through her husband's apparent betrayal, the loneliness and loss of trust in others which resulted from her father's actual betrayal. There are some who will die if they cannot bear even the first loneliness. There are also many who experience catastrophe because they cannot endure the second loneliness. Such may be the fate of the women who have to live cut off from The Mother.

We are deeply touched by the scene in which her hands grow again. She, who has endured and been passive all the way through, tries to hold the baby with her handless arms when it begins to slip from her back. The active deed is channeled naturally through the most impossible point, and it becomes possible. She can grasp her newly born possibility, her child, with her own hands. Here she experiences motherhood deeply as the mother herself. This is her third reunion with motherhood. At this point, no longer the one cut off from The Mother or from the outer world, she becomes a person who can work actively on others.

Naturally, her relationship with her husband is reestablished after her change. Note that she is praying to the shrine deity when her husband finds her. The support of deep religious feeling is absolutely necessary in order that she can continue her life and develop in spite of her severe loneliness. Marie-Louise von Franz, who analyzes Grimm's "The Girl Without Hands" in detail, indicates that only deep religious experience can heal the deep split and hurt suffered by this woman. She compares the experiences of the girl without hands to a hermit's life, pointing out that a man can find the inner, individual connection to God only through loneliness.[2] This applies equally to

"The Handless Maiden" in Japan. The connection between the religious experience and the maiden herself is told in the same way in many variants in Japan and in the West. The poor connection to the outer world enriches the inner affinity. Since she has by nature a strong tie to the inner world, she may have difficulty in outer relations.

The maiden, with hands regained, meets her husband in the end. When they weep with joy, "mysteriously, where their tears fell, beautiful flowers bloomed." This may show that her feelings, sorrows and joys are far deeper than those in our ordinary dimension. Her feeling, which has always been introverted, comes now "in full bloom" to the outside. No longer handless, she regains full relation to the outer world. This theme of blooming may be a residuum of "returning to nature" of which Japanese fairy tales are so fond.

With the happy ending, it is natural that the stepmother and father are punished by the authorities. Here one can also say that the maiden's happiness occurs at the cost of cutting off her own relatives. Even if she were to recover that relation with her newly grown hands, this would be another story.

The Handless Maiden in the East and the West

We have considered "The Handless Maiden" in Japan. As a comparison, we shall look at Grimm's fairy tale, summarized as follows.

A miller becomes poor and has nothing left but his mill and a large apple tree behind it. One day he meets a strange old man who says, "I will make you rich if you will promise me what is standing behind your mill." The miller easily promises as he thinks only the apple tree is there. However, his daughter is also standing behind the mill. The miller becomes rich. Three years later, the Devil (the old man) comes. The daughter is a beautiful, pious girl. As she washes herself clean and makes a circle around herself with chalk, the Devil cannot come near her. Angrily, the Devil orders the father to take the water away from

her. The father obeys. However, her tears cleanse her. The Devil
furiously asks the father to cut off his daughter's hands. The
father protests, but he is afraid when the Devil threatens him
and he tries to persuade the daughter to let him do it. Since she
answers that he can do what he will, he cuts them off. But the
hands are so clean that the Devil has to give in, losing all rights
over her. The father expresses his gratitude and promises to
keep her most handsomely as long as she lives. But she says,
"Here I cannot stay. I will go forth. Compassionate people will
give me as much as I require." And she sets out on her way.

She wants to eat a pear growing in a royal garden. When she
prays, an angel appears and helps her to eat the fruit. Hearing a
report from the gardener, the king meets the daughter the next
day and learns all the circumstances. He sympathizes with her
and takes her into his palace. The king begins to love her and
has silver hands made for her. They marry. After a year, the king
has to go on a journey. Then everything follows like the
Japanese story. The queen has a baby; then the letters between
the king's mother and the king are intercepted by the Devil, and
the queen must leave the palace with her child. When the queen
enters a great forest and prays, an angel appears and takes them
to a hut where it cares for them. The queen gets her hands back
by the grace of God. When he finds out the truth, the king
journeys to seek his wife and child. After seven years, he arrives
at the hut where they live. While he is sleeping, the queen tells
the child that the king is his father, but the boy protests that
"our father in heaven" is his father. Hearing this conversation,
the king asks who they are. He is very glad to know they are his
beloved wife and child. They return to his palace where the
queen and king marry again and live happily ever after.

You can see the close resemblance to the Japanese story. An
obvious difference is that the father plays a larger role in cutting off his daughter's hands in Grimm's tale. The father does
this as a result of his deal with the Devil, whose appearance here
is typical of European fairy tales. It is the Devil who interferes in
the correspondence. The daughter asks the help of the father in
heaven. Fatherhood—i.e., male beings: the father, the Devil,

and the father in heaven—has deep influence in this story in contrast with the importance of motherhood in the Japanese fairy tale. We shall consider this dissimilarity later. If we assume that the story has transmigrated to Japan, we have to note that almost all variants there are concerned with the relation between the stepmother and the daughter, whereas there are many combinations in Europe as I have shown. We can assume only that that kind of pattern is accepted in Japan as it suits the Japanese mentality or another pattern was transmitted but has shifted into a more Japanese mode.

There are many variants in Europe. Sometimes a real mother cuts off her daughter's hands, and a stepmother intervenes in the communications between the young couple. In a variant in the Balearic Islands in the Mediterranean Sea, the father sells his daughter to the Devil, and it is Mary, "the mother of God," to whom the daughter prays for help. Here the image of the mother is stressed rather than the father in heaven. This may stand in-between Grimm's tale, developing around the axis of father–daughter, and the Japanese tale, unfolding around the mother–daughter relationship. When the distribution of the world's fairy tales is investigated more fully, and if we examine it from the perspective mentioned above, we may get a picture of distribution which reflects the cultural differences of each region.

Comparing the Grimm's and Japanese versions of our story, we notice immediately that the heroine has the same qualities— that is, passivity and strength of endurance. Her attitude, which she maintains when her hands are cut off and when she is driven away from home after her marriage, is the same in both stories. The mover who sits behind her is, however, different: "The Father" in Grimm's and "The Mother" in the Japanese story. The differences which appear in the stories may reflect those of the father–daughter and mother–daughter relationships. But if we look at them from the cultural point of view, the variances reflect the woman's way of living in Japan where the maternal principle is strong and the man's way in the West where the paternal principle prevails. If we think that the male figure stands for the ego (either man's or woman's) in the West and the female figure stands for the Japanese ego, "The Handless Maiden" would be more connected with the general way of life of men and women in Japan.

In Grimm's tale, the father unwittingly makes a deal with the Devil at his daughter's cost. In another European variant, the father cuts off his daughter's hands when he becomes infuriated by her dedication to her prayers. Grimm's tale, too, stresses her religious attitude. "The Father" in the West dislikes the attitude which is too inner-oriented. In the story, the father in heaven compensates for this secular father. The extraverted man is going to sacrifice his daughter for money—dealing with the Devil—and accordingly his daughter's unhappiness begins with her father's will to be rich. On the other hand, the heroine's unhappiness in the Japanese version begins with her mother's death. That is, her tie to the mother is *naturally* cut to experience the negative sides of motherhood. The differences of origin —the father's will and the mother's death—reveal the cultural heterogeneity.

In both stories, the father severs his daughter's hands, but he is provoked by the stepmother in one tale and the Devil in the other. The heroine's passive and nonresistant attitude to her misfortune is also common to both. In Grimm's tale, however, she verbalizes her attitude, saying, "Dear father, do with me what you will" or "Here I cannot stay, I will go forth." She is receptive, but her decision is clearly verbalized. On the contrary, the Japanese heroine's hands are cut off while she is sleeping (in the unconscious state). She sets out on the journey feeling resentment. While her intention never becomes clear, her sorrow and resentment do come out.

In Grimm's tale, the angel, a messenger from the father in heaven, appears to help the lonely daughter. The contrast between the angel and the Devil, with the secular father in-between, is portrayed distinctly. The Japanese story clearly contrasts the stepmother and the graceful mother-in-law. They are, however, humans, not the non-human beings of the West. Their humanity has the same connotation as the absence of magic in Japanese fairy tales we pointed out in the last chapter. Mundane and otherworldly events are easily interwoven, and the unnatural or supernatural (in the Western sense) can occur "naturally." This difference is apparent in the scene in which the heroine's hands grow again. In Grimm's, the heroine's hands are recovered by her pious attitude and the grace of God, whereas in the Japanese story her *natural* movement of trying to embrace her child (slipping down from her back) restores them.

The father–daughter bond in Grimm's tale is broken by the appearance of the Devil. The daughter must accept this appearance of evil and, though very sorrowful, separate from her father in order to develop. Here, her father is no longer her protector. Instead, she is protected by the father in heaven. If the balance between the intrusion of evil and the protection by God were shaken, either the daughter would be destroyed by the evil or she could not become independent of her father. The latter situation holds a possibility of father–daughter incest. In a variant in Europe, the daughter leaves home, rejecting her father's incestuous proposal. In our story, the daughter marries the king with the angel's help, but their happiness is short-lived. The king sets out on a journey—here also the man's interest is oriented to the outer world—and they live separately. Then the Devil disturbs their communications.

Unhappiness results from the couple's disrupted communication in both the stories, reflecting a fairly universal truth. A young couple's conversation will be distorted by an evil intervention (which they do not know about) regardless of how much they love and trust each other. One may even say that their naivete causes this tragedy. Both husband and wife are surprised to get the falsified letters, but they do not know to doubt them. This miscommunication may be necessary after all for the psychological development of women. Evil helps to strengthen the human ties by cutting them.

Let us focus on the heroine's mode of living for a while. Instead of doubting the authenticity of her husband's letters, with their unbearable requests, she accepts his apparent wishes and chooses to bear the loneliness. This behavior is diametrically opposed to the deed of the male hero. If he were she, he would inquire into the truth, fight with the Devil, and even subjugate him. However, in our story, everything goes well because of her passive attitude and prayer; she gets her hands back and she meets her husband again.

This is an attitude of great trust in life itself, of waiting for happiness and not fighting for it. It is the process of incubation. Whereas this mode is thought to be characteristically female in the West, it is the common attitude of both men and women in Japan. It may be a universal "truth" that a couple can attain their happiness in the form of "remarriage" through the endurance of indescribable loneliness on each side, provided they love and trust each other greatly. In Grimm's story, the form of "remarriage" is clearly stated: "The King and Queen were married again." Whether or not a couple whose bond has been cut by an almost inevitable intervention of evil can happily remarry is dependent upon how well they can suffer their own loneliness, an endurance supported by deep religious experience. It is quite an impressive contrast that the father in heaven stands behind the whole process in the West, while in Japan it is "Nature."

Happy Marriages

"The Handless Maiden" happily ends in marriage though it has the form of "remarriage." Many of the happy marriages in Japanese fairy tales are found in the twenty stories classified under the title of "Stories of Stepchildren" in CJFT (205-22). We find that about half of these include the happy marriage of a stepchild who endures her or his stepmother's persecution, and the other half primarily relate the punishment to the stepmother (such as the mother's mistakenly killing her own child instead of her stepchild). In the former group are "The Handless Maiden" and "White Bird Sister" (see chapter four), and in the latter are "The Stepchild and the Bird" and "The Stepchild and the Flute." They differ in many ways, including whether they contain the marriage story or not.

The stepchild stories which involve marriages are, in general, long and interesting with several climaxes in their plots, whereas those with the stepmother's punishment are short and plain. One may feel that the stories focus on the persecution of stepchildren by the mothers. I have previously said that scholars in other countries criticize Japanese fairy tales for being similar to legends or for having vague endings. An example would be the stepmother story containing the marriage story which gives us the feeling of a Western mode. Actually, in addition to "The Handless Maiden," we might also cite "Seven Swans" (CJFT 214), "The Old Man's Fur" (CJFT 209), and "Komebuku-Awabuku" (CJFT 205A) as being similar to stories in Grimm's fairy tales such as "The Six Swans" (KHM 49), "Allerleirauh" (Many Different Kinds of Fur) (KHM 65), and "Cinderella" (KHM 21). "Komebuku-Awabuku" consists of two combined stories, its second half corresponding to "Cinderella" (as Seki points out).

These close similarities raise again the question of story transmigration. Even if we accept the possibility, we should notice that Japanese have accepted these kinds of stories and not those of male heroes. One might also conclude, however, that even stories with close resemblances are generated spontaneously in different areas. In any case, we can see that a characteristic group of Japanese fairy tales contain the happy marriage of the stepdaughters who have been persecuted by their stepmothers.

The analysis of "The Handless Maiden" tells us that a woman can become independent through experiencing the negative sides of motherhood: the stepmother promotes the daughter's psychological development. In other words, a mother must show her negative sides to her daughter for her growth. If a mother shows only her "good" sides, her daughters face difficulties in their process of maturation. This kind of wisdom is contained in Japanese fairy tales. As I have pointed out already, the woman figure in "The Handless Maiden" presents the process of development not only for women but also for men in Japan. Then what about male heroes in Japanese fairy tales?

Among all the stepchild stories with the theme of marriage, "Ash Boy" (CJFT 211) is the only one with a male hero. The story should be classified, as Seki points out, under the title of "Marriage Story" rather than that of "Stories of Stepchildren" as far as its pattern is concerned. I shall summarize the story as follows.

The hero, called Mamichigane, is the child of a lord. He is, however, driven away from home by the plot of his stepmother. When he departs, his father gives him splendid clothes and a horse. On the way, he meets an old man from whom he gets poor clothes to wear, and he conceals the nice clothes elsewhere. Becoming a servant of a *chōjya*, he works as a rice cook. He makes himself valuable as he works diligently. One day the *chōjya* asks him to go to the theater with his family. After he declines the invitation, he appears in the theater wearing the splendid clothes, riding on his horse. Everybody thinks that he may be a God from heaven. Only the daughter of the *chōjya* says, "He is my home's *haibo* [ash boy]. I can recognize him as he has a black spot behind his left ear." Upon hearing this, her parents scold her as it is very impolite to say such a thing to a God from heaven. The next time, when Mamichigane is going to change into his fine clothes, the *chōjya's* daughter comes back home, on the excuse that she has forgotten a pair of *zōri* (straw sandals). As she sees the truth, the hero goes to the theater with the daughter on the horse's back. The *chōjya's* family members bow to them saying, "This time the Gods come as a couple."

The daughter suffers from lovesickness. A shaman tells the *chōjya* that in his house lives somebody whom the daughter would like to marry. The *chōjya* asks all of his employees to come into his daughter's room to see her face to face. At the end, the ash boy appears with the fine clothes, riding on the horse. The *chōjya* asks him to be the bridegroom, and they have a great wedding ceremony. Then ash boy wants to visit his own parents. His wife advises him not to eat mulberries on the way. As he does not follow her advice, he dies. The horse brings his dead body to his parents' home. His father puts the body into an old wooden *saké* bucket. The hero's wife comes after him with the water of rebirth by which he is reborn. When she is going to take him home, his father claims that he cannot join another family, as the son is his only child. She then asks her father-in-law to come with them. Mamichigane says, "We cannot take care of two fathers at the same time. Father, please find a proper person to adopt for your son. I shall send money for you. I shall work at my wife's house as she saved my life." Then the couple return to the wife's house and "have lived happily till now."

In this story, it is true that the male hero, ash boy, marries happily through his own efforts. One can easily notice, however, that he is quite different from heroes in typical Western fairy tales. His behavior is nearer to a trickster's than to a hero's. He neither kills a dragon nor averts a disaster but takes an active part in changing his appearance as many tricksters do. It is interesting that the daughter of the *chōjya* sees through his disguise. She falls in love with him and rescues him from death. In the last half of the story, the actual protagonist is the woman. If we consider that ash boy asks his father to adopt a child and he himself lives in his wife's house, we sense all the more that she is the main person. The behavior of ash boy's wife—tricksterish—reminds me of the sister in "The Elder Sister and the Younger Brother," discussed in chapter four. These two stories are found in Oki-no-erabu Island and may have some connection. So their marriage is unlike the marriage of a prince and princess in Western stories.

The story shows the same pattern as "The Handless Maiden" in that the marriage at first does not provide a happy ending. Instead, the couple must be separated for a while, and their reunion is really the happy ending. If we note that the stories with women protagonists have often the pattern of "remarriage," this may be seen as a woman's story. Though its title is "Ash Boy" and his leaving home, compelled by his stepmother, resembles a story of the Western male hero, its development shows that it is about a heroine. This feature may be one of the characteristics of Japanese fairy tales.

We shall look at other marriage stories in which male heroes take active parts. "Mr. Horse Child" found also in Oki-no-erabu Island (CJFT 121 as a variant), "Sleeping Tarō Next Door" (CJFT 25 as a variant), and "The Pigeon Lantern" (CJFT 126) have male heroes with distinctly trickster characters. In "Mr. Horse Child," a poor young man called by that name disguises himself as a rich man, with an old man's help, and succeeds in marrying the daughter of a *chōjya*. This is clearly marriage through deceit. In both "Sleeping Tarō Next Door" and "The Pigeon Lantern," a lazy, poor man marries the daughter of the *chōjya* who lives next door. That these men all become happy in spite of their nasty tricks suggests the Japanese accept this kind of image as almost heroic. It is a peculiarity of Japanese fairy tales—and of the psychology of the Japanese—that we can hardly find typical "heroes" in the fairy tales with "happy marriages." "Heroes" in Japan are rather women of "endurance" such as we have met in this chapter. The Japanese man tends to become a trickster-like being, as he is not separated fully from the mother. The heroes in Japanese mythology, such as Susa-no-wo or Yamato-takeru, have a strong trickster tendency in a way similar to fairy tales.

Let us touch a bit on "Pond Snail Son" (CJFT 134). When I discussed the non-human marriage story in the last chapter, I mentioned that few of these stories lead to a happy marriage. We can say that "Pond Snail Son" may be the only exception to that (the story is not classified under the title of "Non-Human Marriage Story," but "Childbirth" in CJFT). The following is a summary. An old, childless couple makes a vow to the deity of the water of the rice field. Then the deity gives them a *tanishi* (pond snail) as a son. When their *tanishi* son grows up, he wants to marry the daughter of a *chōjya*, but the old man (his father) tells him that he had better give up. One day he stays at the *chōjya's* house. At night, he attaches rice around the mouth of the *chōjya's* daughter while she is sleeping. Next morning, the *tanishi* son falsely accuses the *chōjya's* daughter of stealing his rice and eating it. For compensation, the *chōjya* allows him to marry his daughter. At a spring festival, the son, attached to his wife's head, goes to a shrine. A crow comes flying and causes *tanishi* son to fall down into a rice field. While the wife is weeping, a splendid, handsome young man stands behind her and tells her that he is her husband. He explains that he had taken the form of a *tanishi,* but now he is able to return to his original form as she has served him so faithfully. The *chōjya* is very glad to learn this, and they hold a wedding ceremony again. The young couple becomes a *chōjya* family incomparable to others, and people respect the son as *tanishi chōjya.*

This wonderful marriage is so rare for a non-human bridegroom story. It has as a whole, however, a structure similar to that of "Ash Boy." The title is the man's name; the man gets the woman in a trickster-like way; the marriage occurs early; and true happiness is gained by the woman's activity. ("Pond Snail Son" says, "They hold a wedding ceremony again.") These are the themes they share. (In "Pond Snail Son" some magical transformations are hinted at, but very vaguely.) Again, the figure of "the woman of endurance" comes to the surface: the woman marries a man who tricks her, serves him faithfully, weeps sorrowfully when her pond-snail husband disappears into the rice field. With these considerations, we think that the "mover" of the story may be the woman.

From what we have seen, we understand how important the figure of "the woman of endurance" is. In the marriage stories in which the men take seemingly active roles, we can recognize that there are, standing behind them, "the women of endurance." Here my fantasy continued since chapter one goes as follows. The woman who sorrowfully left this world because the man broke his promise comes back again and again, changing her form, and yet she is driven away each time. She can, however, succeed in gaining happiness in this world by enduring all the suffering with her decision to leave the land of The Mother. This figure of "the woman of endurance" has deep meaning to every Japanese regardless of sexual differences. She stands for the ego of the Japanese. One can never say it is passive or weak for being a female.

A modern man, especially, may be dissatisfied with the figure of a woman who does nothing but endure. The woman in "Ash Boy," however, is neither very passive nor one who simply endures. Her essence lies in her ability to see through to the true nature of ash boy, whereas he tricks everybody else. This woman's wisdom brings her happiness. Her ability of seeing essential nature strongly contrasts with the woman's "hiding the true nature" stressed in the last chapter. In a variant of "Pond Snail Son," the daughter herself says, "If it is so, I would like to be his wife," although the old man (the father) or an employee of the *chōjya* is against his proposal to the daughter. "If it is so" is a vague but meaningful comment. The daughter must have seen the true nature of the pond snail. As she declares, "I would like to be his wife," her active deed, based on the wisdom of women, belongs to a different dimension from the women of endurance. We shall continue to discuss the image of this active woman. Before that, however, we have to investigate the structure of the world to which crane wives return, mentioned at the end of the last chapter.

EIGHT
The Old and the Beauty

To investigate the structure of the world to which non-human wives return, I shall take up "The Dragon Palace Boy" (CJFT 223). In this story, a man invited to the Dragon Palace is given an ugly (or dirty) boy by the beautiful maiden who lives there, and this boy eventually brings fortune to the man. The story describes beautifully the structure of the world under the sea. Kunio Yanagita has written an excellent paper about this story, "The Sea God Boy." Eiichiro Ishida has published *The Mother of Peach Tarō*, focusing on the relation between the small boy and his mother-like woman, introduced here in chapter five.

The Dragon Palace which appears in Japanese fairy tales excellently expresses the depth of the Japanese psyche. In "The Sea God Boy" Yanagita writes that "The Dragon Palace in Japan is a peculiar place. Almost always a young woman there describes the conditions of the sea. Moreover, she carries a mysterious boy in her arms and tries to make contact with this world. The sea is the eternal land of the mother for this nation [Japan]."

What kind of structure has the land of our mother? Let us consider "Hyōtoku," a variant of "The Dragon Palace Boy." A man visits a world down a hole he finds in a mountain, not under the sea. While the mountain and the sea are completely different places, they do not diverge in their psychological meaning—i.e., the depth of the psyche—hence the two stories are classified together.

Hyōtoku

The story begins with "Once there was an old man and an old woman." They have no child, no possibility of new development. In similar situations, an unexpected child sometimes appears, such as Kaguya-hime or Momotarō (Peach Boy) in Japanese fairy tales. In our story, new development comes from the big hole which the old man discovers when he goes to gather firewood on the mountain. The old man tries to plug up the hole with a bundle of firewood, but it is not sufficient. He has to put in all the firewood which he has gathered in three days, because the hole is much wider and deeper than he expected.

This story's beginning describes the phenomenon of regression: the flowing of psychic energy into the unconscious is nicely expressed by the image of putting bundles into the hole. The number three appears here also in the wood he has gathered in three days, suggesting a dynamic possibility of development. In many variants of "The Dragon Palace Boy," the man throws flowers and wood into the sea—dedicating them to the God in the Dragon Palace—then is invited there as repayment. In that situation, the man intentionally throws wood as his offering for the sea God, and it is recognized clearly that the regression is creative.

Regarding the visit to the Dragon Palace, Yanagita comments, "Some explanations are naturally required for the situation in which only one person, chosen from thousands of people, can visit such a wonderful land," and he details two kinds of explanation. One is "the person deserves it": he is invited because of his fidelity to parents or kindness to animals, indicating he is a man of great virtue. The other reason is recognition of one's service to the palace. The former case is exemplified by "Urashima Tarō," who is concerned for his mother and kind to the turtle. Our story belongs to the latter: namely, the old man is invited because he dedicates firewood to the Dragon Palace. About this theme, Yanagita says, "The story called 'The Flower Seller Dragon God' is found exclusively in Japan and its southern islands. The story is told throughout Japan with many beautiful variations. Why is it so much loved and so variously developed? It has been our task to think about it for these twenty years." The story type which Yanagita calls "The Flower Seller Firewood Gathering" is, according to him, unique to Japan and its neighbors.

So far I also have not found in any other countries the story in which the hero is invited to the land under the sea (or underground) because he has thrown something there as a present. In CJFT, AT 555 is nominated as a variant of the story. One of the stories classified as AT 555 is Grimm's "The Fisherman and His Wife" (KHM 19). There, the fisherman catches a flatfish which is actually a bewitched prince. As he sets the fish free, his wishes are fulfilled. This is a story with the theme of animals repaying kindness. Both the Japanese tale and Grimm's share the theme that man's greediness causes a loss of fortune. However, "The Fisherman and His Wife" has nothing to do with visiting the other world. Here we can refer to Grimm's "The Three Feathers" (KHM 63), although the whole pattern of that story differs completely from ours. In that one, the hero goes down to the underworld in order to get something, but is not invited. The focus changes significantly when the underworld invites the hero because of his dedication to it.

Tchistov, a Russian scholar of fairy tales, notably comments on "The Liver of a Monkey" (CJFT 35): "The whole story is developed from the point of view of the undersea land." This may be true for our story. When the hero goes down to the underworld to fetch something, the story is told from the point of view of the land on earth. However, when some being in the underworld (or under the sea) accepts flowers or firewood as a gift and wants to invite the man (who has thrown them voluntarily or involuntarily), the story develops from the point of view of the depths.

Here one of the peculiarities of Japanese fairy tales is evident. Interpreting psychologically, we can say that the eyes by which Japanese look at the world are located in the unconscious depths rather than in the conscious. Since the eyes' function is seeing, however, seeing cannot be fully unconscious, so we had better say "half-closed eyes" to avoid a contradiction. Further, it is not unknown that half-closed eyes can recognize certain things better than fully opened ones.

Let us return to "Hyōtoku." When the old man has put "all the bundles he had chopped and collected for three days" into the hole, a beautiful lady appears and asks him to make a visit inside the hole. When we put psychological energy into the unconscious, some meaningful images appear to us. Perhaps the beautiful lady reminds us of the lady in "The Bush Warbler's Home." However, the man here or in "The Dragon Palace Boy" differs from the man who quite unexpectedly meets the lady in "The Bush Warbler's Home." The former has dedicated flowers or firewood, hence he can descend to the deeper world, accepting the lady's invitation.

Down the hole is a beautiful house, and the firewood is stacked neatly beside it. The old man enters the guest room and meets the noteworthy inhabitants: the lady, the old "man with a white beard" and the child who has such a misshapen face that looking at it is embarrassing and who also fiddles with its navel constantly. This triad of the old man, the beautiful woman and the ugly boy seems quite meaningful, but it does not appear in all variants of "The Dragon Palace Boy." For example, in the one recorded in CJFT, the princess Otohime appears, and the boy called Toho snivels and drivels, but there is no old man. Or, in a variant found in Oki-no-erabu Island, an old man with white hair and a beautiful lady are there, but no boy. What the visitor to the Dragon Palace gets in that version is not a boy but a treasure ball called "Shijiguban" which exists only there. One can live without working if one lays the ball in front of the altar to the ancestors. Among the many kinds of variations, the most frequent pairs are the old man and the beautiful lady or the lady and the boy. In "Hyōtoku," all three appear together.

The boy nevertheless attracts our attention. Yanagita notes with much interest that the Dragon Palace boy has an ugly face and a vulgar name. In some variants, the boy is called Yokenai or Untoku; Yanagita comments, "The meaning of Yokenai or Untoku is not clear. But we can assume that these names are not good ones." In our story, the boy is called Hyōtoku, meaning fire blower, "who is understood as the same being originally as Hyottoko whose mask shows a face blowing fire, pursing up his lips." These boys not only have unpleasant names but also "are very dirty and seemingly not at all precious." Yet, they paradoxically bring great fortune. The productions from the unconscious seem ugly and worthless from a conscious perspective, but they become valuable beyond one's conscious judgment if they are treated properly. In a variant in Higo District, the boy is called the Runny-nosed Boy-*sama* (*sama* is attached to indicate a person in higher positions, usually older). Yanagita says, "To add *sama* for a runny-nosed boy is a difficult thing for common people. It is reasonable that only the old man who is so devoted as not to feel strange about the name of Runny-nosed Boy-*sama* is rewarded." The comment hits the mark. We have to be devoted to this ugly "trivial" being.

The old man treats the boy properly, but the greedy old woman's attitude is wrong. Since gold comes out from the boy's navel, the old woman sticks it, wanting to get more, whereupon the boy dies. In other variants the old man is at fault; his change of attitude causes the boy to vanish. In a variant found in Mitsuke-shi, Niigata Prefecture, the poor man is invited to the Dragon Palace as he has been presenting flowers to Otohime. There the princess gives him a boy called Toho saying, "The boy drivels and snivels, but he can fulfill any wish you have if you take care of him properly. You shall have the boy." Thanks to the boy, the man becomes very rich. However, the child is so dirty that the man no longer can stand it and tells him to "blow your nose" or "change your clothes." When the boy does not obey, the man says to him, "I want to dismiss you. Please go home."As soon as Toho leaves, the man becomes poor again and desperate ("desperate"is *Toho-ni-Kureru* in Japanese, hence the boy is named Toho). The man makes use of Toho at first, but he cannot stand the boy's seeming ugliness as he becomes rich. Then he loses the fortune.

Almost all variants of "The Dragon Palace Boy" recorded in CJFT end with the loss of fortune due to the commonplace thinking of the man or his relatives. Most frequently, the greed of the man's brother or wife causes the catastrophe. The same pattern appears in Grimm's "The Fisherman and His Wife," a moral story which teaches us that a greedy person will lose everything.

Desire itself, of course—to gain something or to make life easier—promotes the development of human civilization. And, in due course, ego consciousness is established. On the other hand, as we well know, too much desire causes misfortune. The balance between "desire" and "no desire" may enable us to lead meaningful lives. Japanese fairy tales seem to lay too much emphasis on the "no desire" side. In "Crane Wife" we saw that the desire generated in the man caused the tragedy.

Another story like "The Fisherman and His Wife" in Grimm's tales, "The Three Feathers," contrasts with "Hyōtoku." Even though the heroes of both stories descend to the underworld, what they do there differs. The hero in Grimm's gets a variety of things from the underworld, and the frog who lives there transforms itself into the most beautiful princess on earth. At every point, the emphasis is laid on this world, as the princess comes from the underworld and begins to live here. In "Hyōtoku," on the other hand, the boy who comes to this world keeps the traits of the other. He hardly meets the "desire" of the "commonplace thinking" of people in this world before he returns to the underworld. In other words, he keeps the qualities of the unconscious, and he will go back to the world of the unconscious unable to bear the force of consciousness to any extent, although he profits it.

The hero in the world of consciousness in "The Three Feathers" journeys to the world of the unconscious and gains something there. He succeeds in integrating something from the unconscious into consciousness. The hero who hardly seems to be a "hero" in "The Dragon Palace Boy" is invited by the world of the unconscious and given something there. He can bring it back to the world of consciousness for a while, but it returns to the unconscious after all. The compelling power of the unconscious is incredibly strong in Japan.

Senex Consciousness

What is brought to this world returns to the one under the sea because of its strong magnetism. The pattern evident in "The Dragon Palace Boy" repeats what we have seen again and again since "The Bush Warbler's Home" in chapter one. If we simply identify this world with consciousness and the other world with the unconscious and compare the Japanese and Western stories, we are tempted to say—as I did at the end of the last section—that the Japanese story shows the strong power of the unconscious or, in other words, the weakness of Japanese ego consciousness.

However, as I mentioned regarding "half-closed eyes," we can take the whole, including both worlds, as a kind of consciousness, avoiding the simple identification of the world under the sea with the unconscious. This whole surely differs from the ego consciousness established in the West, and the structure of "The Dragon Palace Boy" does not have to be interpreted as "the weakness of ego," but may indicate some useful knowledge about a different type of ego. In order to come to know it, we have to know the relationship between the inhabitants in the world under the sea. Let us focus first on the image of the old man.

In "Hyōtoku," the splendid old man with the white beard behaves like the chief of the house. The old man in the Dragon Palace appears sometimes in the variants of "Urashima Tarō" as well as those of "The Dragon Palace Boy." According to the *Kojiki*, in the myth of Toyotama-hime—which has much to do with both fairy tales—the old "God of the sea" lives in the world under the sea. The myth says that the old God of the sea is Toyotama-hime's father. We can presume that the old man and the beautiful lady in the fairy tale are father and daughter. Here we recall another "old man with white hair" who appears in "The Elder Sister and the Younger Brother" discussed in chapter four. Though not a dweller in the undersea land, he too lives in a different dimension and has wisdom beyond this ordinary world.

CJFT contains the following story as a variant of "Urashima Tarō." A man goes to a mountain to gather firewood. There he finds two old hermits (*sennin*) playing *Go*. It takes them a long time. They eat lunch before finishing and share the food with the man. While watching the game, the man leans on the handle of an ax. Finally the game is over. The hermit points out that the handle of the ax has decayed. The man feels strange as such a handle rarely decays even in a hundred years. Returning to his village, he is surprised at the utter change and is told that once upon a time a man went to a nearby mountain to gather firewood and never returned.

In this story a strange experience of time is an important theme. The old hermits playing *Go* (one game takes more than a hundred years!) are also the old men who live in the other world. Each stone piece which they put on the board may have to do with an event in the history of this world during a century.

This strange old man appears, of course, in fairy tales of other countries as well and can be seen as a universal image for mankind. However, the Japanese tales may contain many more instances than the European, although one can hardly verify it statistically. Lerich, a West German scholar, names "the frequent appearance of an old man" as a characteristic of Japanese fairy tales. He might be referring as well to the old man and woman who appear as protagonists in many stories but who differ from the old man we are concerned with now. At any rate, we may count the emphasis on old men as a peculiarity of Japanese fairy tales. Rarely do old men become protagonists in European fairy tales.

We might well think that the old men who frequent Japanese fairy tales are the reflections of the images of the old men living in "the other world." Since an old man is often the main protagonist in these stories, this old figure probably symbolizes a consciousness well-suited to the Japanese ego. When I had been thinking about this for some time in Japan, I was delighted to discover that James Hillman was discussing "senex consciousness," an idea he has been developing since he published the paper "On Senex Consciousness" in 1970. I would like briefly to describe this consciousness according to his thought.

Hillman's interest in the senex stems from his concern with the puer aeternus, a figure which I touched on in chapter five. However, I stressed its negative side at that point, focusing on the bond between puer and mother. Until recently, many Jungians viewed the puer aeternus similarly. Hillman has tried to see this figure from a different angle. If we present his idea schematically, he classifies the young into three groups: son, hero and puer. Both the hero and son are concerned with the mother: the son submits to her, and the hero overcomes her. Here it is necessary, of course, to take "the mother" symbolically. If we rely on the symbolical expressions we have used so far, whether or not one does indeed slay the mother discriminates between a son and a hero. Hillman stresses, on the other hand, that a puer must be considered in relation not with the mother but the senex, apprehending the senex and the puer as one archetype rather than two. Since the puer as an archetype has many attributes of the senex and vice versa, the archetype contains opposites within it.

One may think it impossible or incomprehensible to speak of the coexistence of puer and senex. Nevertheless, this kind of image is quite prolific in Chinese culture. Senex consciousness would be a very useful idea for anyone trying to understand that culture. It has long been familiar to Japanese who are much influenced by China. Mikio Omuro's "A Study of Fairy Tales of *Go*" provides rich examples of the old-and-young tandem. The two hermits in the variant of "Urashima Tarō," introduced at the beginning of this section, play *Go* also. Playing *Go* may be related to the senex. Omuro introduces the following story from "Chuang-tsu" in his book. An emperor who is lost meets a boy and asks him the way. The emperor is surprised at the boy's knowledge. The boy finally teaches him how to rule the country. Bowing to the boy twice, the emperor praises him as the teacher in heaven. The boy has the innocent mind of a child and the wisdom of age. Thereby Omuro concludes that "the boy must be very old."

With this image in mind, we shall think about senex consciousness following Hillman. The first characteristic of the senex is its double nature. On one side, represented by the figure of an old wise man, it tends stubbornly to preserve the rule from the ancients. At the same time, it strongly and immediately moves to destroy that rule, a behavior represented by the puer figure. Accordingly, its figure is cold, hard and permanent, but underneath burns a fire of destruction. The inseparable intertwining of the two opposite qualities creates a powerful tension.

Hillman writes, "We can piece together the major characteristics of Kronos–Saturn as archetypal image of the senex,"[1] and he describes senex consciousness as follows:

> The temperament of the senex is cold, which can also be expressed as distance. Senex-consciousness is outside of things, lonely, wandering, a consciousness set-apart and outcast.... Saturn views the world from the outside, from such depths of distance that he sees it all "upside down", and to this view the structure of things is revealed. He sees the irony of truth within the words, and the city from the cemetery, the bones below the game of skin.[2]

This wisdom, though cold, is unchangeable and keeps rule and order. However, it is so unchangeable that it tends to coagulation. Then it is related to depression. If a young man is intruded upon by this senex consciousness, he will experience extreme depression or apathy and might easily commit suicide.

The characteristics of senex consciousness will become more evident if we compare it with the ego consciousness described in Erich Neumann's theory which we will call "hero consciousness" from now on. Whereas senex consciousness has its viewpoint in the depths, underground, hero consciousness is properly identified with the sun shining in the sky. As the myth of the dragon fight symbolizes, hero consciousness cuts itself off from the mother and separates things distinctly. The hero who has established himself, however, will be thrown out by the next one. Hero consciousness has, therefore, characteristics of "progress and development," contrasting strongly with the coagulation of senex consciousness. Hero consciousness contributes to the development of civilization, whereas senex consciousness has nothing to do with "development." On the other hand, hero consciousness is always threatened by death, while senex consciousness is not so disturbed as it includes death within it.

When the coagulation, the unchangeability of senex consciousness, reaches its peak, self-destruction occurs and anarchy is generated by the sudden functioning of the puer. The Saturnalia, the festival of Saturn held in the ancient Roman era, typically presents the destruction of senex coagulation. According to Hillman, "the festivals of Kronos and Saturn provided for a fantasy of leisure, peace and bounty, food and drink without toil, an end of slavery and property."[3] After such a powerful disruption, senex consciousness recovers its equilibrium, and everything becomes completely the same as before. There is no "progress." Unchangeability and excitement are existing here harmoniously; senex and puer can coexist.

The images of the hero and the senex contrast strongly in regard to their relations with women. The process of establishing hero consciousness requires that one win a maiden after slaying the mother, whereas senex consciousness needs no woman. Actually, the man who takes the role of an old wise man in fairy tales appears often by himself. Saturn "is patron of eunuchs and celibates, being dry, cold and impotent,"[4] as Hillman says. However, in his duality, he is also a God of fertility, represented sometimes by the lecherous goat. Senex consciousness is duplex: sexual impotence *and* uninhibited carnal desire. At the interplay between the dual tendencies, sexual fantasy can emerge.

When senex consciousness has its female partner, she is dark and gloomy. Originally a celibate, Saturn later has a feminine counterpart, Lua. Hillman says that Lua—lues (the plague)—brings evils and illness to this world. She represents the depressive mood which exists behind the wisdom of the old. When such gloominess is combined with uninhibited carnal desire, the senex's female partner will become the one who devours everything into the earth, reminding us of Yama-uba.

In our story, the old man lives with a beautiful lady. We find this kind of pair, an old man and a maiden, in some stories. In a mind otherwise cold, hard and unchangeable, there exists a lovely and sensitive point, an unexpected revelation of vulnerability. The unchangeable senex consciousness may change only through contact with such a point.

Father–Daughter Constellation

As in the case of "Hyōtoku," an old man and maiden pair sometimes appears in fairy tales and myths. In some variants of "Urashima Tarō," Otohime lives with the God of dragons, seemingly her father. In the myth of Toyotama-hime (which is supposed to have connections with these fairy tales), her father appears as the God of the sea. In *Nihonshoki*, Toyotama-hime reports her encounter with the Prince Ho-wori to her parents. However, the other variants in the *Nihonshoki* and the *Kojiki* version describe only her father and mention nothing about her mother. This may reflect the importance of the relation of father–daughter and the triviality of her mother. The father easily allows his daughter's marriage in this myth, but she returns to his land after all. Thus, the tie between father and daughter remains strong.

This father–daughter relation reminds me of Kronos and Aphrodite in Greek mythology. Kronos is the Greek equivalent of Saturn, a personification of senex consciousness. According to Hesiod, Kronos cuts off his father Uranos's genitals, and his semen drops into the sea where Aphrodite is born. Here it is a bit delicate to decide her parentage as Kronos conceives Aphrodite in the sea through the seminal material of Uranos. Psychologically speaking, however, we can consider Kronos to be Aphrodite's father. Her birth from the sea parallels that of Toyotama-hime, daughter of the sea God.

Hillman interprets the story of Kronos and Aphrodite as follows. Senex consciousness has sexual fantasies, but these are cut off by senex-repression and thrown into the unconscious. Sexual fantasies inseminate the sea, and "the images return as the father's daughter: sweet, alluring, aphrodisiacal fantasies bred of the union of sexuality's 'upper' genitals and the emotional depths."⁹ Kronos and Aphrodite give us a fine example of the father–daughter constellation.

One of the psychological meanings of this constellation can be explained as follows: the father–son and mother–daughter constellations represent the extremes of human consciousness. The former denotes the masculine consciousness, and the latter—which would thereby hardly be called "consciousness"—is close to nature's state. Between these extremes, as shown below, the mother–son and father–daughter constellations exist as the intermediate or compensatory states.

The Constellations of Parents and Children

Father—Son
Mother—Son
Father—Daughter
Mother—Daughter

Jung points out that the emphasis upon the father–son constellation in European Christian culture is compensated by the mother–son constellation. The function of compensation hardly works between extreme opposites but often between two beings which have some elements in common and at the same time are in opposition. The mother–daughter constellation is too extreme to work compensatorily for the father–son relation, though the mother–son tandem compensates for the latter relation with mother aspects, while the two constellations share the common possibility of growing sons—the possibility of the establishment of the male ego.

The situation is the same for the mother–daughter constellation. The father–son relation does not compensate it, but the father–daughter tandem can. If we think European male consciousness is the peak of psychological development, we can read the four sets of tandems on page 155 as a schematic presentation of the development of consciousness. Since we need to free ourselves from such a viewpoint, we must recognize the value for each way of consciousness. I will now consider fairy tales in which the father–daughter constellation plays a role.

The Japanese story "Ogin Kogin" (CJFT 207) is a stepmother and daughter story. Here the happy marriage (discussed in chapter seven) does not occur, and the father–daughter relation is stressed in the end. Though this is an interesting story with many variants, we will focus only on the problem of the father–daughter relation without more detailed interpretation.

There are two sisters called O-tsuki (The Moon) and O-hoshi (The Star). The Moon is a stepchild and the Star a blood child of their mother. The stepmother tries to kill the Moon several times, but the Star always saves her sister. They finally leave home and are rescued by the feudal lord who has them live in his mansion. After some time, the two sisters see a blind beggar chanting "Moon and Star, worth far more than even heaven and earth, what's happened with you? If you are still there, why am I striking this drum? Kan, kan. . . ." The two sisters embrace him, realizing he is their father. When Moon's tear enters her father's left eye and Star's tear enters his right, both eyes open and he can see again. The lord is so impressed by this that he has them live happily in his mansion.

The most remarkable thing in this story is its ending with the father–daughter unity, despite the fact that in the first half the daughters try to become independent, leaving their home because of the negative mother's persecution. When the negative sides of the mother are too strong, the father tends to compensate with positive mother mentality. Hence, the relation between the father and daughters here becomes similar to the mother–daughter unity which prevents the daughters from marrying. The peculiarity of this story will become clearer if we compare it with a typical pattern in Western fairy tales in which a father imposes many difficult problems on the daughter's suitor and the young man overcomes them finally to marry her. Our story indicates the strength of the father–daughter tie in Japan.

We assume that the father–daughter constellation may appear often in Asian fairy tales to compensate the mother–daughter constellation which plays such a big role in those cultures. My experience of reading Asian stories convinces me of this. We will take up "Who Is the Provider?" from Pakistan as an interesting example.

A king has seven daughters, all beautiful and chaste princesses. The seventh one is the most beautiful as well as the best cook in her country. The king asks his daughters every day, "Who is the provider of your meal?" Except for the youngest one, each replies, "The king is." One day the king demands an answer from his youngest daughter. She says, "God is." Enraged by her response, he chases her away to the jungle. There she meets a young flutist and takes him for her servant. They travel on together, looking for a home for her. After some time, the man finds some rubies in a stream and thinks this means something must be upstream. Sure enough, there in a castle he finds a captive princess called Red Fairy, who, after refusing to marry a demonic deity, remains his prisoner. Assisted by the young man, she kills the parrot in which the demon has kept his soul. After they rejoin the princess, she and Red Fairy become as close as sisters. Red Fairy builds a palace for her friend, and they invite guests, including the king. Eating what the princess has prepared, he remembers his youngest daughter sorrowfully. He tells Red Fairy how he lost his daughter and that he wishes to see her once more before he dies. The princess comes and speaks to him, "Don't you think it is God who provides everything for us? Although you couldn't even find your lost daughter, I have gotten a palace and treasures." Her father wholeheartedly agrees with her, and they live happily thereafter.

The princess never marries in this story, which ends happily with a strong tie between father and daughter (as in "Ogin Kogin" in Japan). This Pakistani story tells nothing about the mother. Like the case of the Toyotama-hime myth in Japan, this indicates the strength of the father–daughter unity and the absence of the mother or omission of her role. All the daughters, except the seventh, live wholly in the security of the father–daughter unity. But the youngest daughter differs from them. We regret that we cannot be sure what sort of "God" she refers to, but we can assume that, from the context, he is male. With lucid eyes, she can see the father–daughter constellation is one with the heavenly father, rather than with the personal one. This story presents the significance of the former father–daughter constellation.

Although the princess meets an attractive young man, they do not marry. Another typical father's daughter, Athene, never marries. For a woman living in the strong constellation of father–daughter, a young man can be only her follower. (Nevertheless, in the mundane world, such a woman sometimes has a follower called "husband.") The young man in our story is a flutist. Another flutist appears in the Vietnamese fairy tale "The Ugly Boatman," also very much concerned with the father–daughter constellation. In this story, an emperor's daughter falls in love with the young man, attracted by his flute. The story ends sadly as the emperor succeeds in breaking up their love. A flutist is a character in "The Flutist Bridegroom," although the story has nothing to do with the father–daughter constellation. These young men who play flutes are noteworthy. One can hear the sound of their flute over a moat and a fence, penetrating into the daughter's heart in spite of the strong defense her father has put up around her. Because of this penetrative quality, a flutist may appear often in this kind of story. In the Pakistani story, however, the flutist becomes, not the lover, but the follower of the princess.

The young fairy, captured by the demonic deity, can be interpreted as the heroine's alter-self. Here, we think, another form of the father–daughter constellation is pictured. In this typical pattern, the daughter is captured by her "father" and rescued by the young man. Though the pattern is the same as Western stories to this point, the ending differs completely. This is not a story about breaking the father–daughter tie to change into another situation, nor does the story indicate compensation for the father–son or mother–son constellations. It pictures, from beginning to end, the father–daughter dyad in various forms such as the king and the princess, the demonic deity and the fairy, and the heavenly God and the princess. Throughout the story, we find the continued enhancement of the father–daughter relationship. We have to realize that the God appearing here differs from the God in the West, although both are the father. God in the West stands on the axis of father–son, whereas the Pakistani God stands behind the daughter.

The father figure does not merely compensate the mother's negative sides. He is more than protective of his daughter. The father's protection can often deprive her of her liberty, as one can see in the relationship of the demonic deity and Red Fairy. However, a higher fatherhood releases the daughter to sufficient strength to live by herself even against her personal father. She can become happy if she has this higher fatherhood supporting her. Keeping in mind all we have discussed regarding the father–daughter tandem, we shall study the relationships among the dwellers in the underwater land in "The Dragon Palace Boy."

The Triad under the Water

The old man with white hair, the beautiful lady, and the ugly boy live in the underwater world which Kunio Yanagita once called "Eternal Mother Land" for the Japanese. As I pointed out in chapter five, Eiichiro Ishida has discussed the mother–son constellation fully. But in order to understand the structure of the "Eternal Mother Land," we must think about the triad rather than the mother-and-son pair. Though the latter is important to Japanese mentality, the triad is much more suitable here as it includes the father–daughter dyad. If we connect the triad by blood ties, it becomes the grandfather–mother–son constellation in which the woman stands between the two men. The family triad which first comes to mind is of course the father–mother–child constellation, a "natural triad." This "natural triad," however, lacks a blood tie between the father and mother. In this sense, our triad can be called "natural" as all relations are tied by blood. The characteristics of the triad can be assumed easily from what we discussed in the second and third sections in this chapter. We shall make it clearer by comparing other triads in different cultures.

A triad recalls immediately the trinity in Christianity. Understanding its God as the trinity of father, son and holy ghost is essential to Christianity. A non-Christian, however, finds it very hard to "experience" the triad as a unity. I have chosen the word *triad* instead of *trinity* for the title of this section as I do not think that I can understand the undersea triad in Japan as a unity. The *psychological* understanding of the trinity in Christianity was an extremely important task for Jung. Here I emphasize the word *psychological* as it means, as opposed to a theological or philosophical approach to the trinity, that he focused on how a human psyche experiences it.

Saying, "Arrangement in triads is an archetype in the history of religion," Jung mentioned the existence of important triads in ancient religions and myths before Christianity.[6] First of all, he referred to a Babylonian triad: Anu, Enlil, and Ea. Anu is the God of heaven; Enlil, also called Bel, is the storm God and is said to be Anu's son. Ea is the God of water, depth and knowledge. Jung discussed another, later Babylonian triad: Sin, Shamash and Adad—respectively, the God of the moon, the sun and the storm. We can see an interesting correspondence to the Japanese "most precious" triad—Amaterasu, Tsukuyomi, and Susa-no-wo, who are, respectively, the Goddess of the sun, the God of the moon, and the God of the storm.

Jung pointed out that worship of the triad changed its form in Hammurabi's era. That is, worship shifted from the triads mentioned above to the dyad, Anu and Bel, while King Hammurabi ruled his country as the "proclaimer" of the two Gods. Here is implied a new triad including the king who is, hence, combined with the Gods, thus strengthening the kingship.

A similar idea is found in Egypt with the triad of God, king, and *ka*. Since *ka* links God as father and king as son, the Egyptian triad is actually a trinity. And *ka* resembles the Christian holy ghost which also connects father and son. In discussing this Jung introduced a comment by Preisigke that "the early Christian Egyptians simply transferred their traditional ideas about the *ka* to the Holy Ghost."[7]

It seems rather natural that female images are projected on such a mediator. According to a Gnostic interpretation, the holy ghost is the mother. The father-mother-son triad of Sin-Shamash-Adad changed later into Sin-Shamash-Ishtar. Thus Ishtar, the great Goddess in Babylonian mythology, appeared as the third. The relations among these three Gods are not clear as there are so many different traditions. At any rate, we must pay attention to this triad (including the Goddess), as it corresponds to our underwater group.

The Christian trinity characteristically excludes the mother and consists of father-son-holy ghost. The triad of father-mother–child is natural, but it cannot become a unity as the image of a unique God. The homogeneous male beings of father –son are combined by the holy ghost to become the trinity of God, having dared to reject nature. This is characteristic of Christianity as a monotheism, that there should be no contradictions in the image of God as trinity. Homogeneous beings become a unity in which the holy ghost is "breath." Father and son are connected, not through the mother's body, but through the breath, spirit.

As I shall discuss later, Jung pointed out the significance of the female being which compensates the *male* trinity God: his idea of completeness in this context is represented by the image of quaternity. He first of all, however, evaluated European culture which constructs the male God image, reflecting its separation from nature. The holy ghost, which combines father and son, has the power of giving birth or the power of life but also the peculiarity of excluding the mother. Thus, the male relation of father–son is enhanced to a higher stage of the male principle by the breath of the holy ghost. If we look at Christian culture from this point of view, its trinity can be explained from the "history of the development" of human consciousness. Jung gave the following interesting interpretation.

The father is prime cause and creator. If the existence of the son, the counterpart, is not conscious, there is no reflection and the father can only be one. With no room for criticism and ethical conflicts, the father's authority is never impaired. The Other against him is completely split and cannot enter consciousness. Jung mentioned a tribe of negroes on Mt. Elgon, which he investigated, as a typical example of this "father culture." The people believed that the creator had made everything good and beautiful and lived optimistically. After sunset, however, "it was a different world—the dark world of *ayîk*, of evil, danger, fear. The optimistic philosophy gave way to fear of ghosts and magical practices intended to secure protection from evil. Without any inner contradiction the optimism returned at dawn."[8] This is, one can say, the most primordial father culture.

Then comes the world of the son, beginning with awareness of the dark world which had been unconscious through the mechanism of splitting. The father is no longer absolute. With the appearance of his counterpart, doubts arise against him. This world of conflicts yet "[is] filled with longing for redemption and for that state of perfection in which man was still one with the Father. Longingly he looked back to the world of the Father, but it was lost forever, because an irreversible increase in man's consciousness had taken place in the meantime and made it independent."[9]

The third stage, the holy ghost, ends the duality. The third term common to Father and Son, the holy ghost rounds out the Three and restores the One. The unfolding of the One reaches its climax in the Holy Ghost after polarizing itself as Father and Son. If we look at these stages as the development of human consciousness, the first stage denotes the state of unconscious dependency. In order to progress from the first stage to the second, humans must sacrifice their infantile dependency. And they must give up exclusive independence to move from the second stage to the third one.

This idea of Jung's clarifies the process of ego establishment in the West and the significance of the appearance of Christianity in the history of spirit. Nevertheless, we shall not adhere too much to this "developmental" point of view: the Western ego is neither decidedly unique nor necessarily the "best" one. For non-European people, of course, Jung's idea most instructively reveals what lies behind the Western ego. Bearing in mind the *psychological* consideration of the Christian trinity, we shall discuss the underwater triad in Japan.

The triad, grandfather–mother–son, cannot become one being as both sexes are included. Nevertheless, it has a kind of unity because of the blood ties. This triad can be described "developmentally," following what Jung did for the Christian trinity. The stage of the mother corresponds to that of the father in the previous discussion. They resemble each other in uniqueness and absoluteness. However, the father stage is protected by "law" and keeps its absolute goodness by the psychological mechanism of splitting, whereas the mother stage keeps its absolute unity by the nature of the chaotic whole without any discrimination between good and evil. This stage is also optimistic: everything is accepted in the feeling of oneness.

The change from the stage of the mother to that of the son resembles the change from father to son. There occur conflicts between mother and son, or he has doubts about her. Whereas the conflict between father and son is quite sharp, that between mother and son tends to be drawn into the vague whole by the mother's power of containment. A delicate balance maintains the wholeness, containing conflicts, doubts and contradictions in it. Hence it does not need a mediator like the holy ghost in the case of the father-son conflict. The mother-son dyad is, therefore, much more stable than that of father-son. This fact may explain why mother-son dyad Gods appear often in various religions or mythologies.

Even though this dyad is one of the most important keys in understanding the Japanese mentality, its "developmental" description becomes more complete when we add the grandfather, making a triad. Though this dyad is stable, if the son's male traits become stronger, he experiences that stability as restraint. The dyad changes drastically: the son rejects the mother completely or symbolically slays her (the development of the Western ego).

In another, less drastic way, the grandfather is introduced to compensate for the mother's strength. This way felicitously avoids destroying the mother-son dyad, yet the son's weakness is covered by the grandfather who stands behind the mother. The triad of grandfather-mother-son contains the three dyad relations in it: senex and puer, father and daughter, mother and son. You will notice that we have discussed fully all three dyads.

Let us compare the Western and the Japanese egos. The Western hero ego is supported by the God of the trinity in heaven, whereas the Japanese ego is sustained by the triad underwater. As the triad is not a unity, the Japanese ego can sometimes express itself as senex consciousness, or as female consciousness, or as puer consciousness or a mixture. We shall discuss female consciousness in the next chapter. Before that, I would like to touch briefly on the problem of trinity and quaternity.

The Fourth

Jung discussed the psychological meaning of the Christian trinity, evaluating it highly for its epoch-making role in the history of the human spirit. He maintained, however, that psychic wholeness is properly expressed in the quaternity instead, basing this judgment on his studies of world mythologies and religions as well as the structure of the unconscious as revealed by his patients' dreams. Jung believed that the psyche's totality is realized when the fourth element joins the trinity of father, son, and holy ghost. As a psychologist, Jung talked about the image of God—not God per se—which is generated in the human psyche. But he was mistakenly branded as a heretic who criticized the Christian dogma of the trinity. I, as a non-Christian, am not concerned about the problem of heresy, but his theory about the quaternity has much to do with our problem of the underwater triad.

First of all, Jung took up the problem of evil which we are forced to experience. If the monotheistic God is absolutely good, we have the problem of explaining the existence of evil in the world which he created. The theologians explain evil as "privatio boni" in order seriously to maintain theoretical consistency. Jung could not accept such an attitude because of the psychological experiences he valued. Then, through his studies of Gnosis and apocryphal traditions, he reached the conclusion that we have to recognize the existence of Satan who succeeds to the light side of the father. Satan also is a son of God. The conflict between good and evil is reconciled by the holy ghost, according to Jung, as indicated in figure 8.

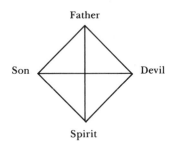

FIG. 8.   *Quaternity (redrawn from C. G.*
Jung, CW 11, §258)

If we face up to psychological reality, we have to realize that we also follow evil no matter how much we try to reject it. It is impossible for human beings only to follow God in the fight between this God of absolute goodness and the Devil opposing him. We need the strength for endurance, for standing between good and evil, instead of searching for absolute goodness. The God of quaternity may rescue us outside our conscious judgment. In the quaternity the "uniting" has highly symbolic meaning. The father–son–spirit side relies on the male principle, whereas the father–devil–spirit side is trying to incorporate evil—that is to say, it is relying on or identifying with the female principle. Thus the image of the God of quaternity becomes complete with the union of the male and female principles. The image of the holy ghost tends to be androgynous as its function is uniting these two principles. The union of male and female has special value in relation to the Christian God of the trinity.

I shall explain this schematically, taking account of the frequent occurrence of marriage in Western fairy tales. The human ego on earth is expressed as a male figure, because the ego's existence is supported by the masculine God of the trinity in heaven. So the human being as a man goes down to the underworld, acquires a woman, and gets married. Thus he brings the woman as the fourth who compensates the heavenly trinity. The theme of marriage often appears in fairy tales to compensate for the Christian God whose powerful masculinity is the formal principle.

The problem of the fourth in Japan is not as simple. In the West, because the only God exists in heaven, everything can be definitely divided into two. So, the compensatory structure appears so clearly. Since the maternal God is superior in Japan, vagueness so predominates that it is difficult even to identify what is formal or traditional. Therefore, it is not proper to use the same schema as in the West. In our story, the young man invited by the underwater triad functions as the fourth to some extent. The Western pattern brings a woman up as the fourth from the underworld, while in Japan a man is the fourth descending to the underworld from earth. The former has the (God of) trinity in heaven, whereas the latter has the triad underwater. Further, in the West, the theme of union appears and the trinity shifts to quaternity, while in Japan the man visits the underwater world, meets the beauty, yet never marries, returning to earth. How should we interpret this?

The plot in which an encounter with a beautiful woman ends with "nothingness" was also found in "The Bush Warbler's Home." I introduced this story at first to show us the common characteristics of Japanese fairy tales. The theme of "nothingness" which I discussed there remains as a base for every chapter in this book. The one absolute God exists in Christianity, but the center point of absolute nothingness in Japan. Male figures embody the Western ego supported by the one God; "nothingness," which might also be considered the condition of non-egos, expresses the Japanese ego. Westerners often say the Japanese (Easterners) "have no ego," a recognition of this difference.

What supports this "non-ego" is not the one God, but the nothingness or emptiness that appears in Japanese mythology. This mythology has a structure whose center is "empty," as symbolized by Tsukuyomi, the focal character of the significant triad Amaterasu–Tsukuyomi–Susa-no-wo. Tsukuyomi is the God who does nothing. Absolute nothing requires no "compensation," unlike the solitary God personalized in the West. Therefore, the theme of union is not so meaningful in Eastern culture. "The nothingness" itself already makes for completeness. Jung presented a square and a circle as the geometrical symbol of totality. But as I pointed out in chapter one, the proper symbol of the totality of "nothingness" would be the circle which has no demarcations for trinity or quaternity. "Nothingness" needs nothing added. Yet, if it needed something, that might be structure. Nothingness, of course, dislikes structure, but to add it daringly is comparable to the enterprise of adding evil to the God of goodness.

In our story, we find the mysterious triad to be the basis for the "nothingness" or "non-ego" on earth. Composed of the old man, young woman and the little boy, this triad has a kind of "structure." As you have seen, these figures often contact humans on earth. We have especially focused on the way the young women behave: struggling to make contact with people on earth, repeating failures, or enduring so much. In a sense, this triad tries to establish senex consciousness or female consciousness in the non-ego world on earth. Isn't it a kind of compensation? This activity endeavors to bring "structure"—a kind of consciousness—into the world of nothingness, and it is utterly antagonistic to nothingness.

In the spiritual history of Christianity, people came to face the task of including the female principle, and the symbol of quaternity appeared to integrate the opposites; then the symbolism of the *mysterium coniunctio* came to have special value. In contrast to that, the effort to unite the underwater triad with the world of nothingness on earth should be made in Japan. As the quaternity Jung insists on has led the West toward the East, similar effort may lead the East toward the West. I shall discuss this further in the next chapter but would like to add one more point here.

Jung's quaternity was attacked so fiercely by theologians because it appeared to oppose Christian dogma. Jung stated that he might have been "burned at the stake" if he had lived in earlier centuries, so fierce was the battle. One of his disciples tried to reconcile this dispute and wrote a paper, but I take Jung's view as follows.

The trinitarian God must be the perfect existence theologically, a perfection from which humans with many evils are clearly separated. Though this existence has no defects at all, it is too perfect to have contact with, especially for us psychotherapists who face the weakness or evil of mankind. Meeting such patients practically, we often need to begin with acceptance of the evil in a human being. To accept it as it is does not mean simply to admit it as good. We try to find an integrative way after a long conflict between good and evil. Accordingly, the image of God conceived by Jung must include evil in itself. Figuratively speaking, the vision of God expressed by innately pious theologians is what they might be seeing in heaven. The image of God conceived by Jung, however, is what could be viewed from hell as he stayed in hell and glimpsed God from that world. Therefore, the God of the theologians has a more brilliant figure of perfection, but that image does not seem helpful for the people in hell.

In Japanese fairy tales, the absolute nothingness is itself complete and needs to add nothing. The most important thing for it is to get rid of "ego," and it seems quite unnecessary to add any consciousness to it. If you value theoretical logic or its perfection, senex consciousness or female consciousness which I discuss in the next chapter may seem like trifles in comparison with absolute nothingness. But when we notice the reality today of the Japanese, who have contacted and are benefiting from modern Western civilization, we cannot help but take account of such considerations. Therefore, despite the completeness of nothingness, I think that making something conscious is important, and it is quite necessary to work toward bringing forth a new symbol out of the various states of consciousness.

In "The Dragon Palace Boy," the hero makes a present to the underwater world and is invited there. This may mean he was not satisfied with this world and hoped to bring back something from the other one. But, in the end, nothing was brought in spite of the contact with that world, and "nothingness" remained in this world. Of course, you can accept "nothingness" affirmatively, and it is difficult to judge if it is good or bad. But such fairy tales may imply that the underwater triad can compensate the world of "nothingness" on earth by introducing some structure. The union of these worlds is hoped for in a different context from that seen in the West. As fairy tales contain the materials of the collective unconscious which can be observed commonly and universally in any culture, they can indicate not only the past and present but also the future perspective in the history of the human spirit. So I would like to introduce in the last chapter the new feminine image who accomplishes union. This image surely has meaning for our future more than our present, going beyond the sorrowful sentiment of the feminine discussed so far in this book.

NINE
The Women of Will

In chapter one I suggested that the female figure best expresses the Japanese ego. I have been discussing the characteristics of Japanese fairy tales from that point of view. In the previous chapter, we saw that the profound difference between the trinitarian God and the God of nothingness grounds the dissimilarity between the Western and Japanese egos. In order to more fully clarify Japanese consciousness, I will present in this chapter the figure which reaches, one might say, the summit in my pursuit of the feminine in Japanese fairy tales. Taking account of the present situation of the Japanese people—as based on clinical experience—this figure is the one which best anticipates the future.

An example of this woman appears in the story known commonly as "The Charcoal Maker *Chōjya*." Distributed throughout Japan, this story is also frequently told as a legend. Kunio

Yanagita's paper "Items about the Charcoal Maker, Kogoro" demonstrates the importance of this tale. I shall introduce some of his ideas in connection with my thoughts.

The Charcoal Maker Chōjya

In CJFT, this fairy tale is classified in the larger category of "Fate and Becoming Rich" with three story patterns: "The Charcoal Maker *Chōjya*" (First Marriage Type, 149A), "The Charcoal Maker *Chōjya*" (Second Marriage Type, 149B), and "The Dialogue of the Deities of Birth" (151A–1). The kernel common to all the stories is that a noble woman proposes to a poor charcoal maker and they become rich after marrying. When their marriage is their first, the story is classified as "First Marriage Type," when their second, "Second Marriage Type." If the story about the heroine's fate is added, it is called "The Dialogue of the Deities of Birth." Typically, the later the story is, the more complicated the plot becomes. In some variants of the "First Marriage Type," we find, however, such passages as "The daughter in Ko·no·ike is called thirteen-houses-bride as her bridegrooms leave her thirteen times" or "The daughter of the *chōjya* in Shimonoseki marries forty-nine times, all of which end with divorce." So they are classified under "First Marriage Type" according to their story pattern, but actually they are not first marriages.

In the version we have selected, the two *chōjya* appear at the beginning, and we are told that they are each going to have a child. The *chōjya* of the west happens to overhear two deities discussing the fates of these two children: the *chōjya* of the east will have a girl with "the rank of one *sho* of salt," while his own child will be a boy with "the rank of a piece of bamboo."[1] As it is the God of the Dragon Palace who bestows the ranks on these children, we sense the secret connection between the heroine and the realm under the sea which we discussed in the last chapter. The *chōjya* of the west tries to overcome his child's poor fate by securing a promise for the two children's marriage. It is quite natural that a father who comes to know his child's future misfortune tries to find a way to prevent it. The power of fate, however, cannot but overwhelm the efforts of a human being.

Although our primary concern will be the heroine's second marriage, we shall first touch briefly on "the newborn's fate," as this has some connection with our theme in this chapter. The idea that a person's fate is already settled when he is born exists in East and West, appearing in many myths and fairy tales. Let us look at "The Dialogue of the Deities of Birth" (A Horsefly and a Hand Ax Type, CJFT 151B). The father learns that his son will die by a horsefly's sting when he turns fifteen or sixteen years old. The father apprentices him to the bucket maker because he thinks his son will have too many chances to be stung by a horsefly if he becomes a farmer. However, when the boy is fifteen or so a horsefly tries to sting him while he is working. Swatting at the horsefly with a tool for bucket making, he accidentally knocks off his own ear, causing his death. Consequently, the father's efforts to avoid a horsefly bring more ill fortune than good. It is well-known that Oedipus's parents' efforts to change their fate caused more harm than acceptance of it would have. Luthi's excellent words "Attempts to avoid fate draw fate all the more" fit so frequently.

The strategy of the *chōjya* of the west to make his ill-fated son happy succeeds only temporarily. The two children marry and live happily for some time, but then catastrophe strikes. In contrast to his wife's faithful attitude toward him, the husband becomes extremely arrogant. This wonderful female figure must be "the woman of endurance" in a marriage in which she of the rank of one *sho* of salt lives with the man of the rank of a piece of bamboo. She changes, however, from "the woman of endurance" to "the woman of will" when she encounters her husband's impropriety of kicking the serving table on which she had placed the first cooked barley of the harvest. She decides to move out, abandoning the house and storehouses to her husband. Leaving him, she will establish another life on her own. This woman differs conspicuously from the female characters discussed so far.

If we interpret the heroine's rank of one *sho* of salt to be a revelation of her secret origin, my fantasy, continued from chapter one, develops as follows. The woman who comes with much difficulty to this world from her original world vanishes, carrying only her resentment, because a man has broken his promise. She returns, even transforming herself into an animal, but in vain. She is finally only able to stay in this world as "the woman of endurance." However, the heroine in our story stops simply enduring and attempts to open a completely new domain in which to stay while in this world. It is a wonderful accomplishment. Here I must not forget that "the woman of will" seems passive at first in marrying the man whom her father chooses. Her shift from passivity to seizing the initiative impresses us. Her ability strikes us all the more vividly when she herself proposes to the charcoal maker Goro and, upon his declining, insists, "This is my own wish. Please make me your wife."

Perhaps there is no such active young woman in European fairy tales. So far, I have not found any direct parallel. Although we have addressed the theme of a woman's proposal, the women we've discussed have not first experienced endurance, and the men have accepted too easily. The man Goro, on the other hand, is conscious of his situation, pointing out the difference in their social status. The marriage nevertheless occurs, transcending that difficulty.

Let us go back to the point at which the heroine decides to leave home. The women leave the men when their own true natures are revealed in a series of stories from "The Bush Warbler's Home" to "Crane Wife." No sooner are they exposed than they depart, but without showing their anger at the men's breaking their promises. The situation differs completely in "The Charcoal Maker *Chōjya*." The heroine's first husband is insensitive to her true nature, i.e., having the "rank of one *sho* of salt." The woman feels the man's true nature in his violent act and resolves to depart. Her ability to see her husband's essence is related to her wisdom to then choose Goro as her true husband. Here she becomes the woman who discovers the man's hidden nature instead of having her nature penetrated by the man. Her active behavior has meaning only when it is supported by this kind of wisdom.

In the story she comes to know about Goro by hearing the deities of the storehouse talking with each other. The deities, of course, may be understood as the manifestation of her wisdom deep within. The God of the Dragon Palace, who gives her her rank, may even have arranged her marriage with the son of the western *chōjya*—if we consider the matter deeply—though the story does not describe the figure of this God of fate. In the previous chapter, the old man "standing behind" the lady emerges as the primary image. The woman has the strength to realize in this world the old man's wisdom. Our fantasy goes so far as to conjecture that she is the woman into whom Otohime in the Dragon Palace transforms herself. Psychologically speaking, the woman is the one who retains the bond with the deep unconscious world.

At the end of chapter seven, I discussed the wisdom of woman which intuits men's true nature. This womanly wisdom often supports the happy marriages in Japanese fairy tales. In the case of "The Charcoal Maker *Chōjya*" it manifests as the personified figure of the deities of the storehouse. In "Pond Snail Son," the woman's words "If it is so, I would like to be his wife" show this feminine wisdom. In "Ash Boy," only the daughter sees through Ash Boy's nature while everybody else is tricked by his disguise. After this penetration to essence, the marriage occurs.

We have to attend to the theme of disrupting the social hierarchy, especially in "The Charcoal Maker *Chōjya*." The ranks the two babies are given by the God of the Dragon Palace are only concerned with inner states, and it is suitable that the children of the two *chōjya* marry. Foregoing this good balance in social position, the heroine wants to marry a charcoal maker who is quite low in social status. To carry through with this challenge to the Japanese social system, she must be very courageous. Her act corresponds to the trials of some brave Western male heroes trying to marry princesses in spite of awesome social differences. In another story, "The Charcoal Maker Goro," a couple marry in accordance with an oracle. The woman is the only daughter of a lord, and Goro is "really the poorest man in the world": the difference in their social positions is extremely distinct. In both stories, the woman who acts without any prejudice for social status is certainly a new person.

The day after this wedding, the couple find much gold in his kilns for charcoal making. There is no explanation about it in the story. We may assume that this treasure results from their accomplishing this unusual marriage. Many variants, however, contain the following episode. When the wife hands her new husband some of her own gold to buy rice, he says, "How can one get rice with such a thing?" When she explains how precious it is, he says there is a lot of such stuff around his kilns. He does not know its value even though he has been living with his kilns full of gold. Here again, the woman's ability to find the hidden value is beautifully revealed. She draws out the treasure which Goro has been keeping (with him) without knowing its value.

Some variants end with their happy marriage, but, as in the story in the Appendix, others describe the fate of the former husband. He becomes poor gradually and even comes to his former wife's house without realizing it. The woman treats him kindly, but he still cannot recognize her. Ultimately he commits suicide because of his shame, realizing that the rich woman is his former spouse. I shall quote Yanagita's discussion of this death in one of the variants:

> The man falls down and dies as he cannot stand his shame and repentance, seeing his former wife. She asks servants to bury the corpse behind the fireplace so her husband will not see it. It is said that the former husband becomes the guardian deity in this house. The deity of the kitchen fireplace stems from this. It seems strange to speak about death and burial in connection with the belief in the hearth deity for whom we have to keep especially pure. [Death or corpses are thought to be the most impure things.] However, in Echigo and Ou in northern Japan, the custom of putting a mask with an ugly face beside the kitchen fireplace is still

widespread. There must be some deep reasons why this custom has been so widely maintained until today.

Yanagita's excellent intuition sees Hyōtoku, discussed in the previous chapter, at the root of this story of the charcoal maker. If we change our viewpoint, the man with the rank of a piece of bamboo may become a valuable being with a secret strong connection to that ugly boy. Unexpectedly, we find that a fairy tale might have a multi-layered structure. We will consider this shortly.

Feminine Consciousness

Neither the specific consciousness of women nor the consciousness that women should have, the feminine consciousness which we are going to discuss is a certain state of ego consciousness that can occur in both men and women. But its characteristics can be more easily represented by the feminine image, and it contrasts with the masculine hero image which, per Neumann, represents modern Western ego consciousness.

Neumann clearly discriminated between patriarchal and matriarchal consciousness. He concluded that both men and women must operate from patriarchal consciousness to live in modern society, while at the same time he recognized the value of matriarchal consciousness and wrote a paper on it. He said patriarchal consciousness is dominant for modern people in general, but at an early age of human history or at early stages in human development, matriarchal consciousness was superior to patriarchal. He also insisted that this can be so even for modern men when they are gripped by a mental crisis or creative process. In short, he placed patriarchal consciousness higher from the developmental point of view, but still admitted that matriarchal consciousness has significance for the "creative process." Though matriarchal consciousness seemed inferior, he commented that a paradoxical reversal of value occurs in the important moment of creation, adding the reservation that it is also a time of mental crisis. To throw feminine consciousness in relief, I will outline Neumann's matriarchal consciousness first.

Neumann related this consciousness to the moon. If the sun symbolizes male consciousness, moonlight symbolizes matriarchal consciousness. It is not glittering daylight but soft radiance. The primary characteristic of matriarchal consciousness is that it does not exist separated from the unconscious but in harmony and resonance with it. It sometimes whimsically changes in response to messages from the unconscious, and those changes sometimes even lead to wonderful ideas or inspirations. Hence, matriarchal consciousness is needed in the creative process.

This consciousness also connects deeply with time and fate. There are waxing and waning times of the moon, as well as an eclipsing time. This sort of time also controls the life of human beings as this world has its own rhythm, a cyclical nature. Patriarchal consciousness, however, tries to demolish the natural rhythm of day and night by, for instance, bringing dazzling lights at night. With patriarchal consciousness, we can work at night as much as in the daytime and can increase "efficiency"; we can invent machines which carry us far away at high speed, far beyond our own innate rhythms. But when we become arrogant, nursing the illusion that we could control the world, tragedy such as a traffic accident occurs and we curse our fate.

Matriarchal consciousness accepts fate rather than cursing it. When one accepts and waits, one's fate can change and good fortune come. This consciousness becomes the more powerful with this ability to wait. Impatient patriarchal consciousness tries to fight and overcome, but matriarchal consciousness waits without struggle. It endures and waits however long the tragedy continues. A human cannot control fate.

Neumann states:

> ... in woman's primal mysteries, in boiling, baking, fermenting, and roasting, the ripening and "getting done," the transformation, is always connected with a period of waiting. The ego of

matriarchal consciousness is used to keeping still till the time is favorable, till the process is complete, till the fruit of the moon-tree has ripened into a full moon; that is, till comprehension has been born out of the unconscious.[2]

The process of "comprehension" by matriarchal conscious-ness might be understood essentially by comparing it with the process of pregnancy. Characteristically, pregnancy is more passive than any other formative activity, beginning with an ac-ceptance of something that invades from outside. It does not act voluntarily. The process from conception to delivery requires total human commitment of both mind and body, and what is created thereby is so self-evident that we do not need any ex-planation or logic. Thus, the comprehension acquired through matriarchal consciousness is so transparent that no explanation is required for those who can share such an experience. But for anyone else, that comprehension is beyond understanding and perhaps even considered worthless. Neumann says: "It [matriar-chal consciousness] behaves more or less passively, without willed ego-intentions."[3] A sense of relativity also characterizes matriarchal consciousness. Neumann mentions: "... it is less oriented to the absolute unambiguity of truth than to a wisdom which remains imbedded in a cosmo-psychological system of ever-changing forces."[4]

Patriarchal consciousness—backed by the one absolute God —insists on absolute universality, using abstractive methods which cut it off from objects, while matriarchal consciousness, related to the unconscious, maintains a bond with objects. It depends on them and becomes relative.

So far I have outlined Neumann's matriarchal consciousness. Now I would like to illustrate the somewhat different feminine consciousness I discuss here with the woman in "The Charcoal Maker *Chōjya*."

To us Japanese, it seems that Neumann first premises the ex-istence of patriarchal consciousness as a base. On that already established basis, he clearly dichotomizes and compares the two styles of consciousness. Therefore, the superiority of patriarchal consciousness is firmly assumed—except for the paradox in the process of creation. Feminine consciousness essentially does not allow such division or opposition, so it is rather difficult to describe it as clearly as patriarchal consciousness would. Apart from that, the feminine consciousness found in the heroine in "The Charcoal Maker *Chōjya*" shares many characteristics with Neumann's matriarchal consciousness.

Both feminine and matriarchal consciousness are closely related to the unconscious. Thus, the heroine's behavior depends upon the opinions of the God of the Dragon Palace or the deities of the storehouses. She is able to discern the voices of the deities of the storehouses. Judging from the outside, her choice to become a charcoal maker's wife instead of the rich *chōjya's* wife seems absurd, a "whim," but the act opens a completely new domain. This story also clearly shows us the connection between time and fate. From the moment of her birth, her fate is given by the God of the Dragon Palace. In a sense, she has just waited for the opportune time, obeying and accepting the intervention of a human being. Notably, however, the mother never appears in the plots connected with "fate." The mother–daughter relationship which would tell us the matriarchal succession is not explained at all. Instead, the God of the Dragon Palace and the deities of the storehouses stand behind our heroine. Though we are not told the sex of these deities, they give us the impression of male figures, reminding us of the senex figure discussed previously. The consciousness derived from the constellation of senex and maiden we call feminine consciousness because the actor is a woman, but we cannot easily classify her consciousness as matriarchal or patriarchal, as is evident in her quick decision and powerful activity.

Though she passively accepts her father's choosing her first husband, she is quite decisive and never returns to her parents' home after her divorce. The wisdom of the storehouse deities supports her decision to go to the charcoal maker, Goro, but remarkably it is she who determines to divorce and leave home —resolute activity, far from matriarchal consciousness. Here we can observe a characteristic of feminine consciousness. Though her initiative arranges her second marriage, she does not persevere in such an attitude by working after the wedding. We might even say she does not work actively or positively because she gets her happiness through discovering the potential treasure in her husband. Her activity includes both passive and active aspects so that it is quite difficult to classify. Remember that in chapter one, we saw that men and women are assigned active and passive roles according to the meaning of male and female derived from the symbolical system in Western alchemy. Feminine consciousness does not allow for such classification.

Such a wonderful feminine image can be found only in Japanese fairy tales, so it must epitomize the consciousness of Japanese, regardless of sex. Realizing that fairy tales always compensate for a culture's formal attitude and that they thus predict the future, this image might be seen as the future orientation of the Japanese mind. If we notice further that the Western modern ego is moribund, this heroine could be presented as a meaningful symbol not only for Japanese, but also for all the people in the world. The fact that this charcoal maker story has been kept in many districts as a legend may indicate its special value in maintaining local independence against the dominant formal attitude. Anyway, what a wonderful image the mind of the Japanese people has created!

Many of the world's fairy tales of heroines include the theme of a transition from passivity to activity, though seldom as clearly as in "The Charcoal Maker *Chōjya*." The theme is related to the "forbidden chamber": the persons who break the taboo about looking are often females in Western fairy tales. The example of "Three-Eyes" (see the Appendix) clearly shows that the lady who obeys her father regarding marriage disobeys her husband regarding the prohibition. This transition is from the unconscious to consciousness rather than from passivity to activity, but it does somewhat resemble the attitude of the heroine in "The Charcoal Maker *Chōjya*." Both women marry at their fathers' command and become unhappy, but end up with happy remarriages. The differences become apparent if we look more carefully. In "Three-Eyes," the heroine's first husband is a monster, who is then slain. This kind of plot indicates that the story is created in a culture where patriarchal consciousness has been established with no connection to the unconscious. In spite of that, the story describes the development of female ego consciousness.

Female consciousness is relativistic like matriarchal consciousness, but its relativity interacts even with the male consciousness which seems to be against it. Thus, the theme of marriage can hardly be avoided. The happy marriage ending "The Charcoal Maker *Chōjya*"—so unusual in Japanese fairy tales—differs considerably from the hero's marriage story in Western fairy tales. Moreover, the relationship between the bride and her previous husband is most delicate, and she never "slays" him as in "Three-Eyes."

The Sacred Marriage

When we carefully read "The Charcoal Maker *Chōjya*" or parallel stories, we see that the story neither sets marriage as the goal nor follows the Western pattern. Though the social status of heroes or heroines in the Western marriage story varies, the partner's position is usually high (king or princess), and the marriage itself means happiness. In contrast, in "The Charcoal Maker *Chōjya*," when our heroine proposes to Goro, his social status is very low—or he is portrayed as poor—and the story then proceeds to their discovery of gold after their marriage. Moreover, the heroine meets her previous husband again in many variants. Marriage here matters differently.

The union of male and female is universal among all creatures, where it matters on the instinctual level of species-preservation. Because marriage resonates in value from instinct to a high spiritual level, its symbolical meaning becomes deep. The connection between male and female is so natural that we need no "story" about it. To become a "story," this connection must be elaborated so that it implicates more than natural phenomena. Marriage is not one of nature's happenings but a task whose fulfillment requires the will and efforts of human beings. In Western fairy tales, this theme appears if the status of the hero or heroine's partner is very high, or he/she must accomplish many tasks, or a heroine must marry the terrible monster. The "death marriage" theme evident in "Beauty and the Beast" occurs frequently in heroine stories.

But in "The Charcoal Maker *Chōjya*," the partner is a *chōjya's* son, so it is at a different level. Although the essential symbolic meaning of marriage is best expressed in the union of differing components, both partners should experience some separation or cutting off before that union in order to fulfill this meaning. The motifs of killing a monster or of metamorphosis reiterate the theme of the "death marriage." Needless to say, killing a monster means cutting off, and in the metamorphosis, we also see a cutting off because rebirth follows the death of the old.

"Female consciousness" must not adhere overmuch to the unconscious since it *is* consciousness. Yet, if it were to separate completely from the unconscious, it would become just like male consciousness. Then, as in Western stories, there would be no room for differentiation. "The Charcoal Maker *Chōjya*" beautifully settles such a dilemma. At first our heroine acts passively, obeying her father, but then she resolves to divorce. She is not only the woman who merely endures; she herself wills a separation. However, her sword is not as sharp as the one in the Western hero story which can wound and kill a monster. Its moderate sharpness allows for contacts with her previous husband. For all that, the female who refuses to endure beyond a certain threshold and who decides to act is remarkable as the new ego figure. Since in the Japan of those days, women were expected to obey men, the existence of such a story is very meaningful.

Contrary to our expectations, there are many such vivid women in Japanese fairy tales. For example, we find a very courageous woman in "The Tako *Chōjya*" (CJFT 124). The plot is as follows: a maiden marries the poor son of "Takoya Chobei" (here we see the same pattern in the heroine's marrying a man of low status), and every night a monster appears in Chobei's house. Chobei and his son, the bridegroom, are frightened, but the bride unperturbedly serves it buns. The monster is so surprised at her courage that he confesses his true color is that of the *koban* (old Japanese gold coins) buried at the corner of the house. So they dig out the *koban* and become rich: the story ends happily. The man who seems to be poor really has the gold but knows nothing of it. The key person who finds the gold is his wife who has decided to marry him. These similarities with "The Charcoal Maker *Chōjya*" illustrate a significant motif. Here in Japan where "courage for men, charm for women" is encouraged, the brave woman remarkably appears in fairy tales.

There is a scene where a woman tests men's courage in "A Maiden Who Eats Babies" (CJFT 123). Each man who sneaks into the *chōjya's* house to propose to his daughter happens to see her with unkempt hair and white cloth take a baby's corpse from its coffin and eat it. Terrified at the sight, the men run away. The one man who looks carefully in spite of his fear finds that the daughter has put on an ogre mask and is eating a doll made of rice cake. So he says to her, "Can I try it?" Then she is so glad and says, "No courageous man but you has come so far. You are the man to be my husband!" And they marry. Though the man is brave, we have to admit the maiden goes one better because she tries his courage. We feel her act means more than a simple test of courage when we remember the figure of Yama-uba discussed in chapter two. The woman who eats nothing marries while disguised and later makes trouble when she reveals herself. But this "maiden who eats babies" takes another tack. Recognizing the true feminine nature that lies deep inside herself, she dares to discover the man who can accept her as she is. We can view her as one of the very impressive cases of "the women of will." Instead of depending on hiding her true nature, she is aware of it and behaves actively on the basis of that awareness.

Though the heroine in "The Charcoal Maker *Chōjya*" seems to have both courage and charm (deserving the rank of one *sho* of salt), let us look at her second husband, the man she decides to marry when abandoning her rich bride status. This story has also become established as a legend, the hero having names such as "Magosaburo" or "Kogoro." Kunio Yanagita comments on it as follows: "Magosaburo and Kogoro are common nicknames among the poor of low status. People had a lot of servants so named in every ordinary house at the time when this story was popular. The reason such names were used lies, for one thing, in the amusement of the success story of the poor. But for another, taking account of the parallels of 'Taijin Yagoro,' these names seem to be pertinent to the relatives of the God of Hachiman."

Yanagita says that we can see in these names both aspects—i.e., the poor and the relatives of the God. Further, he says,

> Today's people may see charcoal maker as a mean occupation, but its purpose was quite different in earlier days. The capacity to treat the metal which may be more solid than stone and to create any forms they wanted was far beyond the ability of average farmers. Only the men who worked a bellows or who had the skill of making charcoal were engaged in this field. So it is not at all strange that there existed people who asserted this was a sacred skill and it was the God who started this activity.

The two aspects of the male figure in "The Charcoal Maker *Chō-jya*" are clearly expressed in this excellent comment. Goro is of low status, but at the same time he could be the God himself.

Although Goro's occupation gives him some contact with the Gods, he possesses almost nothing when our heroine proposes to him. As in the variant I have already introduced, he is even said to be "really the poorest man in the world." Or in many variants, when his wife tells him to buy something, she offers a *koban* and he goes out with it. He comes back after throwing it to a water bird: he knows nothing about its value. The words "he possesses nothing" or "he knows nothing" remind us of the theme which we have consistently pursued in this book. This charcoal maker, Goro, embodies nothingness.

Now our fantasy can proliferate. After being left by the beauty in "The Bush Warbler's Home," the woodsman enters deep into the mountains away from society. There he makes charcoal and is about to settle down to a life of "nothingness." Unexpectedly, the woman invades his world. After going through various experiences, she neither vanishes nor simply endures, but tries to unite herself, as the woman of will, to the consciousness of nothingness. On the other hand, he thinks about the difficulties of married life and becomes prudent so that he does not easily agree to a contract that might be infringed. But they get married at last. The union between the male, embodying nothingness, and the female, embodying female consciousness, is to be the sacred marriage. Its consequence shows as numerous pieces of gold.

The consciousness of nothingness, here expressed by men, differs from the unconscious expressed in the West. In Western stories, a man embodying consciousness invades the unconscious world and procures a woman to marry. Just as we can interpret marriage in Western fairy tales as compensating the culture for the sole God the Father at the top, so we can understand marriage in "The Charcoal Maker *Chōjya*" to compensate the Japanese culture for the God of nothingness. "The woman of will" who appears here contrasts refreshingly with the oversentimentalism that is peculiar to Japan.

Wholeness

Meaningful marriage takes place, and the hero and heroine receive a large amount of gold. Feminine activity does not play the significant role here; instead, the man's latent treasure—its existence unknown to him—is brought out. The woman is not always active. The story also does not end at this point, and interestingly, the previous husband reappears. Especially in the story collected in the Tōnō District, the former husband comes to see her, and to our surprise she invites him to live with them, employing him as a servant. This story is collected in CJFT as "The Charcoal Maker *Chōjya*" (Remarriage Type). During the first visit, the woman gives him some rice, but in the second, she confesses to the charcoal maker Goro. And he says to her, "Tell him to stay here in a casual sort of way" and recommends that he become a servant. Innocently, the former husband is willing to accept the offer and lives all his life in their house. (This story Kunio Yanagita also introduces.) It must be very unique. Their pitying her ex-husband and letting him live with them are foreign to Western fairy tales.

This uniqueness clearly characterizes female consciousness: it tries to recover the relation it once severed. In short, it accepts more than excludes. Yet it is not as completely passive as the matriarchal consciousness Neumann discusses. Jung often contrasts perfection and completeness. Perfection excludes defects or evils, whereas completeness accepts them. Patriarchal consciousness tends to aim at perfection. It cuts off the evil with a sharp sword, while female consciousness tries to accept whatever comes and aims at completeness. To admit whatever comes means to accept even imperfection, including internal contradiction. Here we see the difficulty of completeness. The ex-husband in "The Charcoal Maker *Chōjya*" lives according to his father's will, i.e., to somehow modify inherent destiny. On the contrary, the heroine always lives in deep contact with her fate. In some way she has to accept her former husband who lives antithetically. How hard it is to live with both one's present and former husbands—though the latter is now a servant. If the difficulty is insurmountable, the ex-husband dies in spite of the wife's kind treatment (as in the story in the Appendix). In the intermediate version, the former husband becomes the guardian deity after his death. Japanese fairy tales make every effort to include this pitiful man in the final wholeness.

Nevertheless, this male figure is not highly valued, reminding us of Hiruko in Japanese myths.[5] These myths have the significant triad Amaterasu, Tsukuyomi and Susa-no-wo (the noble deities). Hiruko's function should be called "the fourth," for it resembles that of the former husband in our story. In spite of that, the extreme integrity of Japanese myths excludes the fourth, Hiruko. On the other hand, the fairy tales try so hard to integrate him. The heroine, the God of destiny who hides himself behind her, and the charcoal maker Goro constitute a triad like the three deities in Japanese myths. Therefore, the ex-husband should be the fourth. We would need to refer to all Japanese myths to further discuss this point, so I just note here a similarity between these two figures.

Though Neumann regarded matriarchal consciousness as inferior to patriarchal in human development, he saw it as significant for the creative process—even for adult men. This tells us that patriarchal or matriarchal consciousness is not an immutable stage one has reached but changes in terms of the situation. The individual dominated by patriarchal consciousness does not always stay in that state but transfers himself to another as the occasion demands. Not restricted to one solid consciousness, we can freely alter it according to need. "Female consciousness," especially, seems mutable. I dare say that the image of the sole ego and its integration was born of Western Christian culture, while Japanese can imagine the existence of multiple egos. This multiplicity may be more effective and flexible vis-à-vis future society which will include more diversity. Isn't having all kinds of consciousness—including senex, puer, male and female—the very way to establish wholeness? I know, of course, that this way of saying it carries internal contradiction.

Female consciousness, self-contradictory, cannot easily integrate itself. To be complete without collapsing is extremely difficult. It is impossible for female consciousness to form before we experience a symbol of totality firmly in our psyche. The fairy tale "The Charcoal Maker Chōjya" seems to contain such symbolism. But since totality or wholeness is always changing, the description in this book from chapters one through nine should be viewed as expressing its variations.

All the female figures here must be understood to exist

simultaneously making multiple layers. It is difficult for us human beings to describe or to think of synchronizing phenomena. While this book is also written in a sequential style led by strings of association, the various types of women appearing throughout should be recognized as always changing positions, not as developmental stages. These protean female figures express the Japanese mind: multiple layers creating a beautiful totality. We may liken the composition of this book, the description of its chapters, to a musical score having nine parts in the orchestra. These should be played simultaneously and listened to in the same moment. If a "woman of will" behaves alone without any support from the bass, she and others may suffer.

Wholeness bears a dilemma: if you try to seize it, you lose completeness; if you try to catch completeness, wholeness becomes vague. Human consciousness cannot recognize clearly the God of wholeness. Efforts to describe it suffer from some distortion due to the condition of our consciousness. Jung presented us with the God of quaternity as the symbol of totality. If, following Jung, we recognize four as the complete number, we should take this as the four dimensions—not as a square—to express reality. For human beings "to bring something to consciousness" might be to project the existence of four dimensions on to two. For someone whose consciousness differs from that of Jung's—for example, a Japanese person who expresses wholeness in two dimensions—the form would be different. While these expressions would differ from one another, the original totality would be the same—though no one "knows." For example, I have found the structure of a "triad plus the fourth" in Japanese fairy tales. The components are different, but the structure is similar to Jung's. I presented such a structure composed of four elements in this and the previous chapter, but each structure has a different nuance, and there is no need to select one as the "right" one.

Finally, I would like to reiterate that the feminine figures we have seen in this book manifest the Japanese ego *regardless of sex*.

Of course, you can look for the personal lifestyle of a woman among them, and the resemblance may be meaningful. But my intention is to analyze the Japanese—i.e., to reflect those of us who have undergone the impact of the modern Western ego— so that I have emphasized the cultural aspects. Yet such an analysis cannot help proceeding to the tota⁀ existence of humans as well as to the ego. Since fairy tales eloquently relate to the deep structure of the human mind, the discussion extends from today's situations into the future. Therefore, I hope these feminine images come to have significant meaning not only for the Japanese, but also for people in other countries.

APPENDIX

The Bush Warbler's Home

Iwate Prefecture

Once upon a time, there was a young woodcutter who lived at the foot of a mountain. One day as he went up into the mountain, he was amazed to find a splendid estate which he had never seen before in the middle of a meadow. Although he had been cutting wood for his living around this area, he had never even heard of such a place. He felt quite strange, and so he approached the mansion cautiously. When he entered the grounds, it was utterly silent inside. Not a soul seemed to be around. He went further and soon came upon an immense garden deeply veiled in mist but filled with flowers and the songs of various birds. Finally the woodcutter came to the entrance of the mansion itself. To his surprise, a beautiful woman came to greet him.

"Why have you come?" she asked.

"Well, it was such a beautiful day today that I began walking in high spirits, and so I just happened to come to this place."

The woman looked at him for a while, and she seemed to think he was an honest person.

"You came here at just the right time. Would you do me a favor?" she asked.

"What would you like me to do, madam?" he replied.

"Well, it is a beautiful day today so I, too, would like to go to town now. Would you please house sit for me while I am gone?" she asked.

"That's no problem," the woodcutter replied without hesitation.

"However, while I am gone, do not look into the next room," she said firmly.

The woodcutter accepted her condition also with no hesitation. The woman left for town reassured.

The woodcutter was now all alone in the mansion. He began to get anxious about the next room which the woman had told him not to look in. Soon, however, he lost his resolve. He opened the sliding door and looked inside. There were three beautiful maidens cleaning the room, but as he peeked in they disappeared as though they were birds flying away. He thought that was curious.

Then he opened the second room. There was a tea kettle simmering on a bronze *hibachi*. The sound was like the breeze blowing through pine trees. There was also a golden screen decorated with Chinese-style paintings, but no one was behind it.

As he opened the third room, there were bows and arrows and armor on display.

The fourth room was a horse stable, in which there was a dark-bluish stallion with a gorgeous saddle bordered in gold and richly woven reins. It was kicking the floor. Its mane blew, and it looked like cedar trees in a storm.

In the fifth room he saw displayed a red lacquer table with lacquer bowls, Chinese plates, and so forth.

As he entered the sixth room, there was a white-gold bucket and a gold ladle. From a gold barrel, *saké* was dripping into seven jars underneath. He could not control himself as the wonderful aroma of the *saké* tantalized him. He tried to scoop some up with the gold ladle, and in no time he became tipsy.

The seventh room, spacious and blue, was filled with wonderful aromas of flowers, and there was also a bird's nest. He saw that it held three little eggs. The woodcutter casually picked one up to look at it, but dropped it and broke it accidentally. Thereupon a little bird hatched from the egg, and the bird flew away crying, "Ho Ho Ho Kekkyo!" He dropped the second one and the third one also. Both times, the same as the first: a little bird hatched and flew away with "Ho Ho Ho Kekkyo!"

The woodcutter was dumbfounded, stood there dazed. Just at that moment, the woman came back from town and, seeing the woodcutter, she cried and cried reproachfully, "No one is less trustworthy than a human! You broke your promise and killed my three daughters! How I miss them! Ho Ho Ho Kekkyo..." she cried as she turned into a bush warbler and flew away.

Looking in the direction the bird had disappeared, he picked up his axe beside him and yawned and took a big stretch. It was said that when he regained his senses he found himself standing in the middle of the meadow without a trace of the splendid mansion to be seen.

Faithful John

(Synopsis)

When an old king lay dying, he left the care of his son to his servant Faithful John, who promised not to allow the prince to see the portrait of the Princess of the Golden Dwelling. The prince, however, insisted on being shown inside the one chamber barred to him in the palace, and he fainted when he saw the princess's great beauty. Since he insisted he had to marry her, Faithful John advised him to order the country's goldsmiths to work his five tons of gold into all manner of strange and wonderful objects, as the princess lived surrounded by gold.

The prince—now the king—and his servant disguised themselves as merchants and sailed for the princess's country in a ship loaded with the goldsmiths' art. There Faithful John enticed the princess to the ship with various of the gold items. Once she was aboard and absorbed in looking at the treasures with the young king, the ship set sail. The princess eventually discovered the subterfuge, but the king pled his love and his estate, and she agreed to marry him.

In the meantime, Faithful John overheard three ravens describing perils awaiting the king once ashore. Faithful John could evade these on his master's behalf but would be constrained to silence, as any explanation of his actions would turn him to stone. The first test was a wonderful chestnut horse which John mounted and killed, as it would have carried away the king. The second peril was a wondrous bridal garment John seized and threw into the fire before the king could don it, as it would have burned him fatally. On both occasions, the king defended Faithful John's peculiar actions as ununderstandable but probably beneficial, though his other attendants were murmuring against John.

In the third case, however, the king was scandalized and ordered his servant's execution. John had sucked three drops of blood from the princess's right breast to restore her to life from a dead faint during the bridal dance.

John asked for the courtesy of a last speech and explained all his actions. Distraught, the king forgave him as Faithful John turned to stone.

The stone statue was kept in the king's bedroom and one day answered his master as he wished aloud that he could restore John to life. Despite his horror, the king followed the statue's bidding: he cut off the heads of his young twin sons and smeared the statue with their blood.

Not only was John restored to life but also he revived the children, who were unaware anything had happened. When the queen returned home from church, she agreed that the king had acted properly. And everyone lived happily ever after.

The Woman Who Eats Nothing

Hiroshima Prefecture

I heard that once upon a time there was a man who had been single until his later years. His friends encouraged him to marry, saying: "Isn't it about time to take a bride?"

"I don't mind waiting for a woman however long it takes, but if you find a maiden who eats nothing, please introduce me," he said.

One evening, a beautiful woman arrived at his door who said, "I am a traveler, but I am in trouble as it is getting dark already. I wonder if you would give me a place to stay tonight."

"I wouldn't mind your staying overnight, but unfortunately I have no food in the house," he said, trying politely to refuse her request.

But the woman insisted, "I don't eat anything at all. I am a woman who does not eat. I need only a place to stay."

The man was surprised to hear that and so let her stay. The woman made no sign of getting ready to leave the next morning. She did various house chores for him, so he let her stay longer. And the best thing of all was that she worked hard all day without eating a thing.

Soon, the man became somewhat concerned about her not eating day after day and told her to eat a little something at least. The woman simply refused saying, "It's enough for me just to smell food." He was so proud of her and told his friends that there was no wife better than she. But none of them believed him.

Finally, one of his best friends came to him. "What's wrong with you! You haven't noticed? Your wife is no human being. Wake up!" The friend pointed at him.

"That's impossible," the man gasped.

"You are the only one who doesn't know about it. It's a rumor all over the village. Never! There's no one in the world who does not eat. If you don't believe me, why don't you find out yourself? Just pretend to go away but then climb up to a ceiling beam where she won't be aware of you."

One day, before his trip to town, he told his wife, "I will be back quite late tonight." After going about a mile or so he went back and climbed up onto the ceiling beam and hid himself from his wife.

After she was alone, the woman started to wash rice and made a big fire to cook it. When it was cooked, she made thirty-three rice balls. Then she got three mackerel from the kitchen and broiled them over the fire. And then she sat on the mat with one knee up like a man. He just watched in amazement and wondered what would happen next.

She untied her hairdo and, when her hair fell down, he saw a large open mouth in the top of her head. She tossed rice balls and broiled mackerel into that opened mouth one after another and completely devoured them. Totally frightened to see such a sight, he sneaked down from the beam and ran to his friend's house.

"Ah, that's just what I told you. But tonight you should go home as if nothing has happened," the friend said. So the man did so. When he got home she was in bed suffering from a headache.

"What's wrong?" he asked.

"Well, nothing's wrong, but I don't feel good," she replied in a cat-like voice.

"I'm sorry to hear that. Would you like to take some medicine or call the shaman?" he asked.

"I don't know what to do," she said, and she looked as if she might jump on him.

"All right. I will get the shaman right away for you. Wait a few minutes." He ran to his friend's and brought him back home.

"What sort of curse is on her? A curse with three-*sho* rice! A curse with three mackerel!" his friend shouted.

The woman jumped out of bed and cried, "Grrrr! you must have watched me!" She jumped on his friend and began gobbling him up from his head down. Shocked, the man tried desperately to escape. The woman was already finishing his friend when she caught him, picking him up by the nape of his neck like a kitten. She thrust him up on her head and ran off to the mountain. Through fields and over hills she went, running like a rabbit.

When they came to a forest, he grabbed a branch which happened to reach right in front of his eyes. The woman-who-eats-nothing-*oni* [devil] did not notice this at all. She ran, ran, ran. The man climbed down from the tree and hid himself in some wild plants: mugwort and Japanese wild iris. He kept silent.

Then the devil-woman came back to where he was hiding. "Oh, I know you are in those plants. Wherever you hide, I can find you." She was about to jump on him, but she suddenly jumped back instead.

"Oh, how terrible! Mugwort and iris poison my body. They make my body rot. Oh, how regretful, how bitter! If only these grasses weren't here! I would have eaten you up also."

So the man thought: "Now I'm safe." He threw those plants at the devil. I heard that even the devil could be killed by the poison of those plants.

The Laughter of Oni

Niigata Prefecture

Once upon a time, there was a man of fortune who had a beautiful daughter. Although she was his only daughter, it was arranged that she would wed in a faraway village.

On the day of the wedding, a fine carriage was sent by the groom's family, so the mother and relatives escorted the carriage calling out, "Bride! Bride!" They had to go over hills and mountain ridges. Then, suddenly, a dark cloud hung down from the sky and veiled the carriage.

"What's happening? What shall we do?"

While everyone ran about in confusion, the black cloud stole the bride from the carriage and flew away with her. Losing her dear and precious daughter, the mother became so worried that she was almost losing her mind. But, determined to find her daughter, she prepared some dried, cooked rice, packed it on her back and went out to search.

All over the meadow, all about the hills, she searched and searched without any clue. When night fell, luckily she saw a little temple nearby so she went there and called, "I am in a bit of trouble. May I stay here overnight?" A nun came out and said, "I have neither food nor clothing, but please stay here overnight."

As soon as the mother had entered the hall, fatigue overcame her and she lay down right away. The nun took off her own robe and put it over the mother. After that, the nun spoke softly, saying, "The daughter you have been searching for is being kept at the Oni's mansion on the other side of the river. Because there are large and small watch dogs at the river bank, it's impossible to cross. But sometimes they take a nap during the day, so if you take a chance then it's not necessarily impossible. The bridge is called Abacus Bridge. It has many beads. Crossing the bridge, you must not step on them. If you step on the beads, you will fall to the place of birth. Therefore, you must be cautious."

Next morning she was awakened by bustling noises. She was bewildered when she found neither a temple nor a nun. All she could see was a grass meadow making sad noises in the morning breeze. She had slept there with her head lying on a small, weathered stone pagoda.

She murmured, "How kind you are, Reverend Lady. Thank you so much for everything."

She came to the river bank and, just as she had heard from the nun, one big and one small watch dog were luckily taking a nap. So she crept up on the bridge and tried not to step on the beads. Just as she reached the other side, she heard the familiar rhythm of a weaving loom nearby. "My daughter!" she called. Her daughter looked out, and both ran toward each other and embraced tightly! They were overjoyed.

The daughter hurried to offer her mother supper. Then she said, "It would be a disaster to be found by the Oni," so she hid her mother in a large stone box.

Soon the Oni came home. "I smell a human!" He sniffed around. She told him that she did not know anything about it. Then the Oni went out to check the flowers in the garden. The Oni had a mysterious plant which bloomed according to the number of beings in the house. The Oni found three blossoms. He became furious.

"You must be hiding a human!" He was about to seize her, but suddenly she came up with an idea. "I'm having a baby! That's why three flowers are blooming."

Then, at once, the angry Oni almost flipped upside down and did a headstand with joy. He screamed to all his servants to come. "Bring me drums! Bring me *saké*! Let's beat up the watch dogs!" He skipped and danced around and made loud noises. His servants also got merry. "Oh, *saké*! Bring drums! Let's beat up big watch dog and small watch dog. Kill them! Kill them!"

Soon, all those servants and the Oni got so drunk that they all collapsed and fell asleep. *"Ka ka a!* [wife] I am getting sleepy. Take me to the large wooden box," the Oni said to her. The daughter sighed with relief to hear him say "wooden box," so she placed him in it and closed its seven lids with seven locks.

Then she hurried to the stone box and let her mother out. Both ran away from the Oni's den as fast as they could run. Since the big and small watch dogs had been killed, no one was on guard, so they went to the carriage house.

There they wondered which would be better, the 10,000-mile carriage or the 1,000-mile one. Then the Reverend Lady came. "Neither the 10,000-mile carriage nor the 1,000-mile carriage is good. Take a boat and make a quick escape," she said. So mother and daughter got a boat and tried to escape on the river.

The Oni who was sleeping in the wooden box woke up thirsty. "Wife, bring me a cup of water," he shouted again and again, but there was no answer. He broke those seven locked lids and climbed out, but his maiden wasn't there. He could find no trace of her.

"She escaped! That brat! She must have escaped?!" He shouted for his servants. When they got to the carriage house, they found no boat so all ran to the river. They saw the boat almost disappearing from sight. So the Oni cried, "Dry up the river! Drink up the water!" He and his men eagerly stretched their necks into the water and started to gulp it up. The river gradually lowered, and the boat carrying mother and daughter was drawn backward toward the shore, almost within the Oni's reach.

When both on the boat gave up all chance of escape, again the nun appeared. "Both of you, hurry up and show yourselves to the Oni!" Then all three of them grasped the hems of their kimonos and pulled them up high. Well! Looking at such a sight, all the Oni laughed and laughed, rolling all over the place so they lost all the water they had swallowed.

So, the boat was again pushed far from the shore and their lives were spared. Both mother and daughter expressed their gratitude for the protection the nun had given.

"I am that one stone pagoda in the meadow. Would you please set up a stone pagoda each year beside me? I would enjoy that more than anything else." Saying this, the nun disappeared.

Mother and daughter returned to their home. Since that time, both have never forgotten the nun's favor. They have set up a stone pagoda in the meadow every year.

Three-Eyes

Cyprus

Once upon a time, there was a poor woodcutter who lived with three daughters. One day, as one of his daughters was looking out the window, she saw a farmer passing by. This farmer became interested in her, inquired of her neighbors about her and asked them to be the go-between for him. After her father agreed to his proposal, they were married.

When the daughter came to her husband's house, she felt quite content and happy. Her husband handed her a bundle of one hundred-and-one keys and told her not to open the hundred-and-first room saying, "That room has nothing in it, so it's not necessary to open it anyway. In fact, I will keep this key myself." So he took it with him.

When the young wife opened the one hundred rooms, she found a lot of treasures in each room. Wondering what made him trust her with this great wealth, she could not stop wondering why he did not trust her with the empty room. So she eventually found the key her husband had carefully hidden and opened the door. Entering the room, she looked around and found only four empty walls and one window facing a street. She grew suspicious of this window.

As she sat down by it, she saw a solitary coffin coming toward her. This scene made her weep because she thought when she died her husband would treat her this way. There would be no attending relatives and no procession of mourners for the funeral. After the coffin was buried and the gravediggers had left, she saw her husband coming to the graveyard. When he got there, his head swelled to the size of a large, round bucket. It had three eyes. His arms stretched so long as to embrace the whole world, and his fingers had foot-long nails. He dug up the corpse and started to gobble it. The scene was utterly distressing, yet she had to make sure that he was really eating the corpse. After this, she fell sick and stayed in bed with a high fever.

After a while, her husband returned home, and as usual he went into the locked room to check. He immediately noticed the open window and footprints on the floor. In a fury, he ran to her room and shouted.

"You idiot! You saw that I am three-eyed so I will not let you live. I must devour you!"

Realizing her extreme danger, the young wife plotted her escape. The husband, making a big fire in the kitchen, brought a big skewer in his hand and shouted, "Come here! The hot skewer awaits you. This is the way I've sworn to eat you. Otherwise, I would already have swallowed you."

His wife answered, "Please forgive me, my dear husband. I'm always yours. Please let me live just two more hours, and I will pray and repent. After that you may eat me." So Three-Eyes granted her wish.

This young wife managed to get the key to the room and climbed out into the street from the window. She ran, looking desperately for someone who could help her. Meeting a man with a horse, she begged him to help. He replied, "Three-Eyes will come and eat you, me and my horse. I wonder who could help you? Well, run ahead. You will meet a man with the king's camels. He might be able to help you." So, the wife ran with all her might and caught up with the camel driver. The man felt so sorry for this woman that he pulled a big bundle of cotton down and helped her hide in it.

Meanwhile, Three-Eyes yelled loudly from the kitchen, holding his big red-hot skewer, "Hey, where are you? Come here! Your time is up!" But his wife did not come to him, so he began to search for her. He couldn't find her anywhere. Then finally, he found the window in the forbidden room left open, so he jumped out and started to run, yelling loudly at the man with the horse, "Hey. Wait or I'll eat you and your horse!" So the man stopped. "Did you see a young woman running?" Three-Eyes asked.

"No, I didn't see anyone. But if you go farther you will see a man with camels. He might know."

Three-Eyes ran and saw the camel driver, so he asked him the same question. Then the man answered, "I don't know. I haven't seen anyone." So, Three-Eyes mumbled to himself, "I had better check my house again" and returned.

But he did not find her. So, carrying the red-hot skewer, he rushed back toward the camel driver mumbling, "I'd better check that camel guy again carefully." The driver became frightened but pretended a lack of concern. "Hey, hurry up. Pull those bags down here!"

Three-Eyes pushed the red-hot skewer into each bundle of cotton. He of course stuck it also into the bag his wife was hiding in. Since he had apparently found nothing, he said, "Okay, you may go."

As he moved off, the driver asked the young wife if she had gotten hurt. She answered, "Of course. It wounded my leg badly, but I wiped the blood on the skewer off with cotton so it was clean." "Don't worry," the driver replied. "Let's go to our king for he is very kind and able to take care of your wound."

After hearing the story the king said to the young wife, "Have no fear, young woman. Even Three-Eyes could not hurt you here." Then he called a physician for her. As her wound began to heal, she did not remain idle but started to embroider an exquisite piece of work. She made a portrait of the king, crowned and sitting on the throne, which greatly delighted him. From time to time she showed her finished works to the king.

One day the king said to his queen, "I wonder if there is a bride better than that young woman. Our son might consider her as his bride since she is skillful with her hands, intelligent and beautiful."

The queen agreed with the king, so they called her and revealed their plan. But she started to cry, saying, "I'm very happy to hear this, but why are you thinking of such a plan? If Three-Eyes hears about it, he will devour me and your son. If you want to insist on this arrangement, please build a house with seven steps and dig a deep moat under those steps. Then cover the moat completely with straw mats and smear beef fat all over the steps. Furthermore, the wedding has to be secretly held at night."

So the king ordered everything as she said. The wedding was prepared secretly. But when Three-Eyes caught wind of it, he decided to take revenge. The night of the wedding, after everyone went to bed, he entered the room to eat her up. And he first scattered some dirt from the graveyard over the prince's bed, so he could not wake up. The bride noticed Three-Eyes standing beside her bed, so she poked her husband but he did not stir. Three-Eyes grabbed the bride and said, "Well, get up quietly, young wife; the red-hot skewer is waiting for you. Once I swore to eat you this way, I've got to do it. Otherwise, I would eat you right now."

Then he grabbed her arm and started to go down the steps. At the third step, she said to him, "Would you please go down first, because I'm scared." He listened to her, and when he came to the bottom step, she pushed him off with all her might. There he slipped and fell into the moat where a lion and a tiger waited. Immediately, he was killed and devoured by them.

In the morning, the king got up and waited for the newly-wed couple to come. When they didn't appear, he wondered what had happened. Entering the bedchamber, the king found the prince was almost dead and his bride had also passed out. The court physician was called in and revived both. Then the bride told them what had happened during the night. The king ordered the moat searched, but Three-Eyes had been completely consumed by the lion and tiger.

Then was held a beautiful wedding which lasted forty days and forty nights, filled with merry, joyful sounds. We have just gotten back from bidding farewell to the wedding guests.

White Bird Sister

Kagoshima Prefecture

In the country of Sashu, there lived the Lord of Sashu. After his
son and daughter were born, his wife died. The girl's name was
Tama-no-chu and the boy's name was Kaniharu. The lord lived
patiently without taking another wife for ten years. One day he
called his two children to him and consulted with them.

"Chu and Kaniharu, let's look for a mother. Without a wife
and a mother with us I feel inadequate when I invite a guest or
another lord to visit."

"Father, please take a wife," the children said.

"Your father will bring you a mother, so please take care of
the house for three days," he said and left on a trip.

He looked all over for a lady. There were many women, but
not one of them was suitable to be his wife and a mother for his
children. When he came to Yamadamuchi-muyashi, he saw a
beautiful woman weaving a cloth.

"Excuse me," he called. The woman answered, "Where are
you from? Please have some tobacco."

"I am the Lord of Sashu. My wife died and so I am looking for
a wife. Would you become my wife?" he asked.

"I would be pleased to do so. My husband was the Lord of
Yamadamuchi, and when our only daughter was born he died.
This estate will be transferred to others soon; therefore I am
weaving to make our living now. If you would take me and my
daughter with you, I would be deeply grateful," she said. So it
was decided that the three of them would return to Sashu.

"Chu, your father has brought you a mother. Come and greet
her," he called. Chu heard him and came out.

"As I see her hair, it is like my own mother's hair. Her dress is
like my own mother's dress. Please be our mother," she said to
their new mother.

This new lady took very good care of the children. After a
while, there was a wedding arranged for Chu. She was going to
wed the Lord of Saga. Finally the time came for the wedding.

The mother called Chu and said, "Chu, today go to the Cedar Mountain and get wild hemp. I will make malt."

When Tama-no-chu brought back the hemp, the mother heated to boiling a large pot full of water and placed a screen made of the hemp over it.

"Tama-no-chu, take a bath on this screen," her mother said.

"No, mother, I wouldn't want to. If I fell into the boiling water I would be cooked," she protested.

"Why not? If you are the lady of such a splendid lord, there is no reason why you cannot take a bath over the screen!" So saying, the mother caught Tama-no-chu and threw her into the boiling water. Tama-no-chu boiled to death.

Seeing all this, her brother, Kaniharu, cried so hard he could hardly breathe. The mother told her husband, "You must have had a bad wife. When I was making some malt, her daughter tried to take a bath in boiling water and scalded herself to death."

Hearing her story, the grief-stricken lord said, "She was a daughter already promised to another family. What shall I say to the Lord of Saga at the wedding tomorrow?"

"Don't worry," his wife told him. "We have Kana. We can put Chu's wedding gown on her and let her wed the lord."

But the father went to bed with an unbearable pain in his chest. The next day, an escort was sent by Lord Saga. Since the father was ill and could not travel, the mother, Kana and Kaniharu went and were entertained with a great feast. On leaving, the mother said to the lord, "Kaniharu is Chu's servant. Send him to gather firewood daily. At night, have him give both of you a massage."

When she returned home, she reported to the father. "I changed Kana's name to Chu and offered her to Lord Saga."

"What about Kaniharu?" he asked.

"I told him to stay there for seven days because his sister would be lonely without him," she replied.

The very next day, Kana (who was now called Chu) told Kaniharu, "Finish your breakfast quickly and go get firewood." With this, she sent him to the mountain.

Kaniharu had no idea where the mountain was or how to gather firewood. He decided to go to Cedar Mountain where his sister had been buried.

"Cedar Mountain Spirit, Cedar Mountain Spirit," he called. A white bird flew out from the place where Chu's body had been buried and broke off dried cedar branches and made them into a bundle. Then it spoke: "I am your sister. How have you been?"

"I am having a difficult time, as you can see, trying to gather firewood, making fires and massaging their legs," he said.

"I understand how difficult it is for you. You have only these clothes?"

"Yes, only these," he said.

"When you return home there should be many pieces of thread and some material scraps left around the outer storm door of the weaving room. Collect them and bring them to me and I will make clothes for you,"she said.

Kaniharu left his sister and returned home. He got up early in the morning and went to look around the storm door of the weaving room, and sure enough there were pieces of thread and material. He gathered them up and took them to Cedar Mountain.

"Cedar Mountain Spirit!" he called. The white bird appeared and asked, "Did you find the threads and pieces of material?"

"Yes, I gathered them up," he said.

Then she gave him further instructions: "When you go home after collecting firewood, go to bed saying you have a headache and are not eating supper. Next morning stay in bed and eat only one bowl of rice gruel. Eat only one bowl of it for lunch. If it's just rice, eat only one-half bowl of rice. Then remain in bed for three days. On the fourth morning, say that you are well and eat a lot of rice and come to the mountain." So saying, the white bird made another bundle of cedar branches.

Kaniharu put the bundle on his head and returned home. As the white bird sister had instructed, he went to bed and said that he had a headache. On the fourth morning, he said, "I am well now and ready to gather firewood today," and he left for the mountain.

When he called, "Cedar Mountain Spirit!" the white bird sister flew down and brought a bundle of clothes in her beak.

"I want to give you these clothes," she said, "but do not place this bundle in a nice place. Instead, choose the dirty *tatami* mat in front of the cooking range and hide it underneath. When you awake in the middle of the night you will be chilly, so take the bundle out and put on the clothes. You must take them off before daybreak and return the bundle to the same place. Well, now I will make some firewood for you." Saying this, she gave him another bundle of branches. Then she said, "Today is the last day for me to stay here. Tomorrow is the seventeenth day, and I have to go to the king of the next world, so you must not call me anymore." The brother and sister parted from one another.

Kaniharu hid the clothes under the dirtiest *tatami* mat in front of the cooking range. At night, after a short sleep, he woke up very cold and so he put on the clothes. But that night, the Lord of Saga had difficulty falling asleep. When he called his servant to bring him a fire to light his tobacco, no one responded. He called his wife but she did not answer. The Lord of Saga had to go for the fire himself, and as he approached the cooking range he found the place shining. With his brass chopsticks, he picked up something he thought was fire, but looking at it carefully he saw that it was a bundle of splendid clothes.

"What's happened, lad, where did you get these splendid clothes?" the lord asked, when the boy cried profusely.

"I am not scolding you and I won't beat you. Just tell me your story honestly," he said.

Hearing this, the boy took some of his sister's belongings which he had concealed in his kimono and placed them in the lord's left hand.

"Would you step out? I will tell you everything." They both went out to the road, and the boy told his story.

"Why didn't you tell me sooner? You must cook rice early tomorrow morning, and we will go to your sister," the lord said.

"But tomorrow is already the seventeenth day since she died.

She will already be gone to the next world. She said she wouldn't be coming back."

But the lord insisted, "I've got to go there. My heart would not be consoled for the loss. So cook rice. Eat to your heart's content and make rice balls for two people."

They left before daybreak. When they came to Cedar Mountain, the lord said, "She might not come if she sees me standing here. I'd better hide beside the foot of this tree, and you can cover me up with a branch." After the lord was hidden, Kaniharu called, "Cedar Mountain Spirit!"

Then the white bird sister came flying. "What happened? I had firmly forbidden you to call me again. I was almost halfway to the next world, and I had to come back to you," she said.

Then the Lord of Saga stepped out and asked her, "Is it no longer possible for you to come back to a human form?"

"It was possible till yesterday, but today is the seventeenth day. I have received a notice from the king of the next world. There is nothing we can do. But I will get advice from the king. Anyway, you go home and place an earthenware mortar on the top of two gateway posts. Then please pour some water in it. When you see a white bird bathing in the mortar, you go seek my body around the rocky mound in the garden. You will find my body there. If you don't place the earthenware mortar on the gate pillars, I cannot return to my original form."

While listening to her, the lord tried to catch her. "Don't touch me," white bird sister said.

"How can I live without touching you at least?" he said and then caught her. All that remained of her in his hand were three little flies. Then the Lord of Saga went home.

"Father, mother, the happiness I found this time turned out to be truly meaningless happiness. I have a request. Please let me place an earthenware mortar on the gateposts," he asked, bowing to his parents.

"All your property belongs to you. You may do anything you wish," they told him.

The earthenware mortar settled on the gateposts perfectly. Soon a white bird came down and landed in the mortar and bathed. Then it flew up and down again and again. The lord went to the rocky mound in the garden and saw a beautiful woman so bright that she was shining brighter than the brightest day. He felt like seizing her and drinking her up. She stood in front of the stone-carved wash basin. The lord took her into his carriage and invited her upstairs.

The bad wife was killed by the lord. Having no inkling of what had occurred, the mother was invited to the celebration and given a bundle as a gift before she went home. As she could not walk any farther and had a bad headache, she opened the bundle. There she was shocked to find her daughter's head. Frightened and grief-stricken, she died.

All over again, the lord had a wedding celebration with Tama-no-chu. The three of them, including Kaniharu, went to see their father, the Lord of Sashu, on his sickbed. The father was overjoyed to see all of them in good health. He quickly recovered from his illness. Soon Kaniharu also took a good wife which greatly relieved his father. Sister and brother, helping each other even now, continue to lead happy lives.

Urashima Tarō

Kagawa Prefecture

Once upon a time, a man named Urashima Tarō lived at Oura in Kitamae. He lived with his mother who was over seventy years old, close to eighty. Urashima was a fisherman and was still single.

One day, his mother said, "Urashima, Urashima, please take a wife while I am still in good health."

"Well, I'm still poor. If I took a wife, I couldn't even feed her.

As long as I have my mother, I will just live like this, day to day fishing," Urashima replied.

Time passed until the mother was eighty and Urashima was forty. In the autumn, a north wind blew day after day so he could not go out fishing. No fishing meant no money. Finally, he could not even feed his mother.

"I hope tomorrow will be a fine day," he thought when he was lying in bed. Then the weather seemed to change for the better, so he jumped up and left to fish on his raft boat. Even though he fished just as the eastern sky was getting lighter, he couldn't catch even one fish. Just as the sun was rising and he was thinking "What can I do now?", he got a big bite, so he pulled it in quickly. It was a big turtle. The turtle did not seem to try to go back into the water even when he put its front legs at the edge of the raft.

Urashima said, "What a shame, I expected a sea bream. You are only a turtle. While you are around, no fish will bite. I will let you go, so go quickly." He threw the turtle into the sea.

Smoking pipe tobacco, he tried to fish for some time, but no fish were biting. He was at a loss. Then again, just before noon, he felt a strong tug like a big fish on his line. When he pulled it in again, it was a turtle. "I told it firmly to go away, and yet once again it is a turtle instead of a fish. I'm having terrible luck," he thought. So he let it go. But he could not go home until he caught some fish. He tried hard to fish for two more hours. Again, another big bite. Thinking that this time it had to be a fish for sure, he pulled it up. Again, it was only a turtle so he let it go.

So. After such an afternoon, the sun was setting and still he had no fish. As soon as the sun set, worrying about what he should say to his mother, Urashima started rowing his raft boat when he saw a ship coming across the sea. And for some reason, it was heading toward Urashima's raft. When Urashima turned to the right, it also turned in that direction. When he turned left, it turned that way, too. So, finally, the ship came up right beside the raft. A boatman on the seaworthy vessel said,

"Urashima, please get on this boat. I am a messenger from Otohime, Princess of the Dragon Palace."

"If I go to the Dragon Palace world, then my mother will be left alone. I can't do that."

"Your mother will be well taken care of. So, please, get on this boat," the boatman insisted.

So, Urashima got on it. Soon after that, with Urashima aboard, the boat submerged and sailed down to the Dragon Palace world. Urashima found that the palace was splendid. The princess anticipated he would be hungry, and she had prepared a meal. She said, "Please stay and enjoy this place for a couple of days."

Urashima greatly enjoyed being with the princess, Otohime, and beautiful girls who also changed his clothes and so forth. Soon he had spent three years at the Dragon Palace quite unintentionally. So he thought he had to go home. One day he bid farewell to Otohime. She gave Urashima a casket containing three boxes, one on top of the other, and cautioned him saying, "Open this if you are completely at a loss." And then she seated him in the boat, and it delivered him to a headland.

When Urashima returned to his village, he noticed the shapes of some mountains appeared different and even some trees on the hills were dead or gone. "I was absent only three years. What has happened?" Urashima wondered as he went toward his house. On the way, he met an old man working with straw on a thatched-roof house. After greeting the man, he asked about himself, "Do you know about a man called Urashima?"

"I have heard that in my grandfather's time there was a Urashima. I heard a story that he went to the Dragon Palace, but he never returned although he was long awaited," the old man told Urashima.

So, Urashima asked, "How about his mother? What happened to her?"

The man said, "She died a long, long time ago."

Urashima went to the ruins of his house. Nothing was left but the stone washbasin and the stone doorstep. He was bewildered.

He opened the lid of the casket to the first box and saw a crane feather. When he opened the next box, white smoke rose from it. It turned Urashima into an old man. When he opened the third box, he found a mirror. Looking into it, he saw himself already an old man. Thinking, "What a strange thing!" as he gazed into the mirror, he saw the crane's feather from the first box attach itself to his back. Then he flew up and circled around his mother's grave. Otohime came up to the beach in the form of a turtle to see Urashima.

An Ise folk song, originated from this story, says: "Crane and turtle dance together."

Crane Wife

Kagoshima Prefecture

There was a man called Karoku who lived with his seventy-year-old mother and who made charcoal in the mountains.

One winter, on the way to town to buy a *futon* [folding mattress], he saw a crane struggling in a trap. As he was trying to release the crane, the man who had set the trap accosted him.

"Why are you interfering in my business?"

"I feel sorry for this poor creature and I want to save it. Would you sell it to me? I have some money to buy a *futon*, so please let me buy the crane," he begged.

The man sold the crane to Karoku, and as soon as he had it in his hands he let it go. "It might be cold tonight," he thought, "but it can't be helped." And so he returned home.

"Where is the *futon*?" his mother asked him.

"Mother, I saw a crane in a trap and felt sorry for it. I bought the crane instead of the *futon*. I saved its life," he replied.

"I see. What you have done is just fine," she said.

Next evening just at nightfall, a beautiful woman so dazzling you could barely glance at her came to Karoku's home.

"Would you let me stay overnight?" she asked.

"I have only this unsuitable little hut," he said, trying to refuse.

"Oh, never mind that," she insisted, "just let me stay." So Karoku let her stay.

Then she asked, "I have another request. Please listen to me."

"What sort of request?" he asked.

"Please take me as your wife," she said.

"This is the first time in my life that I have ever seen such a woman, so beautiful and splendid! How could I have a woman like you for my wife when I make only a meager living from day to day?"

"Please don't talk that way. Just take me as your wife."

"Well, well, what a troublesome situation I've gotten myself into," Karoku said.

Karoku's mother overheard their conversation and said to the beautiful woman, "Since you insist so much, please become my son's wife and do your best." So it was settled that the woman was to become Karoku's wife. Time passed and they were married.

One day the wife said to Karoku, "Please leave me in the closet for three days, and be sure that you don't open the door to look inside." So he left her there and didn't look inside, and she came out on the fourth day.

"You must have suffered in there. I was worrying about you so much. Come and have some food," he told her, and she ate a meal as he asked her to.

"Karoku, Karoku, please go and sell the material which I have woven in the closet for two thousand pieces of gold," she said to him. Karoku took the material to the lord. The lord said, "This is gorgeous merchandise. I would pay two thousand, three thousand pieces of gold for this, but can you make another bolt of it?"

"That I must ask my wife. I cannot give you an answer right now," Karoku said.

"You don't need to ask her. If you agree, that will do, won't it? I will pay right now."

When Karoku returned home, he told his wife what had happened.

"Only if you give me enough time will I weave one more bolt. This time, keep me in the closet for a week. You must never peek inside during that time." With this, she entered the closet.

After one week, Karoku was so worried about her that he opened the closet door. Inside it he found a crane with nearly every feather gone, pulling the last fine feather and weaving cloth from it. The bolt was just completed at that moment.

"I have finished the material. However, since you have seen my true body you are surely disgusted with me, so I must leave this place. Truly speaking, I am the crane you saved. Please take this bolt of material to the lord as you have promised." She sat quietly facing the west. Then, suddenly, nearly a thousand cranes came and flew away with the naked crane.

Karoku got a lot of money, but his feeling of loss was unbearable. Wanting desperately to see the crane, he searched all over Japan. When he came upon a beach he just sat there. Then an old man rowing a boat approached the shore. Karoku wondered where he had come from as there was no island in sight. As he was thinking, the boat reached the shore.

"Old man, old man, where have you come from?"

"I came from the island called Crane's Feather Gown."

"Please, would you take me there?"

"Sure." The boat arrived quickly at a beautiful white beach. When Karoku stepped on land, the boat and the old man disappeared.

Beyond the beach, Karoku saw a great pond. In the middle of the pond was a sand dune. There he saw many cranes gathered around the featherless crane, the queen of the cranes. Karoku was treated royally and feasted for a while. Then again by the old man's boat, he returned to his homeland.

The Handless Maiden

Iwate Prefecture

Once upon a time there was a happily married couple who had an only daughter. When the daughter was four years old, her mother died. Later, her father married again, and her step-mother hated her terribly and wanted to get rid of her. Because the daughter was naturally smart, the stepmother found little opportunity.

Even when the daughter had turned fifteen years old, the stepmother's hate toward her continued to grow day by day. She was preoccupied day and night as to how to get rid of her. One day she said to the girl's father, "Father, father, I find it intolerable to live with that smart girl. Please let me leave."

Since the father always listened to what the stepmother said, he answered, "Don't worry. Soon I will take care of it some way." He immediately made up his mind to get rid of the innocent daughter.

One day he invited his daughter to see a festival. "My daughter, come and see the festival with me." He dressed her up in the most beautiful kimono he had ever given her, and both went out to the festival. It was a beautiful day, blessed with good weather.

The daughter was so happy her father had invited her, for his invitation was a rare occurrence. However, she noticed something was wrong. Although they were going to the festival, they went over mountains.

"Father, father, where is the festival?" she asked.

"Go beyond a mountain, go beyond another mountain, and to the festival at a great castle town." Saying this, he walked ahead of her, farther and deeper into the mountains. After crossing two mountains they came to a valley.

"Daughter, let's have lunch," the father said, taking out some rice balls. And so they started to eat. She was so tired from the long walk that while she was eating lunch she began to fall asleep. Seeing this, the father thought now was his chance, and he got his axe from his belt and chopped off her right and left hands. Leaving his daughter crying, he went down the mountain.

"Father, wait for me! Father, I am hurting!" she cried in a pool of blood. Then she rolled down the mountain after him, but he had left without looking back.

"How sad! Why would my own father do this terrible thing to hurt me?" She cleaned her wounded arms in a stream. Being homeless, she survived by eating berries and nuts.

One day, a splendid-looking young man on horseback passed by with a servant.

"You have a human face but no hands! Who are you?" he said to the girl who was moving about in the bushes.

"I am a handless girl abandoned by her father," she wept.

The young man was deeply touched by her pitiful circumstances and said, "You should come to my house." He took her up on his horse, and they rode down the mountain.

He told his mother, "Today I did not find game, but I found a handless maiden in the mountains. She is a truly miserable girl. Please let her stay at our house." He told his mother about the girl's situation.

His mother was a very warm-hearted person. She washed the girl's face and fixed her hair. When the girl was clean and had makeup on, she became the beautiful girl she had once been. The mother was very happy to see her this way and felt close to her as though she were her own daughter.

After some time had passed, the young man asked his mother, "Please let me marry her."

"I think she is a suitable woman to be your bride. I have been thinking about it, too." And since his mother agreed, they had a wedding ceremony right away.

When the young wife became pregnant, her husband had to go to Edo [Tokyo]. He asked his mother, "Please take care of our coming child." His mother promised, "I will send a message right away to let you know about the birth of the baby, so don't worry." And so the young man left for the capital.

Soon a beautiful baby boy was born. The husband's mother

said, "Dear daughter, let us send a message to Edo immediately." She called the neighbor's messenger and handed him a letter for her son reporting the birth of his baby boy.

The fast-footed messenger went over fields and mountains. When he got thirsty, he stopped at a certain house along the way and asked for a drink of water. This house was the former home of the handless maiden. The stepmother asked the messenger, "Where are you going?"

"Where? Well, our next-door neighbors, a rich family, have a handless daughter who has had a baby. I'm delivering a letter to the young father in Edo," he said, speaking quite casually.

Finding her stepdaughter was still alive, the stepmother suddenly became very sweet to the messenger. "My—on this hot day it must be difficult to journey to Edo. Why don't you have a short rest?" Saying this, she offered *saké* to him and soon the messenger became drunk. Meanwhile, the stepmother opened the letter from the letter box and read: "An indescribably handsome jewel, a baby boy, was born."

She was very jealous and changed the letter. "An indescribably ugly snake or devil-like monster was born." She then returned the letter to the box.

"My, my, you have given me such a treat," the messenger said, waking up embarrassed to find he had gotten drunk and overslept. Smiling cheerfully, the stepmother said in a kindly voice, "On the way back, please drop by and let me hear about Edo."

When the young father read the letter in Edo, he was very surprised. "Please take good care of the child until my return —whatever he looks like—be he a snake or a devil," he gravely wrote in his reply and sent the messenger home.

The messenger, unable to forget the treat he had received from the woman along the way, dropped in again expecting the same.

"Oh, now you are on your way home. It's such hot weather. Come in and take a rest," said the stepmother, inviting him inside. Again, she offered him plenty of *saké* and he collapsed.

She then rewrote the letter. "I don't ever want to see such a child. I also don't want to see my handless maiden again. Please cast her out with the child; otherwise, I will never return home. I'd rather stay in Edo." She then replaced the letter in the box.

After the messenger sobered up, he thanked the woman and hurried back to the rich family. When the mother of the new father read the reply, she found it full of unbelievable things.

"What happened? Did you stop any place on your journey?" she asked the messenger.

"Oh, no, I didn't stop anywhere. I ran straight through like a horse and came back," he lied.

The mother thought she would not take action until she talked with her son directly, and so she waited for his return without telling his young wife about the letter. But there was no sign of his homecoming, and so she finally called her daughter-in-law and told her about the letter she had received.

"It is so sad to leave without reciprocating your kindness to me, a poor crippled one, but if this is my husband's wish there is nothing I can do so I will leave home." She was helped to put the baby on her back and departed from the mother and her home in tears.

The maiden had no place to go, and so she wandered here and there, becoming terribly thirsty. Soon she came to a stream. As she knelt down for a drink from the stream, the baby began to slide under the straps and slip from her back.

"Oh, someone, please help!" she cried and tried to hold the baby with her handless arms. Strangely enough, both her hands grew back and caught the sliding baby firmly.

"Oh, how grateful I am that my hands have grown back again!" The maiden was overjoyed.

Soon, the young father returned from Edo, eager to see his child and his wife and his mother, but he found his wife and child gone. When he talked with his mother, he decided that the messenger was definitely suspicious and confronted him about what had happened. He then learned that the messenger had become drunk at the stepmother's house.

"Oh, what a pity! Please look for the maiden and bring her home as soon as possible," his mother said, hurrying to search for the maiden herself.

After searching here and there, the young man came to a shrine by a stream. There he saw a woman beggar holding her child and praying to the shrine deity. The woman resembled his wife, but she had both her hands. He was so curious he called to her, and when she turned he saw that the beggar was the handless maiden.

Both were so happy they sat hand-in-hand and wept. Mysteriously, where their tears fell, beautiful flowers bloomed. As the three of them journeyed home, the grasses and trees burst into beautiful blossoms all along the road.

About the stepmother and father, it is said they were punished most appropriately by the authorities.

Hyōtoku

Iwate Prefecture

Once there was an old man and an old woman. One day the old man went to a mountain to collect firewood and found a large hole. Thinking that some bad things tend to dwell in this sort of hole and that he had better seal it up, he pushed one bundle of firewood into the hole. To his surprise, instead of plugging the hole, the whole bundle slid into it. He pushed another bundle in, and this time also the whole thing slid into the hole. He kept thinking "maybe one more" and "one more" as he put each one in. Finally, he had put all the bundles he had chopped and collected for three days into the hole.

At that moment a beautiful woman appeared from the hole, thanked him for his gift of so much firewood, and invited him into the hole. She insisted so much that he just let her take him along. There was a beautiful house inside, and he saw the firewood which he'd spent three days collecting neatly piled beside it. The beautiful woman told him to come in, so the old man went in and entered a beautiful room. In the room, a splendid-looking, venerable man with a white beard thanked him for the firewood again. When it was time to leave after a wonderful treat, he was asked to take a gift with him as a token of their appreciation. This gift was a little child. This child had such a misshapen face, however, that it was embarrassing to look at, and it also fiddled with its navel all the time. The old man was astonished by the child's looks. But since they insisted on giving it to him, he felt he had to take the child home.

The child was still fiddling with its navel when they got back to the old man's home. One day, when the old man lightly poked the navel with a metal chopstick usually used as fire tongs, a piece of gold popped out from the navel. From then on, it happened three times a day. Soon the old man became very rich, but his wife was a greedy woman and she wanted to get more. When the old man was out, she picked up the metal chopstick and poked the navel with force, piercing it. No gold piece came out and the child died. When the old man returned home and found the child was dead, he wept. The child appeared to the old man in a dream and said, "Don't cry, old man. But make a mask. Make it look like my face and hang it on the post in the cooking place where you will see it every day, and then your family will prosper."

This child's name was Hyōtoku. After this, in the village around the area, it became a custom to hang an ugly Hyōtoku mask made of wood or clay on the post called "Iron-Pot Man" in front of the old brick stove.

The Charcoal Maker *Chōjya*

Kagoshima Prefecture

Once there were two good fishing partners called the east *chōjya* and the west *chōjya*. Every evening they walked along the beach together and had a good time. After a while, their wives became pregnant.

One evening, both went to the beach as usual. Since the tide was still high, they decided to wait for a while. They thought they would take a nap till low tide, so they lay their heads on a large piece of driftwood. The east *chōjya* fell asleep right away, but the west *chōjya* was not quite ready to sleep. He saw the God of the Dragon Palace come out, and he heard the God speak to the driftwood.

"Driftwood spirit, driftwood spirit, let's go to give a rank for the newborn babies of the east and west." The driftwood answered, "I can't go right now; as you can see I have two people using me as a pillow. Would you do my job for me?"

When the God of the Dragon Palace returned from bestowing the ranks, he reported to the driftwood.

"I conferred the ranks. The east *chōjya*'s child was a girl. I gave her the rank of one *sho* of salt. The west *chōjya*'s child was a boy, and I gave him the rank of a piece of bamboo."

The driftwood spirit said, "One *sho* of salt! It's a bit too much, I think."

"Oh, yes, that girl has a character worth that much," declared the Dragon Palace God who then went home.

Overhearing this conversation, the west *chōjya* thought he ought to do something quick since his son had gotten only the rank of a piece of bamboo. He woke the east *chōjya*.

"East *chōjya*, east *chōjya*, I had a dream that at your house and also at mine a baby was born. Let's go home and see!"

So both gave up on fishing and went home. On their way home, the west *chōjya* said, "East *chōjya*, I have some thoughts. If I have a girl and you have a boy, I would have your boy as a son-in-law. If your child was a girl and mine was a boy, then I would give mine to your family as a groom." The east *chōjya* agreed, and they found the east's baby a girl and the west's a boy.

Both children grew up with abundant care. When they reached age eighteen, the east *chōjya* said, "According to the promise on the evening of their birth, I would like to have your son as our groom." And so it was arranged that the child of the west *chōjya* would be the groom of the child of the east's. After the wedding in May, there was a festival day for the harvesting of barley.

The young wife cooked barley and offered it to the ancestor Gods, and then she gave a bowl of cooked barley to her husband saying, "This is the cooked barley which originally was one sack of barley but when hulled became only one tenth of that, then it was pounded and became one *sho* [one tenth of the hulled barley]. Today is harvest festival, so please have some." As she offered it to her husband, he grew angry with her and said, "I eat only rice. I have never eaten anything else except newly hulled rice. You mean to say that I should eat new barley?" He kicked his serving table and the specially prepared bowl. Seeing this, his wife said, "I will not live under the same roof with you. This house and property were inherited by you from my father, so you are free to do whatever you like. I will take this little table and the bowl which you kicked right now and I will leave!" And she picked up every single grain of the scattered barley and left the house.

As soon as she stepped out of the gate, a thin rain started. It so happened that she heard two storehouse deities talking in the rain.

"Even the highest rank barley was kicked and scattered. If we remain here, surely we might be kicked out by the man with the rank of only one piece of bamboo. The charcoal maker Goro who lives in Ushinishi is a hardworking man as well as handsome and good-hearted. Let's go over there."

The wife thought, "Well, I'm glad to hear that conversation, since they are our storehouse deities. I'd better find the house of the charcoal maker Goro somehow." She walked and walked till the next night. Then she saw a tiny light twinkling far away and, walking toward it, reached the hut of Goro.

When she called, "Excuse me, is anyone home? Excuse me!" Goro came out answering, "Ho."

"How can I let such a splendid person as you stay in this tiny hut? It is so small that when your head is in your legs are out, and if you pull your legs in then your head is out. When you go on a little farther, you will come to a big house—so please, go and stay over there," Goro said, trying politely to refuse.

"In this darkness, women like me can't walk any longer. Even under your eaves would be fine with me, so please let me stay!"

After she asked again, he said, "In that case, please come in."

In the house, he made some popped rice tea and offered it to her. After she received the tea, she took out her cooked barley and shared it with him. Then she said, "Please make me your wife."

Goro was so surprised. "Why, I would be punished if a humble man such as I took such a splendid woman as you for a wife."

"No, no, that's not true at all. This is my own wish. Please make me your wife," she insisted.

"If you insist so much, please do become my wife," he agreed. Next morning, his wife said to Goro, "Let's look into all of your charcoal-making kilns from the first one to the one you used today, one by one." Then both of them looked into each kiln. In every kiln they found gold, so they took it out and ordered boxes from the carpenter to put the gold in. This couple became rich quickly.

The man with the rank of one piece of bamboo gradually became poor and peddled bamboo utensils around the villages. One day, he came to charcoal maker Goro's house. Goro's wife recognized him, so she bought things from him. If some of the things cost one measure of rice; she paid two; if something cost two, she paid four. The man of one-bamboo rank thought, "What a stupid woman she is. I will bring a big basket next time and sell it to her." And he made a big basket and brought it to her. She showed him the serving table and rice bowl that she had brought when she had left him. Recognizing them, the man was deeply shamed. He bit his tongue off under the high storehouse to bleed to death. The woman dug a hole under the storehouse for his body and then spoke to him, "I have nothing to offer you, but every May, on the day of the barley harvest, I will offer you some cooked barley so don't ask for anything else. And then, please, don't let any creature climb to the storehouse."

Ever since then, when celebrating the opening of a newly built storehouse, a woman will carry a small sack of grain up into the new structure.

REFERENCES

Notes

ONE

1. *Nihon Mukashibanashi Taisei*, ed. Keigo Seki, 12 vols. (Tokyo: Kadokawa Shoten, 1978–80). Sixty-three tales from this work have been published in English by the University of Chicago Press as *Folktales of Japan* (1963).

2. Antti Aarne and Stith Thompson, *The Types of the Folk-Tale* (Folklore Fellows Communications, 1928).

3. Stith Thompson, *Motif-Index of Folk-Literature* (Bloomington: Indiana University Press, 1975).

4. Erich Neumann, *The Origins and History of Consciousness*, trans. R.F.C. Hull, Bollingen Series 42 (Princeton: Princeton University Press, 1954).

5. Princess Toyotama's husband sees her transformed into a crocodile, giving birth.

THREE

1. *Kojiki*, trans. with an introduction and notes by Donald L. Philippi (Tokyo: University of Tokyo Press, 1967).

2. *Nihongi* [Nihonshoki]: *Chronicles of Japan from the Earliest Times to A.D. 697*, trans. W.G. Aston (Tokyo and Rutland, Vt.: Tuttle, 1972).

FOUR

1. C.G. Jung, *The Collected Works*, trans. R.F.C. Hull, ed. H. Read, M. Fordham, G. Adler, Wm. McGuire, Bollingen Series 20, vols. 1–20 (Princeton: Princeton University Press and London: Routledge and Kegan Paul, 1953 ff.), vol. 16, §427 (hereafter cited as *CW* 16, §427).

2. See C.G. Jung, *CW* 16, §431.

FIVE

1. The Dragon Palace is the undersea home of the "Dragon God," who seldom appears in stories but is the father of Otohime, widely known through the Urashima stories.

2. Karl Kerényi, *Hermes: Guide of Souls*, trans. Murray Stein, Dunquin

Series 7 (Dallas: Spring Publications, Inc.), 23. The long quotation following is found on pages 25–26.

   3. Ibid., 26.

   4. Emma Jung, *Animus and Anima* (Dallas: Spring Publications, Inc., 1957), 46.

SIX

   1. A *chōjya* is the head of a clan or a locally respected or rich person.

   2. The Ise Shrine is the main shrine of the Imperial Family, sacred to Amaterasu, the great Sun Goddess.

SEVEN

   1. Johannes Bolte and Georg Polívka, *Ammerkungen zu den Kinder- und Hausmärchen der Brüder Grimm*, 5 vols. (Leipzig, 1912–1932).

   2. Marie-Louise von Franz, *Problems of the Feminine in Fairytales* (Dallas: Spring Publications, Inc., 1972), 70 ff.

EIGHT

   1. James Hillman, "On Senex Consciousness," *Spring 1970*: 148.

   2. Ibid., 148–49.

   3. Ibid., 150.

   4. Ibid., 155.

   5. Ibid., 161.

   6. C. G. Jung, *CW* 11, §173.

   7. Ibid., §177.

   8. C. G. Jung, *Memories, Dreams, Reflections*, ed. Aniela Jaffé (New York: Vintage Books, 1961), 267–68.

   9. Jung, *CW* 11, §203.

NINE

   1. A *sho* of salt is a measurement of about a quart.

   2. Erich Neumann, "On the Moon and Matriarchal Consciousness," *Spring 1954*: 88–89.

3. Ibid., 93.

4. Ibid., 96.

5. Hiruko is the first offspring of the first marriage of the Gods. Mal-formed ("leech-child" or "sun-child"), he was sent away in a boat made of reeds. See *Kojiki*, trans. Donald L. Philippi, 51, 339.

Selected Bibliography

Baba, Akiko. *Oni no Kenkyu* (A Study of Oni). Sanichi Shobo, 1971.

Edinger, E. F. "Trinity and Quaternity." *The Journal of Analytical Psychology* 9: 103–15.

Eliade, Mircea. *Rites and Symbols of Initiation: The Mysteries of Birth and Rebirth.* New York: Harper & Row, 1965.

Folk Tales from Asia for Children Everywhere, book 3. Sponsored by the Asian Cultural Center for UNESCO. Federal Publication, 1971.

Hillman, James. "The Great Mother, Her Son, Her Hero, and the Puer." In *Fathers and Mothers.* Zürich: Spring Publications, 1973.

Ishida, Eiichiro. *Momotarō no haha* (The Mother of Peach Tarō). Kodansha, 1966.

Iwasaki, Takeo. *Sanshō daiu ko.* Heibon sha, 1973.

Jung, C. G. *The Collected Works.* Translated by R. F. C. Hull and edited by H. Read, M. Fordham, G. Adler, Wm. McGuire. Bollingen Series 20. 20 vols. Princeton: Princeton University Press and London: Routledge and Kegan Paul, 1953 ff., vol. 8.

_____. *The Collected Works,* vol. 12.

_____, and Kerényi, Carl. *Essays on a Science of Mythology.* Bollingen Series 22. Princeton: Princeton University Press, 1949.

Kawai, Hayao. *Mukashibanashi no shinso* (Depth of Fairy Tales). Fukuin Kan-shoten, 1977.

Luthi, Max. *Once upon a Time: On the Nature of Fairy Tales.* Translated by Lee Chadeayne and Paul Gottwald. Bloomington: Indiana University Press, 1976.

Matsumura, Takeo. *Nihon shinwa no Kenkyu* (Study of Japanese Myth), vol. 3. Baifu kan, 1968.

Mizuno, Yu. *Kodai Shakai to Urashima Densetsu,* vols. 1, 2. Yuzan Kaku, 1975.

Origuchi, Shinobu. *Origuchi Nobuo Zenshu,* vol. 2. Chūo Koron sha, 1955.

Ozawa, Toshio, ed. *Sekai no Minwa* (The World's Folktales). Gyosei, 1976-78.

Ozawa, Toshio. *Sekai no Minwa* (The World's Folktales: Marriage between Man and Animal). Chūo Koron sha, 1979.

Sakaguchi, Tamotsu. *Urashima Setsuwa no Kenkyu.* Sogen sha, 1935.

Yanagita, Kunio. "Tōnō Monogatari" (Tales of Tōnō). In *Teihon Yanagita Kunio shu,* vol. 4. Tsukumashobo, 1963.

_____. *Teihon,* vol. 8.

_____. *Teihon,* vol. 9. Imo no chikara.